Monographs of the Association for Asian Studies
Delmer M. Brown, Editor

Association for Asian Studies
Monographs and Papers

XIII. *Conciliation and Japanese Law*
Tokugawa and Modern

Conciliation and Japanese Law
Tokugawa and Modern

Conciliation and Japanese Law
Tokugawa and Modern

by
Dan Fenno Henderson

Volume II

Published for the Association for Asian Studies by

UNIVERSITY OF WASHINGTON PRESS
Seattle

UNIVERSITY OF TOKYO PRESS
Tokyo

K
. H45
v. 2

Publication of this volume has been made possible by a generous grant to the Association for Asian Studies by the Ford Foundation.

University of Tokyo Press
Tokyo, Japan
University of Washington Press
Seattle, Washington 98105
Library of Congress Catalog Card Number 64–18425
Printed in Japan. All rights reserved

200606

Contents

Volume I

Contents

Volume II

Appendices

Bibliography

Charts

Volume I

Charts

Volume II

Conciliation and Japanese Law
Tokugawa and Modern

CHAPTER VIII

Modern Japanese Analogies to Tokugawa Conciliation

THE MODERN skyscraper is not the necessary lineal descendant of the pre-historic mud hut, but by analogy the functional similarities between Tokugawa conciliation *(atsukai* and *naisai)* and three aspects of modern dispute resolution in Japan—(1) Informal Conciliation (sometimes called *jidan),* (2) Conciliation *(chōtei),* and (3) some of the code Compromises *(wakai)*—suggest considerable continuity[1] in the Japanese approach to law, lawsuits, and lawyers. But the changes in the character of Japanese conciliation itself, in moving from pre-war, didactic to present-day, voluntary Conciliation *(chōtei),* are quite as important as the continuity, and both aspects will be given close scrutiny in this chapter.

TERMINOLOGY AND DEFINITIONS FOR TOKUGAWA AND MODERN TYPES

In following the growth of modern conciliation from its Tokugawa antecedents, some specific preliminary attention must be given to defini-tions and language equivalence. There is not only the awkward problem of selecting English terms suitable for labeling novel Japanese institutions, but also the Tokugawa and the modern Japanese conciliation practices themselves, as well as their respective Japanese terminology, are quite distinguishable from each other. Since their distinguishing characteristics are important parts of our story, the terminology must reflect both the historical distinctions and the different types of modern conciliatory practice.

Informal conciliation: What we have called the first stage of didactic conciliation *(atsukai* or *naisai)* in the Tokugawa period—the informal

---

[1] See Henderson, "Patterns and Persistence of Traditional Procedures in Japanese Law" 1–9 (1955). During the last few years, several Japanese scholars have given the historical continuity between Tokugawa and modern conciliatory practices some atten-tion, but up to 1955 most of the Japanese writings on chōtei were rather uncritical of its limitations and also apparently unconcerned or unaware of its historical, social origins predating the legislative history of the statutes. For examples of recent Japanese writings noting the historical continuity, see Yamazaki Tasuku 山崎佐, *Nihon chōtei seido no rekishi* 日本調停制度の歴史 (History of the Japanese conciliation system) 12–63 (1957); Ryōsuke Ishii, *Japanese Legislation in the Meiji Era,* tr. Wm. J. Chambliss, 490–93 (1958).

settlement discussion on the local level—persists in Japan today as a social practice outside of the courts, unfettered by technicalities and conducted in much the same way as it was centuries earlier, except, as we shall see, lawyers and police officers now have significant roles as conciliators. We shall refer to this modern usage as "Informal Conciliation." With reference to its volitional aspects in the bargaining stage, it may still be in some degree didactic even today, depending on how practicable litigation may appear to the parties as an alternative in any particular case. For if the parties are legally minded, either of them can go to court at his option, or once an informal agreement has been reached, it is accorded the formal, legal status of an enforceable contract under the modern Japanese Civil Code, Articles 695–96.[2]

Conciliation (chōtei) : In chapter IX we will trace in detail the appearance of the most significant type of present-day conciliatory procedure, *chōtei*, in the formal Japanese law. At this point then it is sufficient to know that it is primarily a prelitigation procedure, conducted in the regular courts by a three-man conciliation committee composed of two laymen and a judge appointed for each case. Conciliation proceedings as such may be voluntarily filed by either of the parties to a dispute; the parties may legally discontinue conciliation and start a lawsuit at their option.

The term *chōtei* is used in at least five different technical senses[3] in the Japanese legal material:

    1. The institution or whole system of conciliation.[4]

    2. The conciliation procedure.[5]

    3. The act of conciliating itself.[6]

---

[2] Note that this usage of "wakai" is only one of several found in the codes. Civil Code arts. 695–696; for English translation, see Supreme Court (tr.), Civil Code arts. 695–696 (1959); also a translation of a number of important Japanese laws, including the "six codes" may be found in the translation compendium entitled *EHS, Law Bulletin Series Japan,* ed. Nakane Fukio (1955). Hereafter cited as *EHS.* Volume II contains both the Civil Code and the Code of Civil Procedure. Civil Code, arts. 695 and 696 are translated in the Supreme Court version as follows:

    Article 695. A compromise becomes effective when the parties have agreed to terminate a dispute between them by mutual concessions.

    Article 696. If, in cases where it has, by a compromise, been admitted that one of the parties possesses the right constituting the object of a dispute or that the other party does not possess such right, it has afterwards been established that the former party did not possess the right or that the other party did possess the same, such right shall be treated as having by virtue of the compromise been transferred to the former party or extinguished as the case may be.

[3] Miyazaki Sumio 宮崎澄夫, *Chōteihō no riron to jissai* 調停法の理論と実際 (The theory and practice of conciliation law) 84 (1942).

[4] Civil Conciliation Law (1951), art. 23; for author's translation see appendix III.

[5] Civil Conciliation Law (1951), art. 2.

[6] Civil Conciliation Law (1951), art. 5 (1).

4. The substance of the agreement or compromise embodied in writing.[7]

5. The "meeting of the minds" in making the agreement (like Compromise, *wakai*).[8]

Hereafter we will use the term *chōtei*[9] to indicate the entire institution, as in number one listed above, and other Japanese usages will be distinguished as necessary in the context.[10] Chōtei is similar to some of the practices in the United States[11] called "conciliation"; however, as mentioned

[7] Civil Conciliation Law (1951), art. 20 (2).

[8] Civil Conciliation Law (1951), art. 16.

[9] "Chōtei" has been translated officially as "conciliation." "*The Official Gazette*" [*Kampō*] (no. 1560) 36–41 (June 9, 1951) contains the first official English translation. *The Official Gazette* was translated into English in 1946–51, but the translation was discontinued at the end of the allied occupation; another Japanese government English translation of the Civil Conciliation Law of 1951 may be found in Supreme Court, *The Law of Civil Procedure* (hereafter CCP) 209 ff. (1959); see appendix III for the present writer's English translation; the official Japanese text may be found in Ōkurashō Insatsu-kyoku (ed.), 大藏省印刷局 *Hōrei zensho* 法令全書 (Complete compilation of laws and ordinances [another name for the Kampō, classified and bound]) 212–16 (June 9, 1951). Generally Japanese practitioners and students use some version of the ubiquitous *Roppō zensho* for Japanese texts of the six codes and also other important statutes and regulations; a reliable version revised and reprinted annually is *Roppō zensho* 六法全書 (Complete collection of the six codes) ed. Wagatsuma Sakae 我妻榮 and Miyazawa Toshiyoshi 宮澤俊義, 1964. See *id.* at 1309 for the Japanese text of the Civil Conciliation Law of 1951; hereafter we will simply cite the *Roppō zensho* by code or statutes and the articles thereof.

[10] For historical comparisons, see Ryōsuke Ishii, *Japanese Legislation in the Meiji Era* 491–97 (1958); another recent detailed treatment is found in Yamazaki Tasuku, *Nihon chōtei seido no rekishi* 1–126 (1957).

The problem of terminology is considered carefully by Maki Kenji, "Kinsei bukehō no wakai oyobi chōtei" 近世武家法の和解及び調停 (Conciliation and compromise in the law of the military houses of the recent era), in *Saitō hakushi kanreki kinen, hō to saiban*, 203–4 (1942). He uses Conciliation as equivalent to *atsukai* and Compromise as equivalent to *naisai. Atsukai* is the procedure; *naisai* is the resultant settlement itself. Kobayakawa uses the same equivalents: Kobayakawa Kingo, *Kinsei minji soshō seido no kenkyū* 84 (1957); Kaneda Heiichirō, "Tokugawa jidai ni okeru soshōjō no wakai," 1 *Shien* 174 (1928) uses *wakai* for *naisai*, but makes the important distinction between *naisai* in and out of court. *Koji ruien*, 3 *Hōritsu no bu* 1006 uses *wakai* without indication of its exact equivalent or any indication that it is not a Tokugawa term, for that matter.

[11] See California Code of Civil Procedure, arts. 1730–1772; also the old North Dakota procedure (repealed 1943) was rather similar to the Japanese chōtei, and it used the term *conciliation. Supplement to the 1913 Compiled Laws of North Dakota (Annotated 1913–1925)* section 9192 (a) (1)–9192 (a) (15) (passed 1921; repealed 1943). Labor law furnishes several relevant definitions: see CCH *Labor Law Reporter* (4th ed.) 6901 quoting Secretary of Labor of United States, *Annual Report* 9 (June 30, 1936): "Conciliation is an attempt by a third party to bring about an amicable solution of the differences involved, but without power to settle them."

The distinction in labor law (see Forkosch, *A Treatise on Labor Law* 838–44 [1953]) between conciliation and mediation is that, although both imply a third party, in mediation his role is active and in conciliation it is passive; whereas such a distinction is rather the opposite to the difference observed in international diplomatic usage of the terms (see chapter I). Also see Burke, "The Conciliation Court in Los Angeles," 42 *A.B.A.J.* 621 (1956).

in chapter I, there is little uniformity in the American usage,[12] and mediation would also be an acceptable rendition perhaps.[13]

Compromise (wakai): For us the most important meaning of the multi-purpose,[14] modern Japanese legal word, *wakai*, is the process whereby the judge encourages the parties to a lawsuit to compromise the dispute which is being tried before him in the court. But like *chōtei*, *wakai* is used in a number of different ways in the modern Japanese law. For example, as mentioned above, *wakai* is a contractual agreement embodying a private compromise, as provided for in the Civil Code (Article 695). *Wakai*, in the Code of Civil Procedure (hereafter CCP) Article 136,[15] is also a method used by the judge to induce compromise in a lawsuit being tried before him. Such a compromise agreement when written into the protocol of the court is given the force of a final judgment (CCP Article 203).[16] Disputants may also apply to a summary court (CCP Article 356)[17] to make a com-

---

[12] See Elkouri, *How Arbitration Works* 3 (1952). Conciliation does not imply a third party, whereas mediation does.

[13] Ishii, *Japanese Legislation in the Meiji Era*, tr. Chambliss, 308 (1958) uses both terms, *conciliation* and *mediation*. But for the early use of "conciliation," see Wigmore, "Materials for the Study of Private Law in Old Japan," 20 *T.A.S.J.* (Supp.) 75 (1892). Wigmore was probably the first westerner to emphasize this traditional feature and translate it "conciliation," perhaps following Simmons, although both Wigmore and Simmons also used the term *arbitration* (*id.* at 118). Considering the fact that in some of these primitive situations didactic conciliation blends into primitive or "anthropological adjudication," this use of "arbitration" is not as wrong as it might appear from modern uses of the term. Compare, for example, compulsory arbitration with didactic conciliation.

[14] Kaneko Hajime 兼子一, *Minji soshōhō taikei* 民事訴訟法体系 (Outline of the Code of Civil Procedure) 304–10 (1956) gives a useful short explanation of the various kinds of code compromises; also, Miyazaki Sumio, *Chōteihō no riron to jissai* 88 ff. (1942) gives a variety of meanings of the term *wakai* in various sections of the codes.

[15] CCP art. 136: At whatever stage the action may be, the court may endeavor to effect a compromise, or require a commissioned judge or requisitioned judge to do so.

The court or a commissioned judge or requisitioned judge may order the parties themselves, or their legal representatives, to appear with a view to arranging a compromise.

See Nakamura Hideo 中村英郎, "Saibanjō no wakai" 裁判上の和解 (Compromise in court), *Minji soshō zasshi* (no. 7) 177–243 (1961).

[16] CCP art. 203: When a compromise or the waiver or admission of the claim is entered in the protocol, such entry has the same effect as an irrevocable judgment.

[17] Note that CCP art. 356 compromises are often simply contractual arrangements wherein the parties have obtained court action to give the contract the effect of a judgment before a dispute ever arises. See note 18 below for the citation to an article critical of this practice.

CCP art. 356: A party to a civil dispute may make an application for a compromise to the summary court of the place where the general forum of the other party exists, stating the gist and grounds of the claim and the actual circumstances of the dispute.

On a compromise being arranged, it must be entered in the protocol. In default of a compromise, the court, on the application of both

promise, even without having a lawsuit pending before the court, and if such a compromise agreement[18] is concluded and embodied in a protocol of the court, it becomes effective as a final judgment.[19] Hereafter we will use "compromise" to indicate the process wherein the judge attempts to settle cases before him in court, and the other usages will be explained in context where required.

How precisely do these modern conciliatory practices—Informal Conciliation *(jidan)*, Compromise *(wakai)*, and Conciliation *(chōtei)*—relate to the Tokugawa conciliation [*naisai* and *atsukai*]? Certainly the present-day informal conciliation, however different its milieu, is a lineal descendant of the Tokugawa village practices, although the relative accessibility of the courts as an alternative today is indeed significant (see chapter X). Current compromise and chōtei legal procedures are, however, quite distinguishable from the Tokugawa practices in the Shogunate courts. Compromise is a German borrowing apparently; chōtei was devised in Japan piecemeal during the 1920's and 1930's. Despite the differences, however, we suggest that there is a strong functional similarity between these procedures and the Shogunate court practices as seen in chapter VI.

The earlier Japanese jurists[20] writing about modern chōtei seem to have given little attention to the possible underlying continuity of these modern conciliatory practices. Several of the recent legal historians, however—Kobayakawa Kingo, Kaneda Heiichirō, Maki Kenji, and Ishii Ryōsuke[21]—have mentioned in passing the significance of a study of the continuity between modern and Tokugawa conciliation practices. The continuity is

---

parties who have appeared on the date for negotiations for compromise, orders oral proceedings in the action to be entered upon forthwith. In this case, the person who has made an application with a view to arranging a compromise is deemed to have instituted the action at the time when such application was made, and the costs of the (intended) compromise constitute part of the costs of the suit. Should either the applicant or the other party fail to appear on the date set for negotiation for compromise, the court may deem compromise impossible.

[18] Yamakido Katsumi 山木戸克巳, "Wakai tetsuzuki no taishō" 和解手続の対象 (The object of compromise procedure), 2 *Kōbe hōgaku zasshi* 1–24 (1952) deals extensively with CCP art. 356 proceedings, and he notes the way this article is used by contracting parties to make their agreements effective like a judgment even before a dispute or charges of nonperformance arise. Yamakido raises the question whether Article 356 legally contemplates the use of *wakai* procedure before there is a dispute in existence.

[19] Koyama Noboru 小山昇, "Soshōjō no wakai to chōtei" 訴訟上の和解と調停 (Compromise during trial and conciliation), *Shihō* (no. 9) 104–15 (1953); Koyama Noboru, "Saibanjō no wakai" 裁判上の和解 (Compromise in court), in 3 *Sōgō hanrei kenkyū sōsho: Minji soshōhō* 42–130 (1961).

[20] For example, Miyazaki, Ikeda, Onogi. See bibliography for writings.

[21] Kobayakawa Kingo, *Kinsei minji soshō seido no kenkyū* 78 (1957); Kaneda, *op. cit. supra* note 10; Maki, *op. cit. supra* note 10; Ishii, *Japanese Legislation in the Meiji Era* 491–97 (1958).

sometimes particularly difficult for a modern Japanese lawyer to see because the conciliatory tendency is largely of social origin,[22] and its present legislative embodiment tends to prevent inquiring for its origins beyond the date of enactment. Nor should we overlook the developmental significance of the legislative embodiment; this sort of conciliation is now in court.

The massive reconstruction of the Japanese legal system along foreign lines between 1868 and 1900 tended to preoccupy the Japanese jurists with exegetical tasks and to obscure the functioning of the continuing conciliation process, especially until the 1920's, and to some extent obscures the informal conciliation even now. So far apart were the social practices and the new Meiji legal codes, which presumed to change them at the turn of the century, that in order to fathom the reasons for this continuing hiatus, it is worthwhile to consider briefly the way the massive reception of foreign legal institutions came about.

MEIJI RECEPTION

It is well known that the Meiji reception of western law was inspired as much by diplomacy and oligarchic pride as by popular zeal for legal codification on the part of any substantial Japanese social group at the time.[23] In the crucial Treaty of Amity and Commerce between the United States and Japan (signed 1858), Townsend Harris reluctantly[24] included a provision[25] extending extraterritoriality to United States citizens in Japan in order to get the treaty ratified by the Senate. This provision was preceded by a similar one in the Dutch treaty (1856). It is fair to assume that few Japanese understood at the time the reasoning behind the foreigners' demand for extraterritoriality, which derived from the vast differences between the Tokugawa and western legal systems. Nevertheless, the Meiji political authorities resented this feature in the early treaties, and by the late 1870's it had become a major goal of successive Japanese foreign ministers to negotiate new treaties in which the western nations would relinquish their extraterritorial rights. Before the western nations would agree to subject their nationals to the Japanese law and courts, it was necessary for Japan to reconstruct its whole formal legal system; eschewing the details, one can say that the reconstruction was accomplished by

---

[22] Kawashima Takeyoshi 川島武宜, "Shakai kōzō to saiban" 社會構造と裁判 (Social structure and litigation), *Shisō* (no. 432) 1–17 (1960).

[23] Kenzō Takayanagi, *Reception and Influence of Occidental Legal Ideas in Japan*, 11–12 (1929).

[24] Chitoshi Yanaga, *Japan Since Perry* 26 (1949).

[25] For a convenient copy of the treaty, see *The Complete Journal of Townsend Harris*, ed. Cosenza, appendix IX (rev. ed. 1959); the extraterritoriality provisions are found in Article VI, p. 581.

1899, and in the same year the new western treaties relinquishing extraterritoriality became effective.

The resulting statutory changes amounted to a monumental reception of foreign codified law, mostly German. A new Meiji Constitution (1889) and five new codes (criminal, 1882; civil, 1898; commercial, 1899; criminal procedure, 1882; civil procedure, 1891), modeled mostly after the German and French codes, were enforced. A judiciary was established which was to a degree independent from the administration; a German-type system of multiple appeals on both the law and facts was provided in a highly centralized hierarchy of courts, composed of summary courts, district courts, high courts, and a Supreme Court;[26] a rudimentary professional bar was recognized; criminal and civil jurisdictions and procedures were distinguished; torture was abolished; and a token system of judicial review of official action was provided through a separate administrative court.[27]

The contrast between the new code system and the Tokugawa legal system—generally decentralized, with only the beginnings of a recognized bar, with no separate bench, and with a fusion of civil and criminal procedures—was indeed striking. Therefore, without detracting from the magnitude of these Meiji accomplishments, it is enough to recognize that the reception of foreign law was to a large extent externally inspired and

[26] The outline of the present Japanese court system is as follows:

Name	Number of courts	Jurisdiction
(1) Supreme Court *(Saikō saibansho)*	1	Largely appeals from high courts.
(2) High Courts *(Kōtō saibansho)*	8	Largely appeals from district courts.
(3) District Courts *(Chihō saibansho)*	49	(1) Appeals from summary courts and (2) original trial jurisdiction in cases over ¥100,000 ($278).
(4) Family Courts *(Katei saibansho)*	49	Domestic relations cases.
(5) Summary Courts *(Kan-i saibansho)*	570	Original trial jurisdiction over all cases involving less than ¥100,000.

[27] See generally Ishii Ryōsuke (ed.), 2 *Meiji bunkashi (Hōseihen)* 明治文化史法制編 (History of Meiji culture, part on legal institutions) 36–43 (1954); in English also, Ishii, *op. cit. supra* note 21, 268–320 (1958). Other works covering this important development are: Kobayakawa Kingo 小早川欣吾, *Meiji hōseishi ron* 明治法制史論 (A treatise on the legal history of the Meiji era) (1940); Hoshino Tōru 星野通, *Meiji mimpō hensanshi kenkyū* 明治民法編纂史研究 (A study of the history of the Meiji compilation of the civil code) (1943); Hoshino Tōru, *Mimpōten ronsōshi* 民法典論爭史 (History of the Civil Code dispute) (1944); Nakagawa Zennosuke 中川善之助 and Miyazawa Toshiyoshi 宮澤俊義, *Hōritsushi* 法律史 (History of law) 33–98 and separate following pagination 1–59 (1944); important other newer works include: Ukai Nobushige 鵜飼信成, Fukushima Masao 福島正夫, Kawashima Takeyoshi 川島武宜, and Tsuji Kiyoaki 辻清明 (editors), *Nihon kindaihō hattatsushi* 日本近代法発達史 (History of the development of modern Japanese law) published between 1958 and 1961; Suzuki Yasuzō 鈴木安藏, *Hōritsushi* 法律史 (History of law) 110–70 (1960).

that the social efficacy of the alien codes has been understandably gradual and only partial among the populace.

As might be expected, it was several decades after 1900 before sufficient jurisprudence had been accumulated by the courts and jurists to make the system a thoroughly indigenous product. During this period of concentrated exegesis of the new codes, a working understanding of the internal consistency of the codes as a system was achieved by the universities and jurists, but the populace at large was slower to understand and even slower to act in accordance with the new legislation. The social efficacy of the law was difficult to appraise because penetrating academic studies of social compliance with the codes or empirical inquiries into the jural life of the people were rare. But it is no doubt a fair assumption that the people went about their affairs for some time after the enactment of the Code of Civil Procedure in much the same way that they had before 1890.

Fortunately, since 1945 Japanese interest in the sociological aspects of the law has increased at an encouraging rate.[28] In the meantime, the interaction between the code system and the society has also had its effect on both. Yet, as we shall see, lawsuits based upon the codes are still a relatively small part of social control or dispute settlement in Japan even today.

Informal conciliation practices continued to function underground immediately after the codes were adopted, but conciliation procedures began to appear in the legislation to an increasing extent after 1920. In order to see their total effect, we will examine the several conciliatory methods of settling civil disputes—informal conciliation, chōtei, and compromise—as they have come to operate in present-day Japan since the enactment of the Law for Adjustment of Domestic Affairs (1948) and the Civil Conciliation Law (1951). It is important to understand not only their relationship to each other but also their relationship to formal Arbitration[29] *(chūsai)*

[28] For examples of sociological studies related to conciliation, see Sasaki Yoshio 佐々木吉男, "Minji chōtei ni okeru 'gōi' no kentō" 民事調停における「合意」の検討 (Inquiry in "agreements" in civil conciliation), 9 *Kanazawa hōgaku* 1–31 (Dec. 1963); Sasaki, "Minji chōtei ni okeru hōteki handan no jian no kaimei" 民事調停における法的判断と事案の解明 (Fact determination and decision in accordance with law in civil conciliation), *Minji soshō zasshi* (no. 7) 143–76 (1961); Kawashima Takeyoshi, *op. cit. supra* note 22; Taniguchi Tomohei 谷口知平, "Kaji chōtei iin no shakai kaisō to shisō" 家事調停委員の社會階層と思想 (The social class and thought of family conciliators), 30 *Hōritsu jihō* 293–98 and 64 (1958); Hironaka Toshio 廣中俊雄, "Shimin no kenri kakuho to minji saiban" 市民の権利確保と民事裁判 (Civil adjudication and upholding the rights of the urban citizenry), 32 *Hōritsu jihō* 1002–8 (1960).

[29] Note that modern arbitration is quite distinguishable in that the decision is made by a third party. See Kawashima, *op. cit.* supra note 22, at 16, note 16; also see Ikeda Enjirō 池田寅二郎, *Chūsai to chōtei* 仲裁と調停 (Arbitration and conciliation) 55 (1932) for one of the earliest works by a former Supreme Court judge; and Koyama Noboru, "Chōteihō, chūsaihō" 調停法仲裁法 (Conciliation law and arbitration law), 38 *Hōritsugaku zenshū* 1–208 (1959). For German origins of modern Japanese arbitration, see Ishii, *Japanese Legislation in the Meiji Era* 501 (1958).

and Lawsuits *(soshō)*. Together, these several types of procedures constitute the major methods for resolution of civil disputes in Japan, and we
will seek to identify the combined quantity of disputes settled by the various conciliatory practices as opposed to lawsuits in contemporary Japan.

INFORMAL CONCILIATION

Although few experienced observers would doubt that the Japanese
have an unusually pronounced tendency to avoid litigation and, conversely, an equally pronounced tendency to obtain settlements informally,
nevertheless the informal and confidential handling itself makes such a
process very illusive to the investigator. We cannot measure the extent of
this phenomenon by direct statistics, but indirectly and inferentially[30]
we can get an inkling of its magnitude and importance by the following
types of evidence.

Police counseling: It has become quite common for Japanese police
officers to act informally as conciliators in civil disputes arising within
their area, and the larger police offices usually maintain facilities for conciliating disputes brought to them voluntarily in the context of a disturbance. National statistics are not available, but in 1958, there were 21,596
civil disputes brought to the Tokyo police for conciliation, and 39 per cent
of them were apparently settled in one way or another. In the Tokyo
district court area there were only 6,815 cases filed for formal conciliation.
Hence it seems that for Tokyo the police alone received more cases for
informal conciliation than the courts handled[31] by formal, chōtei proceedings.

Divorce by agreement (kyōgi rikon): Article 763 of the Japanese Civil Code
authorizes married couples to divorce themselves by registering their
signed divorce agreement at the proper registry office. No court action is
required. Most significantly, the vast majority of Japanese divorces are
accomplished in this manner. For example, in 1955, over 90 per cent
(68,514 out of 75,267) of all divorces which became effective in Japan

---

[30] A direct survey to try to discover in concrete terms just what precedes the actual
filing of a suit in modern Japan might do a great deal to show the difference in attitude
and atmosphere surrounding an American and a Japanese lawsuit. One would probably
discover that a lawsuit is a last resort to a much stronger degree than in American
practice. But by the same token, since litigation has been traditionally considered to be
an unworthy public demonstration that the parties are unable to settle their disputes with
dignity and in private, the prospects of getting answers regarding such inner workings are
not very promising. The results of such a survey have turned out rather well in one instance, however. See below, note 32.

[31] See Hironaka Toshio, "Keisatsukan no hatasu hōteki kinō ni tsuite" 警察官のはたす
法的機能について (Concerning the legal functions performed by police officers), *Jurisuto*
(no. 78) 31–35 (1955); and *id.*, "Shimin no kenri no kakuho to minji saiban", 32 *Hōritsu
jihō* 1002–8, 1004 (1960); also see Kawashima *et al.*, 28 *Hōritsu jihō* 182–83 (1956).

were divorces by agreement.[32] We cannot say with precision how many of these divorces were arranged by informal conciliation, especially since Japanese marital relationships are changing rapidly in the postwar period in accordance with changing social conditions and the individualism expressed in the 1947 constitution. No one, however, would doubt that many divorces by agreement still occur only after interfamily conciliation involving also the go-betweens, who customarily assist in the marriage arrangements in the first place and who are often consulted regarding subsequent marital storms. We can assume that, through the go-between, family members, and friends of both spouses, the informal conciliation process operates extensively in the arrangement of these numerous divorces by agreement, quite outside of the judicial process.

Survey: Two interesting recent surveys bear rather directly on our inquiry into the extent of informal conciliation, since they show the methods which the persons surveyed state that they would use to settle a civil dispute, should they become involved in one. The surveys were conducted by Yoshio Sasaki in Osaka (1960–61) and in Shimane prefecture (1958).[33] In Shimane the survey covered four city areas, five farming villages, eight mountain villages, and two fishing villages. Questionnaires were sent to twenty-five hundred persons requesting anonymous answers to the following question: "In case a civil dispute arose and despite discussions with the opponent you could not settle it, what would you do?" Chart VIII indicates the results:[34]

CHART VIII
EXPRESSED PREFERENCES AS TO DISPUTE-SETTLEMENT PROCEDURES

Types of Answers	City Areas	Farming Villages	Mountain Villages	Fishing Villages	Total
1. There would be no way to solve the problem; I would accept the solution.	12	12	15	2	41
2. I would use the court (either a lawsuit or *chōtei*).	120	116	101	40	377
3. I would ask a suitable person to settle the matter and if he failed there would be no solution.	29	58	99	32	218

[32] Tanabe Shigeko 田辺繁子 and Ōhama Eiko 大浜英子, "Kyōgi rikon no jittai chōsa" 協議離婚の実態調査 (An empirical study of divorce by agreement), 30 *Hōritsu jihō* 337–41 (1958); for a lucid, concise explanation of divorce by agreement and some of its social implications, see Kawashima Takeyoshi and Steiner, "Modernization and Divorce Trends in Japan," 9 *Econ. Dev. and Soc. Change* (no. 1, pt. 2) 222–25 (1960).

[33] Comparisons of the results of both surveys are found in Sasaki Yoshio, "Minji chōtei ni okeru 'gōi' no kentō," 9 *Kanazawa hōgaku* (nos. 1 and 2) 1–31 (Dec. 1963); see earlier Shimane survey only, Sasaki Yoshio, "Minji chōtei ni okeru hōteki handan to jian no kaimei," *Minji soshō zasshi* (no. 7) 43–176 (1961).

[34] *Id.* at 165 (1961).

4. I would ask a suitable person to settle it, and if he failed, I would resort to the courts.	331	459	420	119	1329
5. Other answers	31	38	44	11	124
Total answers*	523	683	679	204	2089

* Persons consulting the Japanese version of the chart, Sasaki Yoshio, "Minji chōtei ni okeru hōteki handan to jian no kaimei," *Minji soshō zasshi* (no. 7) 165 (1961), will see that the "Total Answers" line was substituted by this writer for a "Valid Answers" line in the original, the figures of which do not correspond with the sums of the columns. Sasaki explained by letter that many valid answers contained more than one usable answer so that the sums of the columns are understandably larger (2,089) than his "Valid Answer" figures (1,852). But the figures for valid answers are confusing under the circumstances, so they were omitted here.

It was assumed in the questionnaire that initial efforts would be made to settle the matter between the parties themselves. In interpreting the results we would eliminate groups one and five, totaling 165, and, of the 1,924 persons who say they would take specific further action, 1,547 (about 80 per cent) would invoke the assistance of an informal conciliator, and only 377 (about 20 per cent) would go to court directly. In addition, forty-one others would drop their claim without even asking for informal conciliation. Even those who would invoke the court's aid might, although this is not specified, first ask the court's assistance in a chōtei proceeding. Even if they filed a lawsuit, as we shall see later, a considerable number of suits would be settled by compromise procedures or chōtei during trial.

Concentrating on those persons who would invoke informal conciliators, and if the conciliation failed, either drop the claim or sue (i.e., items 3 and 4 respectively), a further question was asked: "Who would you request to handle the conciliation?" The anonymous answers appear in chart IX:[35]

CHART IX
EXPRESSED PREFERENCES AS TO CONCILIATORS

Answers	City Areas	Farming Villages	Mountain Villages	Fishing Villages	Total
1. Relatives	119	195	165	69	548
2. Organizational superiors (bosses)	24	49	58	10	141
3. Judicial scriveners	58	85	41	22	206*
4. Lawyers	179	137	131	45	492
5. Police or the police station	19	64	86	27	196
6. Others	66	106	129	22	323
Total answers	465	636	610	195	1906

* The author has been informed that *209* in the Japanese text, Sasaki, "Minji chōtei ni okeru hōteki handan to jian no kaimei," *Minji soshō zasshi* (no.7) 165 (chart12) (1961), is a misprint for *206*.

[35] *Ibid.*

The figures show that 492 persons (25.7 per cent) would ask a lawyer to settle the case, and this pattern is not unlike the normal course followed in the United States. But some of those might have decided in advance not to proceed to court, either by lawsuit or chōtei (number 3 above). The data do not give us such a breakdown.

One other point should be mentioned: the lawyer in Japan is mainly a court lawyer, and the Japanese Judicial Scrivener *(Shihō shoshi)* in some of his functions, such as drafting and registration, does the work of an office lawyer in the United States. So if those who would ask the judicial scrivener to intervene are added to those who would request lawyer's intervention, the number becomes 701 (36.6 per cent). Still, the survey shows that between three fourths and two thirds of those questioned would resort to informal conciliation of the traditional type, little known in this country, in order to settle their civil disputes out of court. There is some significance to our inquiry in the fact that relatives, bosses, and village officials still serve in the capacity of informal conciliators much as they did in Tokugawa times. Conversely, the extent to which the lawyers and judicial scriveners enter into the process nowadays is indicative of the increasing role of the modern legal order.

Of course the Shimane survey covered only one rural prefecture, and it shows only what those responding felt they would do prospectively. Nevertheless, it represents a balanced cross section of the rural prefecture surveyed. The Osaka survey showed substantially similar results on the points, reported above, although as might be expected the urbanites of Osaka tended to use courts and lawyers somewhat more. (The Osaka results seem to confirm the general impression which one obtains from the practice of law in Tokyo.)

Contractual relationships: Another phenomenon noticeable in the Tokyo law practice which bears on the extent of informal conciliation in present-day Japan is the general reaction of Japanese businessmen to the inclusion of dispute-settlement provisions as standard clauses in their contracts. It is not unusual for the foreign lawyer to propose an arbitration and a governing law clause, especially in international licensing, sales, construction, supply, agency, transportation, or joint venture contracts. But except for those firms especially experienced in foreign trade, the Japanese party will usually feel uncomfortable about including such provisions.[36] Instead, he will often suggest a clause to the effect that if a dispute should occur under the contract, the parties will try to settle the matter amicably by mutual discussion.

From a legal point of view, the non-Japanese party may regard this

---

[36] See Hironaka, *op. cit. supra* note 31, at 1005 (1960), which notes this characteristic of Japanese businessmen.

as nothing more than an unnecessary provision for a novation or an agreement to agree on future changes, if they should be considered advantageous at the time; if changes are not deemed desirable by both parties in the future, he would expect the contract to be enforced in its terms. This view, though legally sound perhaps, misses the Japanese party's meaning. The Japanese will probably regard the contract as a functioning relationship requiring mutual accommodation to future contingencies by the parties rather than what it is in positive law: a written embodiment of strict rights and duties enforceable in court. To the traditional Japanese, the relationship is what is important, and it is governed by status and by mutual accommodation of the parties rather than by reference to any generalized external principles of law. Hence, the idea of having a judge, or even a voluntarily selected arbitrator, intervene in such matters is rather embarrassing to contemplate. The remarkably infrequent use made of the elaborate provision for arbitration existing in the Code of Civil Procedure since 1890 confirms the fact that the intervention of an outsider to decide a dispute at his discretion, rather than to facilitate mutual agreement, is unusual in Japan. Indeed, it is only in international transactions and, to an increasing extent, in domestic urban transactions (where the close-knit, rather Confucian social relationships of the family and village are not available to supply the status bearers necessary for the traditional process of settling disputes) that, in Japanese terms, the embarrassing confrontation with sterile, universal principles of law and unrelated outsiders occurs in the settlement process. As mentioned, adaptation to the code law by those Japanese concerned with international transactions is occurring rapidly, in step with the post-1945 rehabilitation of Japanese industry and the growth of foreign trade; consequently, these businessmen may come to rely less on informal conciliation in the future, perhaps even among themselves.

Lawyers per capita: Two other indications of the heavy reliance on informal conciliation in present-day Japan are of a rather negative sort. First, the paucity of lawyers per capita, and second, the comparative scarcity of litigation would seem to indicate that other means must be used to dispose of civil controversies. Comparative figures[37] for lawyers in private or business practice in the United States, Germany, and Japan for 1964 appear in chart X.

[37] The German figures are from 12 *Anwaltsblatt* 115 (May 1962); Japanese figures are for 1964 and were furnished by Judge Tao of the Legal Training and Research Institute; and the United States figures are from "US Lawyer Population at New High of 296,069," 9 *American Bar News* 1 (April 15, 1964). For comparability, the 200,586 figure for the United States is obtained by excluding government lawyers (29,314 or 14.6 per cent), retired lawyers (12,024 or 6 per cent), and lawyers in private industry (26,492 or 13 per cent), because Japanese lawyers seldom accept a salary with the government or a private company, and seldom fully retire.

CHART X

COMPARISON OF LAWYERS PER CAPITA

	Population	Lawyers	Persons per lawyer
Japan	95,000,000	7,136	13,300
Germany	55,000,000	18,700	2,900
United States	190,000,000*	200,586	950

* World Almanac estimate for 1964.

We would expect a higher ratio of lawyers to population in the United States than in Japan, of course, because of a higher standard of living[38] and a higher degree of industrialization, but even so the ratio disclosed by the figures is rather startling.[39]

There are fourteen times more practicing lawyers per capita in the United States than in Japan and not quite five times as many in Germany as Japan. The Japanese lawyer is primarily, though not exclusively, concerned with dispute settlement, whereas among the two hundred thousand practicing lawyers in the United States, many engaged primarily in private practice do largely counseling and other office work; therefore, a statistical comparison of the United States and Japan is an extremely difficult one. Unfortunately, the data available prevent division of the United States bar into court work and office work. Nevertheless, even if only half of the average American lawyers' time is concerned primarily with dispute settlement, the per-capita ratio would still be seven or eight American lawyers to one Japanese.

This sort of comparison is further distorted by two other factors. First, we find that to a remarkable extent Japanese parties, even when they go to court, do so without employing a lawyer. In 1962 the statistics show that in 60.4 per cent of the cases concluded in the district courts[40] and in 89.2 per cent of those concluded in the summary courts,[41] one or both of the parties appeared personally without counsel. Secondly, there may be a significant difference in the case load which a Japanese lawyer can handle in a given period of time as compared with his American counterpart. We cannot do more than advert to this possibility because empirical data required for such a comparison are unavailable, but Japanese procedural

---

[38] In 1963 Japan had an annual per capita income of $509 as opposed to $2,310 for the United States and $965 for West Germany. *Nihon keizai shimbun* ("Japan Economic Journal") 5 (July 14, 1964).

[39] See Sawa Eizō 澤榮三, "Soshō no chien to hōsō jinkō" 訴訟の遅延と法曹人口 (Delay in lawsuits and jurist population), *Shōji hōmu kenkyū* (no. 94) 2–5 (1958), for other comparative figures.

[40] Saikō saibansho jimu sōkyoku minjikyoku 最高裁判所事務總局民事局, "Shōwa sanjū shichi nendo minji jiken no gaikyō" 昭和三十七年度民事事件の概況 (General view of civil cases in 1962), 15 *Hōsō jihō* 1789 (1963).

[41] *Id.* at 1798 (1963).

and clerical conditions are such that one might suppose that the Japanese lawyer could litigate fewer cases annually.[42]

The vast differences between the lawyers' roles in the United States and Japan, the tendency to litigate without lawyers, and the comparative case loads which lawyers can handle in the two countries are factors which require difficult adjustments in the use of statistical comparison of the lawyer populations. The net result of the adjustments, however, would probably be to reduce greatly the stark fourteen-to-one disparity produced by a simple comparison of the number of lawyers in private practice in the United States and Japan. Still, the difference is striking and doubtless reflects a vastly different attitude toward litigation in Japan and a corresponding heavy reliance on informal conciliation for the settlement of civil disputes.

Court proceedings filed per capita: A comparison of the number of lawsuits per capita filed in the United States and the lawsuits, plus code compromises and chōtei cases,[43] filed in Japan shows a much higher incidence of formal filings in the United States, supporting the inference that, perhaps, many Japanese disputes are settled informally. Again, however, the difference in the economic development and living standards of the two

---

[42] Other contributing factors which might tend to increase the annual work load per Japanese lawyer are (1) Japanese private settlements may be effected more expeditiously precisely because the piecemeal trial procedures are so slow and therefore the parties are impelled to settle the cases at an early stage, and (2) the Japanese lawyer does less preparation before trial, relying on the judge to clarify issues of law and fact during the intermittent trial hearings under the judge's power granted by CCP art. 127. Both the pre-war and postwar trends of the precedents interpreting CCP art. 127 are discussed in Muramatsu Toshio 村松俊夫, "Shakumei-ken" 釈明權 (Authority to clarify), in *Sōgō hanrei kenkyū sōsho, Minji soshōhō* (pt. 1) 98–161 (1958).

   CCP art. 127: In order to make clear (elucidate) the relations involved in the action, the presiding judge may question the parties on matters of fact and points of law, or may require them to furnish evidence.
   The associate judges may adopt the measures specified in the foregoing paragraph after informing the presiding judge (of their intention to do so).
   The parties may request the presiding judge to put any necessary questions.

[43] Compromise (CCP art. 356) and chōtei cases have been added to the Japanese figures on lawsuits because we are trying to show, by the dearth of all cases of whatever sort *filed* with the court, that a quantum of disputes presumably arise but never come to the attention of officialdom because they are settled informally. An interesting comparison of Japanese filings (summary and district courts) and German civil filings *(Amtsgericht* and *Landgericht)* was done in 1957 showing about thirteen times as many suits per capita in the German *Amtsgericht* than in the Japanese summary courts and 2.24 times as many suits in the German *Landgericht* as in the Japanese district court. See Mikazuki Akira 三ケ月章, and Nakata Junichi 中田淳一 (ed.), *Kēsu bukku minji soshōhō* ケースブック民事訴訟法 (Casebook on civil procedure law) 246 (1961).

countries might make one expect less litigation.[44] Such an inference is also based, of course, on an unverifiable premise that disputes occur in both societies in equal numbers per capita. We suspect, without attempting to demonstrate it at this point, that they actually occur less in Japan. Consequently, although the statistical comparisons in charts XI, XII, and XIII have some corroborative value to show that the Japanese rely less on the positive legal order and more on informal conciliation to settle their disputes, they also probably prove less than the striking ratio of filing statistics seems to indicate.

CHART XI

Civil Suits Filed in California (1959/1960 Fiscal Year)*

State courts		594,566
Justice courts	94,951	
Municipal courts	402,884	
Superior courts	96,154	
Supreme Court and		
district court of appeal	577	
Federal courts		2,965
Total		597,531

These California filings are a composite of state and federal statistics. See Judicial Council of California, *Eighteenth Biennial Report* 135–46 (1961) and *Annual Report of the Director of the Administrative Office of the United States Courts* 228 (1960). Both state and federal statistics are for the fiscal year June 30, 1959 to July 1, 1960.

* It is quite impractical, because of the diversity of statistical method in the various states as well as the scarcity of statistics in some states, to attempt to work out a figure showing filings in civil suits per capita in the United States generally. Instead, we have used California and New York as illustrative states because they have fairly adequate statistics and considerable foreign trade as well as urban areas somewhat comparable to Japan. We have used California to illustrate the way we have selected a body of civil filings comparable to those appearing in the Japanese statistics. The New York figures which follow in chart XII were selected by the same process except as indicated in the notes. Also it is important to note that because of the way the New York statistics are reported, in seeking statistics for "cases filed," we have had to use the figures for cases "noticed for trial" rather than those for "summons served." So there were actually more suits "filed" in New York by Japanese standards than appeared in the statistics. This fact also probably explains the difference between New York and California.

----

[44] A lack of tort suits in Japan, tending to reduce the total filings, arises not only from a tendency to settle tort cases by informal conciliation, which is the subject of our inquiry, but also from a lack of development of refined tort concepts in the substantive law and from a lack of claims-consciousness among the populace. However, this area of the law will probably develop rather noticeably in the near future. See the symposium entitled "Kōtsū jiko to kōtsū hōsei" 交通事故と交通法制 (Traffic accidents and traffic legal system), 34 *Hōritsu jihō* 4–35 (1962). Especially see page 20, where it shows that traffic violations have increased 700 per cent in the 1951–61 period. See also note 56 below.

CHART XII
STATISTICS ON CIVIL SUITS, COMPROMISES, AND CHŌTEI
FILED IN JAPAN (1959 CALENDAR YEAR)

Lawsuits district court	65,648*	
Lawsuits summary courts	90,718†	
Total lawsuits		156.366
Summary court court compromises		
(*wakai* under CCP art. 356)	18,434‡	
Chōtei district court	8,644§	
Chōtei summary court	62,095‖	
Total compromise and chōtei		89,173#
Total lawsuits, compromise, and		
chōtei at first instance		245,539

* 1 Saikō saibansho jimu sōkyoku, *Shihō tōkei nempō* 司法統計年報 (Annual report of judicial statistics) 102 (1960). Care has been used to exclude appeal statistics which are included as "cases" in many of the Japanese consolidated statistics on filings; also nearly all domestic relations and probate matters are not included because most of them are handled differently as to courts and procedures in Japan; and administrative cases have been excluded also, because they are statistically insignificant (736 in all Japan).

† *Id.* at 348.

‡ *Ibid.*

§ *Id.* at 322. Of these 8,644 disputes, 5,903 were apparently handled first as a lawsuit then transferred to the chōtei procedures by the judge's authority [*shokken*]; hence these 5,903 disputes may have been counted twice, first as a lawsuit, then as a chōtei proceeding, but whatever duplication there may be would lessen rather than exaggerate the point we are making by use of these figures. Also, after transfer these cases are apparently not counted in the statistics as a conciliation case until the conciliation is completed; and the delay in physically transferring the data from one place to the other explains the difference between the lawsuits settled by conciliation, hence withdrawn (*torisage*; 4,987, *id.* at 137), and the conciliations referred from the court (*shokken*; 5,903, *id.* at 322). Judge Yamaki of the Legal Training and Research Institute in Tokyo was helpful in clarifying this point.

‖ *Id.* at 433. At least 51,598 of these cases constitute disputes separate from those covered by the statistics on lawsuits, but 10,497 may be duplicate listings. See note § above.

There are also a few conciliation cases in the high courts of Japan, but they are statistically unimportant. E.g., 1 *Shihō tōkei nempō* 96 (1961) shows only 205 new cases filed in the eight high courts throughout Japan in 1960, and 203 of them were transferred to chōtei on motion of the court itself.

Even if we assume that there may be a lesser number of disputes occurring in Japanese society (because it is less developed economically, or more harmonious or collectivistic, or for whatever reason), still it seems unlikely that this difference would be anywhere near the fourteen-to-one ratio between California and Japan. If only Japanese lawsuits (chart XIII, no. 1) as such are considered, the ratio is twenty-three to one.

In summation, considering the extensive police conciliation; divorce by agreement; the present-day Japanese attitudes reflected by the above-mentioned personal questionnaires; the attitudes of Japanese businessmen toward modern arbitration and contractual relationships; the relative infrequency with which the Japanese populace resorts to the courts; and the small bar that this diminutive flow of litigation supports, we can fairly suppose that the social process of traditional informal conciliation centering around family and village dignitaries is still employed to considerable extent to settle civil disputes in Japan today.

CHART XIII

COMPARISON OF FILINGS PER CAPITA

Jurisdiction	Population	Filings	Persons per filing
1. Japan (lawsuits)	93,000,000	156,366	595
2. Japan (lawsuits plus chōtei and compromises)	93,000,000	245,539	378
3. California	15,700,000	597,531	26
4. New York	16,782,000	344,152*	48

* These New York statistics are or the fiscal year ending June, 1960. New York statistics are the most adequately classified of any kept to date in the United States, although even they do not have the refinement of the Japanese statistics. But, incoming cases are not counted when the case is filed and a summon is served, but only after the case is "noticed for trial." The jurisdictional tangle in New York makes it tedious to select a body of comparable civil cases from the whole system. See State of New York, *Sixth Annual Report of the Judicial Conference of the State of New York* 171 ff. (1961); and *Annual Report of the Director of the Administration Office of the U. S. Courts.* For jurisdictional problems, see State of New York, *Temporary Commission on the Courts* (1955). William A. Bulman, Jr., assistant counsel at the Judicial Conference of the State of New York, was kind enough to confirm that the figure appearing in the text is a generally accurate expression of the total number of civil cases "noticed for trial" throughout various courts in the state of New York in 1959–60.

FORMAL CONCILIATION IN THE PROCEDURAL LAW

In our survey of the scope and functioning of modern conciliation, we must finally consider the formal conciliatory practices which have been enacted as statutory procedures and in which the Japanese courts participate. Chart XII indicates that, broadly speaking, there are two methods of accomplishing conciliatory settlements at first instance through the facilities of either the summary or district courts: compromise and chōtei. Additionally, from the beginning, the Code of Civil Procedure has provided for Arbitration *(chūsai)* ;[45] but as we have noted, only in the sense that the parties agree to submit to arbitration is it voluntary, and the solution is imposed by the decision of a third party, the arbitrator, without reference to its acceptability to the parties. Such a solution is as foreign

[45] CCP arts. 786–805.

to the traditional Japanese preference for voluntary settlement as litigation itself, and the Japanese have consequently made little use of the arbitration procedures. We need not be concerned with arbitration further here.

Compromise and chōtei, as the heirs of Tokugawa trial practices, play prominent roles in the settlement of civil disputes which come within the cognizance of the courts both as to cases which the parties have commenced in the courts voluntarily[46] as chōtei proceedings, and as auxiliary procedures employed by the judges to handle cases that have already advanced to the status of a formal lawsuit. We will therefore consider the natures of chōtei and compromise and their relationship to each other, first procedurally, and second in terms of their respective percentages of the total number of disputes disposed of in the court system.

Procedural relationships between chōtei, compromise, and lawsuits: Since chōtei is to be examined in detail in the next chapter, we need only say here that as a practical matter it is a court procedure whereby lay committees, maintained in each court and nominally headed by a judge, meet with the parties and attempt to work out settlements mutually agreeable to the parties. Also if he deems it proper, the judge may act as sole conciliator[47] unless the parties specifically request a lay committee. It is important to note that there are two main types of chōtei in the modern system: conciliation of ordinary civil disputes in the 570 summary courts or 49 district courts under the Civil Conciliation Law (1951), and conciliation of family matters in the 49 family courts as provided in the Law for Adjustment of Domestic Affairs. Under the latter law preliminary conciliation is made a prerequisite to later court action in certain cases in the district courts. At this stage it is also important to know that the chōtei proceeding may be commenced in the summary or district courts in two ways: either by a complaint by one of the parties before a lawsuit is filed, or, during the pendency of a lawsuit, by motion of the court when it feels that conciliation is an appropriate way to settle the suits before it.[48] In such a transferred case, the court also has the power to refer the case to a chōtei com-

---

[46] Actually conciliation under the Civil Conciliation Laws of 1951 (or the Law for Adjustment of Domestic Matters of 1948) contains a substantial element of compulsion, in that the proceeding can be initiated by one party, and the other party (and also third parties, if summoned under Civil Conciliation Law art. 11 [2]) whether they wish to conciliate or not, must appear in response to a summons or incur a penalty (art. 34). See Hironaka, "Shimin kenri kakuho to minji saiban," 32 *Hōritsu jihō* 1002–8, 1003 (1960) where he classifies this procedure as Semi Compulsory Conciliation *(han kyōsei chōtei)*; also see discussion of this point in Nakagawa Tsuyoshi 中川毅, "Kyōsei chōtei no ikensei" 強制調停の違憲性 (Unconstitutionality of compulsory conciliation), 8 *Hanrei taimuzu* (no. 2) 164–67 (1957), where he even questions the constitutionality of "semi compulsory conciliation" of the Civil Conciliation Law, art. 17 (1951); and see Kaneko *et al., Jurisuto* (no. 20) 29 (1952).

[47] Civil Conciliation Law, art. 5 (1). See translation thereof in appendix III.

[48] Civil Conciliation Law, art. 20 (1).

mittee, or to act as sole conciliator himself,[49] unless the parties specifically request a committee.[50]

Under CCP Article 136 the judge also has a similar power to try to obtain a compromise between the parties at any stage of a trial. Consequently, like chōtei, there are two ways that compromise can be effected: during trial, and before a lawsuit has even been filed, for under CCP Article 356, a proceeding may be commenced on application to the summary court for a compromise as such before a suit is filed.[51] In addition such a proceeding may be converted to a lawsuit on application of both parties. Hence, both chōtei[52] and compromise[53] settlements may be commenced as such and later converted to a lawsuit or vice versa (chōtei, Article 20; compromise, CCP Article 136). One final point needs to be noted regarding the relationship between lawsuits, chōtei, and compromise: a compromise during the trial entered in the protocol has the effect

CHART XIV
Cases Settled by Compromise and Chōtei

A. Disputes settled by compromise:

1. Compromise (Dist. Ct. CCP art. 136)*	11,474	
2. Compromise (Sum. Ct. CCP art. 136)†	25,765	
3. Compromise (Sum. Ct. CCP art. 356)‡	18,493	
4. Total cases settled by compromise		55,732

B. Disputes settled by chōtei:

1. Conciliation (Both separate and transferred proceedings, Dist. Ct.) §	8,673	
2. Conciliation (Both separate and transferred proceedings, Sum. Ct.) ‖	62,366	
3. Conciliation (Family courts) #	45,111	
4. Total cases settled by conciliation.........................		116,150

C. Total disputes settled by compromise and conciliation............ 171,882

* 1 *Shihō tōkei nempō* 136–37 (1960); these "CCP 136" compromises took place during the trial of lawsuits pending in the district courts.
† *Id.* at 382–83; these "CCP 136" compromises took place during the trial of lawsuits pending in the summary courts.
‡ *Id.* at 348.
§ *Id.* at 322. Unfortunately, the disposition (as distinguished from the filing) statistics do not give a breakdown of chōtei cases filed separately or transferred from litigation.
‖ *Id.* at 433.
3 *Shihō tōkei nempō* 3 (1960).

[49] Civil Conciliation Law, arts. 5 (1) and 20.
[50] Civil Conciliation Law, arts. 5 (2) and 20.
[51] Note that Article 356 compromises are often merely contractual arrangements wherein the parties agree to obtain court action under Article 356 before a dispute ever arises so that execution may be obtained without going through the procedures of a lawsuit, in case of nonperformance later. See Yamakido, *op. cit. supra* note 18.
[52] Civil Conciliation Law, art. 19, and note, however, that it requires a separate filing of a complaint.
[53] CCP art. 356, and note it requires the application of both parties.

of a final judgment,[54] and a chōtei settlement recorded in the protocol becomes effective "like a compromise during trial" (i.e., it has the effect of a final judgment).[55]

Comparative work loads of chōtei, compromise, and litigation in the formal dispute-settlement procedures: Because of the overlap during trial of these conciliatory proceedings, it is necessary to look to the number of cases settled by each type of procedure, rather than the filings, in order to determine the number of disputes settled by each type and their relative work load in the entire dispute-settlement process. Fortunately, the Japanese statistics are reported in such a way as to make it possible, within limits, to make such determinations, as shown in charts XIV and XV for cases disposed of in the courts of first instance in 1959.

CHART XV

CASES SETTLED BY LAWSUIT

1. Litigation in district courts*

a. Judgments *(hanketsu)*	27,059	
b. Rulings *(kettei)*	292	
c. Orders *(meirei)*	1,000	
d. Abandonment of claims *(hōki)*	30	
e. Acknowledgment of claims *(nindaku)*	556	
f. Withdrawal *(torisage)*, excluding cases withdrawn for chōtei	19,166	
Total district courts..............................		48,103

2. Family court decision after conciliation .... 4,055†

3. Litigation in summary courts‡

a. Judgments	32,163	
b. Rulings	981	
c. Orders	2,362	
d. Abandonment of claims	18	
e. Acknowledgment of claims	454	
f. Withdrawal, excluding cases withdrawn for chōtei	21,809	
Total summary courts.............................		57,787

Total disputes settled by litigation 109,945
Total disputes settled by court compromise and chōtei........... 171,882
Total disputes settled in the courts 281,827

* 1 *Shihō tōkei nempō* 136–37 (1960).

† 3 *Shihō tōkei nempō* 44 (1960), but note that these family court dispositions in cases that have been conciliated first are premised upon the fact that the parties have ceased to dispute the points covered therein. Hence inclusion of this figure is arguable, since the disposition is rather similar to an agreed settlement. See Law for Adjustment of Domestic Affairs, art. 23, but by including these cases the ratio of conciliation is weakened rather than exaggerated.

‡ *Id.* at 384–85 (1960).

[54] CCP art. 203.
[55] Civil Conciliation Law, art. 16.

The statistics in charts XIV and XV cast some light on the relative performance of lawsuits as compared with the conciliatory practices of one sort or another in the total dispute-settlement process. The ratio is about 38.9 per cent for lawsuits as such and 61.1 per cent for chōtei plus court compromises after filing.

Two points must be noted in the comparison, however, because they bear upon the degree of overlap between Japanese lawsuits and these conciliatory practices and are also related to the normal settlement tendencies during the pendency of an action, as we know them in the United States. First, roughly 40 per cent of the dispositions credited to litigation (see chart XV, items 1f plus 3f) were withdrawals by the parties for undisclosed reasons. But it is quite possible, indeed probable, that in many cases the parties had concluded a settlement by informal conciliation, as opposed to chōtei. Perhaps if we knew the facts behind these withdrawals, we would find that these cases should be credited to the informal conciliatory practices subsisting in society apart from the positive legal order, as described at the beginning of this chapter.

Second, roughly 55 per cent of the settlements credited to the combined performances of compromise and chōtei had already been filed by the parties as lawsuits in one of the summary or district courts. This 55 per cent probably tells us as much about judicial pressure to obtain private settlements as it does about the inclination of Japanese litigants to conciliate. Perhaps the pretrial conferences may approximate this sort of result in our system. We shall have more to say about both of these points in evaluating the conciliatory practices of Japan in chapter X. It may be that both of the above phenomena—the 40 per cent of the Japanese lawsuits settled by withdrawal and the 55 per cent of the conciliatory settlements which originated as lawsuits—are functionally a part of the normal settlement ratio to be expected in the course of processing an average work load of lawsuits through the courts of any jurisdiction.[56]

---

[56] New York courts only dispose of about 25 per cent of the filed cases on the merits; the other 75 per cent are settled privately during pendency. See New York, *Sixth Annual Report* (table 12) 214–15 (1961). Comparison of Japanese and New York settlement after filing is difficult. Yet New York is the only large state that publishes statistics which are refined enough to show at what stage and precisely how disposition of cases takes place, and unfortunately the New York Supreme Court, with a reputation for a severe policy favoring settlement, is not typical of the United States practice.

The procedural differences between the United States' so-called concentrated trial and the Japanese multiple-hearing trial method also make comparison of dispositions which must be correlated with various procedural phases unusually complex. Also the types of cases forming the grist of the judicial mill are different and some types, such as personal injury claims, are numerous in the United States state courts and are more susceptible of negotiated settlement perhaps. For example, personal injury suits in the New York Supreme Court are about 62 per cent of the total work load compared to about 4 per cent for Japan. See Franklin, Chanin, and Mark, "Accidents, Money and the Law: A

Considering all of the Japanese procedures (lawsuits, court compromise, and chōtei) available in the positive law as separate methods for the settlement of civil disputes, we find then that of a total of 281,827 cases settled by the courts, only 38.9 per cent (109,945) were settled by judgments or orders in a lawsuit as such, and 61.1 per cent (171,882) were settled by conciliatory proceedings commenced separately or invoked after filing a lawsuit. And about 40 per cent of the lawsuits as such were simply withdrawn, probably after conclusion of a settlement by informal conciliation in many instances.

A certain portion of the cases formally conciliated or compromised after filing (93,815), however, should doubtless be ascribed to the normal settlement probabilities during the course of litigation; at the same time the small number of Japanese filings would give rise to the inference that the proceedings finally filed would probably involve those disputes where amicable agreement had proved impossible, and that many could not be settled without considerable pressure from the judges to induce the parties to compromise or conciliate further.

SUMMARY

To gain an over-all perspective of the role of modern conciliation, we have dealt in some detail with the several aspects of present-day Japanese conciliatory practices and their relationship to the litigation process. It remains now to summarize the findings. The initial basic impression that emerges from the statistics on Japanese lawyers and lawsuits is that the Japanese courts are still relatively little used by the populace in litigation for the positive vindication of substantive rights conferred by the law. The figures in chart XIII show that including chōtei and code compromises in the Japanese figures there are still fourteen times as many proceedings per capita filed in the state of California as there are in Japan and about eight times as many cases per capita noticed for trial in New York as there are filed in Japan. Making all allowances for the difficulties of comparison, this differential remains impressive; it suggests by negative inference, supported by the other evidence noted, that many of Japan's civil disputes are still settled by traditional informal conciliation practices which never reach the courts. In addition we find that 61.1 per cent of the adversary cases that are filed in the courts are settled by chōtei or compromise, either by separate proceeding or in the course of a lawsuit; and an addi-

---

Study of the Economics of Personal Injury Litigation," 61 *Col. L. R.* 1–39 (1961). The Japanese "tort" claims are found in 1 *Shihō tōkei nempō* 136 (district court) and 382 (summary court) (1960), but the Japanese classification there is probably more inclusive than "personal injury" in the New York classification.

tional 40 per cent, of the remaining 38.9 per cent credited to court disposition by judgment or other decision, are withdrawn, with the strong probability that many of them were also settled privately.

CHAPTER IX

Modern Statutory Conciliation

WE HAVE seen that the Japanese penchant for handling civil disputes by conciliatory procedures did not expire with the Tokugawa Shogunate in 1868, nor was it legislated out of existence by enactment of the Code of Civil Procedure in 1890. Rather, as shown by the statistics reviewed in chapter VIII, it is clear that the regular trial procedures are relatively little used, and instead conciliatory practices of one sort or another *(jidan, wakai,* or *chōtei*—for family and civil cases) are still effective to settle the majority of civil disputes in Japan today. In this chapter we will review briefly the statutory development of the most elaborate and perhaps the most important of the modern conciliatory procedures, chōtei. In addition we will describe its practical functioning and review some of the recent criticism addressed to its social performance as a method of settling disputes.

Our attention will be concentrated hereafter on the proceedings under the Civil Conciliation Law (1951), but it must be remembered that the Law for Adjustment of Domestic Affairs (1948) provides (Articles 17 and 18)[1] that certain types of adversary family matters, including divorce (for limited exceptions see Article 18 [2]), will initially be referred to the special family court for conciliation, and only after conciliation has failed may they be prosecuted in the regular courts as a lawsuit. It should be remembered that in 1961 there were 42,485[2] conciliation cases filed in the family

---

[1] *Kaji shimpanhō* in *Roppō zensho* (1964); English translation *EHS* Vol. II. See Akiyama Kazuo 明山和夫, "Kaji chōtei seido kanken" 家事調停制度管見 (Views on the system of family conciliation), *Kēsu kenkyū* (no. 80) 31–41 (1963); and Yano Teruo 矢野照男, "Kaji chōtei to pāsonaritī rikai o meguru shomondai—sono shinriteki apurōchi" (shiryō) 家事調停とパーソナリティー理解をめぐる諸問題—その心理的アプローチ—資料 (Some problems centering around family conciliation and comprehension of personality—psychological approach to them [materials]), *Chōtei kiyō* (no. 5) 97–107 (1964); Kurihara Yukio 栗原幸男, "Rikon chōtei jiken tōjisha ni taisuru tankikan no kaunseringu (Short-term counseling) no kokoromi" 離婚調停事件当事者に対する短期間のカウンセリングの試み—ケース研究 (An attempt to do short-term counseling for persons concerned in a conciliation divorce case—case study), *Chōtei kiyō* (no. 5) 61–69 (1964).

[2] 3 *Shihō tōkei nempō (Kaji-hen)* 16 (1963).

courts throughout Japan, and 42,584 cases (some of which were pending from prior years) were successfully settled or withdrawn.[3] Hence, domestic relations conciliation procedures are a substantial part of the total chōtei system under the post-World War II statutes.

DEVELOPMENT OF STATUTORY CONCILIATION

In summarizing the growth of modern conciliation,[4] the period after the restoration (1868–1961) can be divided into four phases: (1) the period between the Meiji restoration and the promulgation of the new Code of Civil Procedure (1868–90); (2) the period up to the first special Law of Conciliation (1890–1922); (3) the period ending with the codification of the various special laws into a general Civil Conciliation Law (1922–51); and (4) the decade of practical experience under the new law (1951–61).

First period (1868–90): Although these years were generally characterized by a flux of forms in the court system and administrative structure, the carry-over of Tokugawa practices into the Meiji society was direct and inevitable.[5] As mentioned in chapter VIII, perhaps the chief immediate motivation for the sweeping, formal changes in the Japanese law and courts was the desire to construct a legal system acceptable to modern western standards in order to induce the western powers to relinquish their extraterritoriality granted by the treaties in 1858. After an initial reactionary reversion to ancient *Ritsuryō* (702 A.D. and 718 A.D.) administrative models,[6] the first reform efforts were expended in establishing courts,[7] appeals, a bar association, and procedures mainly along the lines

[3] *Ibid.*

[4] For the history of chōtei, see Yamazaki Tasuku, *Nihon chōtei seido no rekishi* (1957), which gives details and source materials for the Tokugawa and Meiji chōtei practices; and see Saikō saibansho jimu sōkyoku 最高裁判所事務總局, *Wagakuni ni okeru chōtei no enkaku* わが国における調停の沿革 (Development of the conciliation system in our country) (undated, but about 1951), which, with respect, we suggest overemphasizes foreign analogies and slights the Tokugawa origins of Japanese conciliatory tendencies; Koyama Noboru 小山昇, *Minji chōteihō gaisetsu* 民事調停法概説 (General survey of civil conciliation law) 1–45 (1954) has one of the best short histories of the development of chōtei legislation after 1922.

[5] Ishii Ryōsuke, *Japanese Legislation in the Meiji Era* 298–306 (1958).

[6] Nakagawa Zennosuke 中川善之助, and Miyazawa Toshiyoshi 宮澤俊義, *Hōritsushi* 法律史 (History of law) 5–15 in 5 *Gendai Nihon bummeishi* 現代日本文明史 (History of contemporary Japanese civilization) (1944); Suzuki Yasuzō 鈴木安藏, *Hōritsushi* 法律史 (History of law) (1960).

[7] See Osatake Takeshi 尾佐竹猛, "Shihōken no dokuritsu" 司法權の独立 (Independence of the judicial power), 1 *Rekishigaku kenkyū* 321–27 (1934); Osatake Takeshi, *Konan jiken* 湖南事件 (Southern lake incident) (1951), for an account and interpretation of the judicial importance of the incident wherein the Russian Crown Prince (later Nicholas II) was wounded by a policeman near Lake Biwa (1891). The court trying the offender was subjected to some executive pressures, but stood its ground. Dandō Shigemitsu 團藤重光, "Shihō seido no kakuritsu" 司法制度の確立 (Establishing the judicial system), 58 *Kokka gakkai zasshi* 148–83 (1944); also *Nihon kindaihō hattatsushi*, ed. Ukai Nobushige *et al.*, particularly see Vols. 2 (1958) and 6 (1959).

of French institutions initially, through the influence of Boissonade.[8] In the 1880's, however, with the assistance of the German advisers residing in Tokyo, particularly Otto Rudorff (courts), and Mosse and Techow (procedure), the German influence became very strong, and ultimately it was Techow's much revised draft of the Code of Civil Procedure, based largely on the then new German code of 1877, which prevailed instead of Boissonade's draft based on the French code.[9] The new code was promulgated in revised form in 1890 and enforced in 1891.

Of specific concern here is the appearance in the formal procedural law of a type of conciliation known as Encouraging Settlement *(kankai)*. Probably the first mention of the procedure for encouraging settlement in the decrees of the Ministry of Justice was in 1875,[10] although the term was used as early as 1871 in a set of local rules for settling disputes.[11] Also, of course, informal conciliation may be assumed to have subsisted throughout this period. In civil cases after 1876, the regulations were interpreted to make procedures to encourage settlement obligatory as a first step in civil dispute resolution in much the same way that conciliation is made a prerequisite to most adversary divorce suits today under the Law for Adjustment of Domestic Affairs (1948). In 1884 special officials [*kankai kakari*] were appointed to supervise the settlement negotiations. The pattern of these proceedings was, as one might expect, similar to the Tokugawa practice in the Shogunate courts.[12]

An 1875 ordinance (Dajōkan Ordinance 108, Article 3) is important to justify the customary practices formally. It provided that in the absence of law to govern a civil case, custom would be applied, and in the absence

---

[8] Shihōshō 司法省, *Shihō enkakushi* 司法沿革誌 (History of the development of the judiciary) 2–123 (1939); Maki Kenji 牧健二, "Meiji hachinen minji saiban no gensoku" 明治八年民事裁判の原則 (General principles of civil litigation of 1875), 17 *Hōgaku ronsō* 349–62 (1927); Onogi Tsune 小野木常, "Meiji shoki no minji soshō" 明治初期の民事訴訟 (Civil procedure in the first part of the Meiji period), 49 *Hōgaku ronsō* 169, 313, 432, 605, and 659 (1943).

[9] Ishii, *Japanese Legislation in the Meiji Era* 493–501 (1958); and in Japanese, 2 *Meiji bunkashi (hōseihen)* 416–17; Kaneko Hajime 兼子一, "Minji soshōhō no seitei—tehyō no sōan o chūshin to shite" 民事訴訟法の制定—テヒョウの草案を中心として (Establishing the Code of Civil Procedure—centered around Techow's draft), in *Tokyo daigaku gakujitsu taikan* 223–34 (1942).

[10] Ishii, *Japanese Legislation in the Meiji Era* 308 and 492 (1958); cf. Nakagawa and Miyazawa, *Hōritsushi* 17 (separate paging for part on Judiciary [Shihō] by Nakagawa); Maki Kenji, "Meiji shonen ni okeru minji saiban no kannen" 明治初年に於ける民事裁判の觀念 (The concept of civil litigation in the first years of Meiji) 12 *Shirin* 85–93 (1927).

[11] For the text, see Yamazaki, *Nihon chōtei seido no rekishi* 68 (1957).

[12] Ishii, *Japanese Legislation in the Meiji Era* 492 (1958); and Yamazaki, *Nihon chōtei seido no rekishi* 94–95 (1957). Note that Rudorff, who advised the Japanese government on the judicial institutions, spent considerable time studying Tokugawa law and institutions. Rudorff, "Tokugawa-gesetz-sammlung," 5 *Mittheilungen der deutschen Gesellschaft für natur- und-völkerkunde Ostasiens in Tokio* (Supp.) (1889).

of custom, Common Reason *(jōri)* should govern the decision.[13] The system for encouraging settlement was abolished with the enforcement of the Code of Civil Procedure in 1891, and instead provisions for compromise (Article 221 of the 1890 code, similar to Article 136 of the present law) and arbitration (Articles 786–805, present law) were included in the Code of Civil Procedure.

Second period (1889–1922): This is the lean period for conciliation in the formal law, although pioneering chōtei systems were established in several Japanese colonies, including Taiwan (1904) and Korea (1910). Also in 1911, Takagi Masutarō introduced an important bill in the Twenty-seventh Diet to establish a chōtei system. The bill did not get through the Diet, but as a precedent it is important, because the bill itself[14] and Takagi's statement in support of it[15] make it clear that he had drawn upon the colonial practices as well as the Edo tradition in devising his proposal. This bill is therefore an important link in the growth of chōtei, particularly since it was in turn consulted in the drafting of the first of the special chōtei laws (1922).

As Takayanagi Kenzō has emphasized,[16] Japanese lawyers and jurists clearly forsook tradition and reality throughout this period in their zest for German exegesis of the new codes. In many ways the imported procedural codes, like the codified substantive law, established norms which sought to transform Japanese society, but were not supported initially by Japanese social practices. Indeed, a need for reform in the Code of Civil Procedure was felt in some quarters[17] almost as soon as it was enforced, but a revised code was not promulgated until 1926. In the meantime social practices regarding the resolution of civil disputes changed gradually, and two or three decades of scholarly analysis of the codes was a necessary first step in the process of understanding and adapting them to the Japanese milieu. Needless to say, considering the codes generally, the consumers of the law—the people themselves—were still unable to follow the scholars in their flights of exegetical refinement during this period of study, but with the passage of time the codes have had a considerable effect in gradually changing the Japanese attitudes and social practices regarding dispute resolution, particularly in the period since 1945.

Third period (1922–51): This era saw the emergence of chōtei in Japan

---

[13] Ishii, *id.* at 307; also Ishii, 2 *Meiji bunkashi (hōseihen)* 422 for the Japanese text.

[14] Miyazaki, *Nihon chōtei seido no rekishi* 112–18 (1957).

[15] *Id.* at 119–20.

[16] Takayanagi Kenzō, *Reception and Influence of Occidental Legal Ideas in Japan*, in series, *Western Influence in Modern Japan* 14 (1929).

[17] For example, Takagi (see notes 14 and 15 above); also see Katō Masaharu 加藤正治, *Kaisei minji soshōhō gaisetsu* 改正民事訴訟法概説 (General survey of the revised code of civil procedure) (1937).

proper in a statutory form considerably different in detail from the Edo practice. But no analysis of the role of conciliation procedures within the framework of modern constitutionalism can ignore the consistency of chōtei theory and function with the collectivistic Tokugawa practice,[18] especially in the war years (1941–45). It is interesting from the standpoint of legal development to note, for example, that the revival of chōtei procedures by special enactments in the procedural law took place in a piecemeal fashion, beginning in 1922 with the Land-Lease and House-Lease Conciliation Law. Most of these special laws were addressed to problems arising out of aggravated inconsistencies between the substantive law of the codes and the subsisting, traditional "law" and practices. We are told that the old landlord and tenant relationships particularly were at odds with the substantive property law of the Civil Code (1898) based on concepts of freedom of contract and free alienability. These variances were not raised to the level of social or political problems until modern urban mobility developed with Japanese industrialization, especially in the 1920's.

Traditionally, changes of Japanese residences were relatively few, and house owners, house tenants, or farm tenants had rather fixed rights[19] to

---

[18] Kobayakawa Kingo, *Kenkyū* 87 (1957); or Kobayakawa, "Kinsei minji saiban no gainen to tokushitsu," 45 *Hōgaku ronsō* 632 (1941) for the traditional and collectivistic meaning of chōtei, and its relation to the family system.

We do not intend to assert that modern statutory chōtei dating from 1922 is not a significant step in the institutionalization of conciliation in the formal law. In fact, by lending the facilities and power of the courts to the conciliation process, conciliation has been recognized as a dispute-settlement procedure in the positive-law order. However, we suggest here that this legislation must be understood as largely a codification of the long standing social tradition of conciliation among the populace rather than a new conception or a system based primarily on foreign analogies. Some confusion may arise from the references to conciliation systems found in North Dakota and elsewhere in the United States and in Germany, Denmark, Norway, and other European countries, which in fact seem to have had little influence in the legislative consideration of the Japanese statutes. The early work of Ikeda Torajirō 池田寅二郎, *Chūsai to chōtei* 仲裁と調停 (Arbitration and conciliation) (1932) followed by Saikō saibansho jimu sōkyoku, *Wagakuni ni okeru chōtei seido no enkaku* (undated, about 1951) and Ōhashi Seiichi 大橋誠一, *Ōbei no chōtei seido* 欧米の調停制度 (The conciliation systems of Europe and America) (1957) may have tended to overemphasize the legislative innovation of statutory chōtei as well as possible foreign influences. In fact, the conciliation commissioners of North Dakota and Denmark were abolished in 1943 and 1952 respectively. See North Dakota 1943 *Session Laws*, Chapter 228, and Danish Law No. 220, June 7, 1952. Yamazaki Tasuku, *Nihon chōtei seido no rekishi* (1957) has placed proper emphasis on the continuity of traditional conciliation in the growth of the modern Japanese system.

[19] See Ishii, *Nihon hōseishi gaisetsu* 512–23 (1960) for descriptive material on the law of land ownership and tenure in Tokugawa times, and note that it was illegal to transfer rice lands or to subdivide them beyond a minimal holding prescribed by the law, but in fact fictional foreclosure devices were fairly common to effect transfer. These traditional relationships between landlord and tenant dating from the Edo period are sometimes referred to as "feudal," but unless "feudal" is understood loosely to mean everything of Tokugawa origin, the term is misleading (see chapter II). Hence we prefer to refer to

remain in their residences or on the lands which they cultivated, as long
as they paid their rents and taxes. With the quickening of industrialization
and urbanization, however, especially during and after World War I, the
provisions of the Civil Code, which distinguished between the landowner's
right and the tenant's or houseowner's right and furthermore provided
that these relationships were governed by freedom of contract, was applied
to situations where a later transferee of land did not recognize a tenant's
customary "rights." The Civil Code was also applied to situations where
a contract term expired, evicting a tenant whose connection with the land
predated the Code. Also, if the term were indefinite, the land or house-
owner could terminate the tenant's rights after a fixed period of notice
(Civil Code 617). In Tokyo, especially after the great earthquake of 1923,
this type of case was common because of the destruction and shortage of
housing and because of the disputes arising over attempts by tenants to
rebuild. The problem finally reached political proportions when tenants
organized into pressure groups and asserted the impropriety of the Civil
Code provisions, for often the Civil Code had been little understood by
these tenants, whose relationship to the land or housing in question either
antedated the Code, even though it had then been effective for some thirty
years, or had been established later in accordance with the older customs
and in ignorance of the changes wrought by the Civil Code.

Although the foregoing is only a brief summary of the background of
the Land-Lease and House-Lease Conciliation Law (1922), it serves to
illustrate the broader problem of the occasional friction between Edo
traditions and the new substantive law of the Codes, and particularly the
role of conciliation as a social and political mediator in the procedural law,
and, in a sense, as a temporary substitute for legislative reform in the
substantive law. Significantly, in the discussions leading up to the enactment of the Land-Lease and House-Lease Conciliation Law, the government did not emphasize the inadequacy of the substantive law, but rather
pointed out that chōtei, leading to a harmonious solution, was more suitable to the Japanese personality and tradition, and that litigation, which
seeks to vindicate rights and individualism, was an inappropriate method
for settling this sort of dispute in the Japanese context.[20]

After the Land-Lease and House-Lease Conciliation Law was enacted,
the Conciliation Law for Tenants (1924), the Conciliation Law for Commercial Matters (1926), the Temporary Law for Conciliation of Monetary
Obligations (1932)—all three statutes were also, in a sense, reform mecha-

---

these relationships as simply traditional in the sense that they predate the reception of
code law, and leave the peculiar nature of the Tokugawa institutions to speak for
themselves.

[20] Koyama Noboru, *Minji chōteihō gaisetsu* 5–6 (1954).

nisms—the Conciliation Law for Personal Affairs (1939), the Mining Industries Law, Articles 126–64 (1939, revised 1950), and the Special Law for Wartime Civil Matters, Articles 14–19 (1942) were all passed in succession, and together they constitute the growth of chōtei by special statutes for special types of subject matter between World War I and World War II.[21]

In several of these chōtei laws, there was a significant provision permitting the court to issue an order dispositive of the dispute, even though chōtei between the parties had failed. This feature, referred to as Substitution of Trial for Conciliation *(chōtei ni kawaru saiban)*,[22] has raised the important constitutional question as to whether such a disposition does not in fact deprive the parties of a judicial trial guaranteed by Article 32 of the new Japanese constitution. It has therefore received some well-deserved attention by the Supreme Court in recent years in cases carried over from the period when the old chōtei laws were still operative. We will reserve comment on the important litigation concerning this constitutional point until a more adequate description of the operation of the chōtei system has been presented.

Finally, these special laws were codified into two general codes of significance in the present system of adjudication. The first was the Law for Adjustment of Domestic Affairs (1948),[23] which replaced the Conciliation Law for Personal Affairs (1939) and made chōtei a prerequisite of most lawsuits of an adversary nature regarding family relations. Second, even as early as 1940 the Japanese bar association had recommended including a general code for chōtei as a chapter of the Code of Civil Procedure. Nothing came of this effort, and finally in 1951 the Civil Conciliation Law[24] was enacted as a separate statute outside of the Code. This new

[21] Miyazaki, *Chōteihō no riron to jissai* (1942) includes texts of all of these laws except the Special Law for Wartime Civil Matters and the 1950 amendments to the mining law, for which see Saikō saibansho jimu sōkyoku minjikyoku 最高裁判所事務總局民事局 (ed.), *Chōtei kankei hōkishū* 調停關係法規集 (A collection of regulations concerning conciliation) 69 (1953). See Saikō saibansho jimusōkyoku, *Wagakuni ni okeru chōtei seido no enkaku* 95–101 (1951) for a detailed chronological list of the laws and regulations established on conciliation from 1920 onward.

[22] Miyazaki Sumio, *Chōtei no riron to jissai* 54–61 (1942).

[23] *Kaji shimpan hō* in *Roppō zensho* 1217 (1962); see the collection of articles entitled "Kaji chōtei no kagakuka" 家事調停の科學化 (Rendering family conciliation more scientific), 30 *Hōritsu jihō* (no. 334) 4–77 (1958); and Ichikawa Shirō 市川四郎, *Kaji shimpanhō gaisetsu* 家事審判法概説 (General survey of the law for settling family affairs) (1954) for a treatment of family conciliation. Also Terajima Yoshimatsu 寺島由松, *Kaji chōtei kaisetsu* 家事調停解説 (Explanation of conciliation of family affairs) (1952). There is also a periodical devoted to this practice and emphasizing case studies: *Kēsu kenkyū*, published by the Katei Jiken Kenkyūkai 家庭事件研究會.

[24] *Minji chōteihō* in *Roppō zensho* (1964); or *Chōtei kankei hōkishū* 3 (1953); for discussions and reports in the Diet at the time the law was enacted, see *Daijukkai kokkai sangiin kaigiroku* 第十回國會參議院會議録 (Records of the meetings of the House of Councillors

Civil Conciliation Law repealed the other piecemeal laws on civil chōtei and provided for voluntary chōtei proceedings in all civil matters except domestic relations and labor disputes. Labor conciliation, like chōtei for domestic relations, has its own machinery and special features for settling labor disputes. For example, in labor conciliation judges do not participate, and the result does not have the effect of a "compromise during trial."

CHART XVI

TRENDS IN FILING STATISTICS: LAWSUITS AND CHŌTEI (1948–61)

Year	Lawsuits*	Chōtei	Family Chōtei	Percentage of Lawsuits to Total Filing
1948	42,294	42,216	32,384	36%
1949	50,255	44,919	38,229	38%
1950	74,215	56,300	41,412	43%
1951	87,435	58,794	37,920	47%
1952	97,066	60,661	38,186	49%
1953	110,815	65,766	38,351	52%
1954	145,573	54,837	40,023	61%
1955	158,485	78,955	43,109	56%
1956	162,232	76,790	42,711	57%
1957	167,914	73,992	43,358	59%
1958	179,599	76,590	45,900	59%
1959	175,439	70,929	46,038	60%
1960	166,518	64,936	43,325	60%
1961	153,398	58,049	42,485	60%
1962	150,220	55,172	43,587	60%

* These figures for lawsuits include appeals filed in the courts for review of lower court decisions. In chapter VIII we subtracted the appeals out, but for purposes of following the general trend it is unimportant to do so, since the ratio of appeals is fairly constant at roughly 15 per cent of all summary court judgments appealed to the district courts and 32 per cent of district court judgments appealed to the high courts. See 1 *Shihō tōkei nempō* xxiii (1960).

---

of the Tenth Diet) 1046–48 (1951); *Daijukkai kokkai shūgiin kaigiroku* 第十回國會衆議院會議録 (Records of the meetings of the House of Representatives of the Tenth Diet) 718–21 (also *furoku* 附録 86–87) (1951). There was practically no recorded discussion in the main meeting of the Diet when this law was passed, hence the committee records are more interesting; 1 *Daijū kokkai shūgiin iinkai kaigiroku* 第十國會衆議院委員會會議録 (Reports of the committee meetings of the House of Representatives of the Tenth Diet) (1951); *Hōmu iinkaigiroku* 法務委員會議録 (no. 20) 3–7 (May 9, 1951); 2 *Daijū kokkai sangiin iinkai kaigiroku* 第十國會參議院委員會會議録 (Records of committee meetings of the House of Councillors of the Tenth Diet), *Sangiin hōmu iinkai kaigiroku* (no. 17) 1–6 (May 22, 1951); (no. 18) 9–15 (May 24, 1951). There are English translations of the main Diet discussions on this law, but no English translation of the more important committee discussion. See the Tenth Session of the National Diet, *The Official Gazette Extra* 4 (June 1, 1951); *The Official Gazette Extra* 8–9 (May 18, 1951) (a copy is located on the fourth floor of the Diet Building).

Fourth period (1951–61): More than ten years have passed since the promulgation of the Japanese constitution in 1948 and the end of the allied occupation of Japan in 1952. This means that the first decade of experience under the codified Civil Conciliation Law (1951) and the Law for Adjustment of Domestic Affairs (1948) has coincided roughly with Japanese experience with independent government limited by law and judicial supremacy. During this period, especially since 1956, several Japanese legal scholars as well as the Supreme Court judges have had an opportunity to review the role of chōtei in a democratic legal order, and we will revert to these problems later. Here we will only indicate the trend in the statistics[25] on chōtei proceedings filed under the new laws as compared to lawsuits filed in the same courts.

From the figures in chart XVI it can be seen that the total filings of both lawsuits and combined (civil and family) chōtei proceedings have been declining somewhat since 1958, and that the ratio of lawsuits has increased steadily since 1948. This trend bears watching in the future for it may mean that the Japanese populace is growing relatively more accustomed to formal litigation in the postwar period.

Starting with conciliation as the core of the whole adjudication system in the Tokugawa period, it is possible to trace the persistence of private settlement techniques through the period of Meiji conciliation *(kankai,* 1872–90) and the lean period of compromise and arbitration (1890–1922), finally to the period of modern chōtei in the special statutes (1922–51) and the last decade of experience under the Civil Conciliation Law (1951–61). Also, the continuous and extensive uses of various focal points of authority in the community to settle disputes locally and privately, by informal conciliation quite apart from the formal law or the modern court system and the extensive use of compromise, are important parts of the story (chapter VIII).

It is interesting to note the conservative role of this new statutory chōtei as envisaged by the legislators and jurists when the laws were under legislative consideration. During this period one of the clearest statements of the primary importance of chōtei for preserving the Japanese tradition is found in the report of the Special Investigation Commission on Legal Institutions *(hōsei shingikai),* appointed in 1919 to consider revisions of the substantive law of the Civil Code on family relations and succession. In its report (June, 1922) the commission notes that before the substantive law could be revised, procedures for settling family disputes should be revised to avoid lawsuits inappropriate to the tradition:

---

[25] 1 *Shihō tōkei nempō* 2 (1962).

...as the study progressed as to the revisions which should be made in the various parts of the Civil Code, especially the chapters on relatives and succession, in order to maintain the Virtuous Ways and Beautiful Traditions *(jumpū bizoku)* of our country, it was recognized that to cleave to the type of lawsuit such as is used in the present system for family disputes would not preserve the virtuous ways and beautiful tradition from the past, but rather it was recognized as extremely important to establish a special system to solve them amicably with compassion and based on morality. We recognized that the decision on this system had an integral relationship to our main problem, the revision of the provisions of the Civil Code. In fact, it is a problem which must be solved first.[26]

Although the Conciliation Law for Personal Affairs was not enacted by the Diet until 1939, the same sort of rationale was also found in the discussion there.

But it is in the works of certain jurists under the strain of the war period —for example, Yasuda Mikita, Onogi Tsune, and Miyazaki Sumio—that the new role of chōtei is spelled out in sufficient detail to show that, unless properly limited to an auxiliary role, chōtei can serve as a ready handmaiden for authoritarian, official discretion. In varying degrees these authors abandoned the sounder treatment of this point by earlier writers, such as Hozumi Shigetō, Miyake Shōtarō, Ikeda Torajirō, Nakajima Kōdō, and Kaneko Hajime.[27]

Yasuda's position even had a certain affinity to Nazi ideas on the administration of justice, as can be seen from his theory, propounded in 1933, to the effect that chōtei proceedings should be based on "the Sense of Justice in the New Society" *(shinshakai no seigikan)*:

> Conciliation must be thought of as conducting an equitable *(kōhei)* trial in "reality" according to equity, that is the new sense of justice based on the standards of society, instead of a trial by proper law based on norms fixed by an existent legal order in turn based on rules; that is, on ideas of liberalism.[28]

---

[26] Saikō saibansho jimu sōkyoku, *Wagakuni ni okeru chōtei seido no enkaku* 45–46 (1951).

[27] Hozumi Shigetō 穂積重遠, "Chōteihō" 調停法 (Civil conciliation law), in 38 *Gendai hōgaku zenshū* 現代法學全集 (Complete collection on jurisprudence) 289 (1931); Miyake Shotarō 三宅正太郎, "Chōteihō," in 12 *Shinhōgaku zenshū* 26 (1937); Ikeda Torajirō, *Chūsai to chōtei* 3 (1932); Nakajima Kōdō 中島弘道, "Chōtei jōkō to kore ni kansuru ichikōsatsu" 調停條項とこれに關する一考察 (Conciliation provisions and a view concerning them), 12 *Hōritsu jihō* 2 (1940); Kaneko Hajime, *Minji soshōhō gairon* 民事訴訟法概論 (General discussion of the law of civil procedure).

[28] Yasuda Mikitō 安田幹太, "Shihō tenka no dankai to shite no chōtei" 私法轉化の段階としての調停 (Conciliation as a step in transforming the private law), 51 *Hōgaku kyōkai zasshi* 1253 (1933). Also see *id.* at 1250–51:
> Nay, in the settlement of disputes by conciliation, what I am claiming is that there is a fundamental principle which is founded on the sense of justice in the new society which serves to rationalize the requirements of the new society.
See also Friedmann, *Legal Theory* 260 (1949) for the Nazi law of 1935 which empowered the judge to punish acts which deserve punishment, according to the "healthy instincts of the people." Also see Schlesinger, *Comparative Law Cases and Materials* 339–41 (1950).

Miyazaki developed at length the theory that chōtei was a superior method of dispute settlement for purposes of Realizing-the-Law *(hōjitsu-gen)*. By his definitions realizing the law turned out to be a process whereby the individual was integrated into the Citizen's Cooperative Structure *(kokumin kyōdōtai)*, which, needless to say, is a concept weighted heavily in favor of the state.[29]

Onogi, relying heavily on German writers, elaborates at length the irrational elements hidden in the formal process of adjudication. He tries to demonstrate that adjudication and chōtei are not so different as may be supposed, but he fails to evaluate properly the effect in adjudication of requiring judges to rationalize their decisions, that is, to make their decisions understandable and acceptable to others in terms of legal standards previously given. After showing that both adjudication and chōtei are heavily dependent on morality, he ends by exhorting officials to strive to be wise and good.[30]

The Civil Conciliation Law of 1951 removes most of the excesses born of wartime expediency, at least so far as the new legislation itself is concerned. There are, however, some substantial criticisms of the system with respect to the extensive role it has assumed since 1945 and to the way it actually operates in context. Before referring to these criticisms, we will present an outline of the main features of the chōtei proceedings as conducted under the Civil Conciliation Law of 1951.

---

[29] Miyazaki Sumio, *Chōteihō no riron to jissai* 19–30 (1942). Miyazaki's book shows the pressures of war, as he notes Yasuda's excesses (80, note 3) but with all due respect, it seems to this writer that he slips into some of them himself. His "realizing the law" seems to mean complying with the discipline of the authoritarian state:

> Therefore, the above "law" is not the same as statutory law. As opposed to "law" a statute is a norm established by a legislature. Statutes are simply one method of "realizing the law...." Conciliation is then defined as not only a method of resolving a dispute, but also a means of "realizing the law" (p. 21).

[30] Onogi Tsune, "Chōtei to saiban" 調停と裁判 (Conciliation and adjudication), 44 *Hōgaku ronsō* 442 (1941). Onogi is one of the most extensive writers on conciliation both before and after the war. See Onogi Tsune, review of Miyazaki Kyōju, *Chōteihō no riron to jissai* 宮崎教授調停法の理論と實際 (Miyazaki's The theory and practice of conciliation law), 46 *Hōgaku ronsō* 646–61 (1942); and also Onogi, *Chōteihō gaisetsu* 調停法概説 (General survey of conciliation law) (1942) and Onogi, *Minji soshōhō oyobi chōteihō kōgi* 民事訴訟法及び調停法講義 (Lectures on the law of civil procedure and the law of conciliation) (1949). For a fuller list by Onogi, as well as a general bibliography on conciliation and an interesting list of cases on various legal points, see Koyama, *Minji chōteihō gaisetsu* 237–41, and for cases, p. 242 (1954).

MODERN CIVIL CONCILIATION

Chōtei[31] as provided in the Civil Conciliation Law[32] of 1951 (see translation, appendix III) may be invoked to settle a civil dispute by simply filing a proposal (Article 2) by one or both of the parties and paying a small fee (Article 10). Jurisdiction is in one of the 570 summary courts throughout Japan, unless the parties designate one of the forty-nine district courts (Article 3). Chōtei is then conducted by the court through a chōtei committee (Article 5 [1]) composed of a judge, designated by the court (Article 7 [1]), and two or more conciliators (Article 6) appointed for the particular case by the court, usually from a list of conciliators made up each year by the court itself (Article 7 [2]); but the judge may instead (Article 7 [3]) appoint an appropriate conciliator. The judge alone may act as conciliator (Article 5 [1]), however, if he considers it to be appropriate[33] and if the parties do not request a committee (Article 5 [2]). The parties may by agreement designate a district court to handle the chōtei and they may also designate the conciliators. As mentioned in chapter VIII, chōtei procedures may also be invoked by the judge during a pending lawsuit, where he considers it appropriate (Article 20).[34] When the judge acts alone this device is functionally quite similar and may be considered as an alternative to efforts to compromise as provided by Article

---

[31] Koyama Noboru, *Minji chōteihō gaisetsu* (1954) is still one of the best general treatments of the new law; also see Koyama, *Chōteihō* in 38 *Hōritsugaku zenshū* 1–50, separate pagination (1958); Koyama, "Soshōjō no wakai to chōtei" 訴訟上の和解と調停 (Conciliation and compromise—during suit), *Shihō* (no. 9) 104–15 (1953); and Sasaki Yoshio, "Minji chōtei ni okeru gōi no hōteki seishitsu ni kansuru ichishiron" 民事調停における合意の法的性質に關する一試論 (Discussion concerning the legal nature of mutuality in civil conciliation), *Shimadai hōgaku* (no. 7) 31–54 (1962). Also see the following collections of articles: "Chūsai to chōtei no hōri" 仲裁と調停の法理 (Legal theory of arbitration and conciliation), 6 *Sōgō hōgaku* (no. 3) 2–31 (1963); "Chōtei tokushū" 調停特集 (Special collection on conciliation), *Jurisuto* (no. 20) 2–31 (1952); "Minji chōtei—genjō to hihan" 民事調停—現情と批判 (Civil conciliation—present condition and criticism), 28 *Hōritsu jihō* 148–211 (1956); "Kaji chōtei no kagakuka" 30 *Hōritsu jihō* 276–349 (1958); and Imai Dōkan 今井道鑑, "Chōtei (saibanjō no wakai o fukumu) no kashi to sono kyūsai" 調停 (裁判上の和解を含む) の瑕疵と其の救濟 (Defects in conciliation [including court compromises] and its relief), 37 *Minshō-hō zasshi* 667–87 (1958); Tsuneda Bunji 恒田文次, "Minji saiban seido ni okeru chōtei no shimei" 民事裁判制度における調停の使命 (The task of chōtei in the civil trial system), 1 *Aoyama hōgaku ronshū* (nos. 1 and 2) 113–34 (1959).

[32] The most convenient source of chōtei law generally is *Chōtei roppō* 調停六法 (The conciliation six codes), 1964.

[33] Actually in 1960, which was a typical year, only 2,292 cases out of 55,396 chōtei cases (about 4 per cent) concluded in the summary court were handled by the judge without a committee. 1 *Shihō tōkei nempō* 442 (1961).

[34] In 1960 out of 56, 582 new chōtei cases filed in the 570 summary courts in Japan, 9,194 (or 16 per cent) were commenced by the judge transferring the case to conciliation under Article 20. 1 *Shihō tōkei nempō* 437 (1961).

136 of the Code of Civil Procedures. The chōtei hearings take place in a number of sessions, often extending over a period of several months.[35]

The negotiations before the committee may then result in several alternative dispositions. The most desirable result is that the parties reach an agreement by chōtei (Article 16). The agreement is then carefully embodied in written form [*chōsho*]; copies are given to each party, and one copy is filed with the court. The settlement then becomes effective (Article 16) in the same way as a compromise during trial, i.e., like a final judgment (CCP 202). If there is no prospect for agreement, or if the agreement reached is regarded as inappropriate by the committee, the chōtei proceeding may be terminated (Article 14). Also, if the committee deems the purpose of the petition inappropriate or the case, because of its nature, unsuitable for chōtei, the chōtei may be terminated (Article 13). Furthermore, in case there is no prospect for agreement, the court may hear the opinions of the committee and, after complying with other standards, issue a decision (see Article 17). If neither of the two parties files a protest against this decision within two weeks (Article 18), it becomes effective in the same way as a compromise during trial (Article 18 [3]).[36] If settlement is reached in a lawsuit transferred to chōtei from the regular trial docket by authority of the court, the suit is considered withdrawn (Article 20 [2]) and the settlement has the effect of a compromise during trial (Article 16). If chōtei fails, or if a decision under Article 17 loses its effect because of a protest, the parties may file a lawsuit within two weeks; if such a filing is made, the petition will be considered as filed on the date chōtei was originally requested (Article 19).

The Supreme Court is given rule-making power to implement the statute.[37] Penalties are provided for failure to respond to a summons (Article 34), for violation of court restraints on personal action or on property (Article 35), for improper disclosure by a conciliator of information concerning the proceedings, the opinions or votes of members (Article 37), or the private affairs of the parties (Article 38). Where no special rules are specified, Article 22 provides that chōtei is to be governed generally by the Law of Procedure for Noncontentious Matters. This brief outline of the legal provisions indicates the general legal relationship of the chōtei system to the formal court system of Japan.

[35] In about 22 per cent (12,889) of the cases (57,688), more than five meetings were held. For average numbers of hearings per case and average lapsed time between filing and disposition of conciliation cases in 1960, see 1 *Shihō tōkei nempō* 442–43 and 446–47 (1961).

[36] In 1960, out of a total of only eleven cases handled by court decision under Article 17, none were avoided by a protest under Article 18 (3) 1 *Shihō tōkei nempō* 437 (1961).

[37] Rules issued by the Supreme Court under Article 19 may be found in *Roppō zensho* 1225 (1962); or *Chōtei kankei hōkishū* 16 ff. contains complete regulations to date.

Concretely, chōtei hearings usually take place in a small room in the court building with the committee and parties seated about informally.[38] The meetings are not public. In fact, as mentioned above, penalties are provided against disclosure by the conciliators of information elicited at the proceedings.[39] The general rule is that the principals will appear in person, along with a lawyer if the party decides to retain one. In case of real necessity, a representative or an Assistant *(hosanin)* may appear alone on behalf of a party, but if the representative or assistant is not a lawyer, permission of the committee is required for his appearance.[40]

Ideally, the meeting opens with the introduction of the persons assembled by the chairman (a judge). He explains the spirit and purpose of chōtei proceedings and emphasizes the difference between chōtei and a lawsuit. Usually he then explains that the conciliators will be fair and unbiased and emphasizes that information disclosed will be held in confidence. Actually, the hearings are very informal, but most often the plaintiff is first asked if he has any comment; the chairman may question the plaintiff if he feels it is necessary to do so to get all of the pertinent facts. The other committee members may have further questions, and if so, they are allowed to put them to the plaintiff. Then the other party is heard, and he is also questioned where it is deemed necessary. Sometimes a party is heard while the other party is not present because animosity between them may make it difficult to clarify the facts.[41] When both parties have stated their troubles before the gathering, they are dismissed, and the committee then decides[42] its course of action.

Unless they decide to terminate the proceeding, the committee members will devise among themselves an appropriate settlement (or preferably, several alternative suggestions). Usually, during the course of several

[38] Photographs of chōtei sessions may be seen in Saikō saibansho jimu sōkyoku, *Wagakuni ni okeru chōtei seido no enkaku* (frontispiece, undated) and 30 *Hōritsu jihō* 1 (1958).

[39] Supreme Court Regulations Rule No. 10 authorizes the committee to allow observers, if the committee considers it appropriate. In making this study, the writer received cordial and generous assistance from the bar and bench both in terms of official materials and permission to observe the proceedings. Judges Niimura and Tanabe of the Mito District Court (1962), Judge Asano of the Nagano Summary Court (Tokyo) in 1958, Judge Kondō of the Family Court of Tokyo (1955), Chief Judge Ono of the District Court at Fukuoka (1954), the Sapporo Summary Court (1953) were particularly helpful on various occasions in obtaining permission for the writer to observe chōtei proceedings.

[40] Supreme Court Regulation Rule No. 8. In the early laws on chōtei, lawyers were barred from accompanying parties or acting as conciliators. See Ōhashi Seiichi, "Chōtei o meguru zadankai" 調停をめぐる座談會 (Discussion meeting involving conciliation), *Jurisuto* (no. 20) 17 (Oct. 15, 1952). Lawyers were first allowed as conciliators in the Temporary Law for Conciliation of Monetary Obligations (1932).

[41] Trial of facts may be referred to the district court. If tried by the committee, the rules for taking evidence of the Code of Civil Procedure are to be followed. Supreme Court Regulations Rule No. 12.

[42] Supreme Court Regulations Rule No. 18.

subsequent hearings, the parties are persuaded to make concessions to each other with a view to reaching a mutually agreeable solution. If such an agreement is finally reached, it is recorded as a protocol of the court, which then becomes enforceable by the court.

Considerable effort is made by the Japanese government, through the courts and administrative offices, to educate the conciliators in the purpose and technique of chōtei; the government sponsors the conciliators' association,[43] lectures, and meetings. Although conciliators receive only nominal fees (travel, hotel, expenses, plus a daily stipend),[44] many people are anxious to serve for the prestige that goes with the position, and apparently this is particularly the case in the rural areas, where the persons of most prestige in the community frequently serve as conciliators. As we shall see later, there has recently been considerable criticism addressed to the fact that the conciliators are too often chosen from certain social strata and that their background colors the operation of chōtei in favor of traditional institutions.

A fairly typical lecture to conciliators by Judge Togashi Mitsusaburō,[45] chief of the Hachiōji branch court, emphasized various points in two main aspects of the proceedings—the hearing, and drafting the settlement. Some of the main points may be summarized as follows.

In conducting the hearing it is necessary to avoid raising the voice, becoming angry, showing agreement with one side, refusing to transmit even unreasonable views of one party to the other, advising a party that he has no chance to win a lawsuit, or becoming professional and forgetting the informal nature of the meeting and the newness of the procedure to the parties. It is particularly important to distinguish the chōtei proceeding from a lawsuit. Sincerity[46] is encouraged instead of wit. Private investigations, meetings at either of the parties' houses, and acceptance of drinks or other favors, as well as visits from the parties after the hearings, are

---

[43] See Kanesue Tashio 金末多志雄, "Minji saiban chien to sono taisaku—chōtei zenchi-shugi jisshi no teishō," 民事裁判遅延とその対策—調停前置主義実施の提唱 (Delay in civil trials and countermeasures therefor—a proposal to require preliminary conciliation), *Chōtei jihō* (no. 35) 15–19 (1963), and (no. 36) 14–16 (1963); and Nihon chōtei kyōkai rengōkai 日本調停協会連合会, *Chōtei tokuhon* 調停読本 (Conciliation reader) (1954); there are several pamphlets printed by the courts as guides to chōtei. Among others, see Saikō saibansho jimu sōkyoku minjikyoku (ed.), *Chōtei no tebiki* (A guide to conciliation) (1951); and Tsuda Susumu 津田進 (ed.), *Chōtei no arikata* 調停のあり方 (The nature of conciliation) (1953).

[44] See Civil Conciliation Law, art. 9.

[45] *Tokyo chihō saibansho* 東京地方裁判所 pub., *Chōtei no tebiki* (A guide to conciliation) 1–25 (1952). This is a lecture given by Judge Togashi Mitsusaburo 富樫光三郎 to a meeting of conciliation committee members at Niigata in 1949.

[46] One case is said to have been settled because the conciliators personally climbed all over a hillside to survey the land in dispute, which so impressed the parties that they could not bear to let the committee down.

strictly forbidden. The good conciliator should not push a single specific suggestion for settlement too far. He should devise alternatives and avoid trying to apply stereotyped solutions learned in prior disputes to similar cases that might arise later in his experience.

It is important to call in other members of the family or friends of the parties, who might help to get the whole situation clarified in the minds of the committee and promote a solution. Especially in family affairs, the conciliators must distinguish between emotional and pecuniary aspects of the case. Little will be accomplished by making money proposals if the real issue is pride, or emotional or sexual maladjustment. The committee members are encouraged to disqualify themselves for bias in proper cases and to maintain secrecy. They should avoid gaining a reputation as a private conciliator by refusing to help settle quarrels out of court.

Once settlement is agreed upon, the job of the committee is to see that it is thoroughly understood and acknowledged[47] and that it is embodied in written form sufficiently clear to avoid misinterpretation and precise enough to enforce specifically in court, if it is not performed later. One rather common type of chōtei case involving a money claim originated as a lawsuit in Fukuoka,[48] and the judge, considering it to be appropriate, ordered (Article 20) the suit transferred to chōtei and settled there. A Tokyo firm had sold picks to a small coal mining firm from northern Kyūshū, producing about fifteen hundred tons per month, and the suit was for payment overdue on a note executed by the coal mining firm for 48,500 *yen* in consideration for the picks. The real situation, as it developed at the chōtei meeting and as it had probably appeared at the trial, was that there was a depression—the defendant could not sell his coal; therefore, he could not even pay the wages of his two hundred workers. Though his request had little basis in law, the judge granted him the privilege of working out a compromise solution by chōtei. An amicable agreement was then reached whereby the defendant would pay the full amount of the claim at a deferred date, April 10, 1955 (hearing was July 29, 1954). The general similarity between the plight of this defendant and Chūbē in 1808 (see chapter VI) is obvious, and for such a routine claim, where the chief problem is simply inability to pay, the conciliated solution is doubtless better than a strictly legal but futile judgment followed by an unproductive compulsory execution procedure.

---

[47] Judge Togashi suggests that the members formally congratulate the parties, and in family affairs he suggests that the parties inform the spirits of their ancestors of the happy solution.

Usually the court records of conciliation cases consist simply of a formal proposal (*mōshitatesho* 申立書) and the document of settlement (*chōsho* 調書). See Supreme Court Regulations Rule No. 2 (proposal) and No. 11 (document of settlement).

[48] With permission, the writer observed the chōtei hearing at the Fukuoka district court.

PROBLEMS OF PRACTICAL OPERATION

Up to this point chōtei has been viewed largely through the legal provisions and the official literature portraying the ideal operation of the system. It remains to consider four interrelated problems[49] arising out of its actual performance in context: (1) procedurally there is some question whether the operations always comply with the provisions of the Civil Conciliation Law itself; (2) the relevant substantive law is largely disregarded as a standard in formulating compromises by the conciliators;[50] (3) worse than disregarding the substantive laws, some scholarly comment asserts that conservative conciliators tend to apply the repealed standards of the old civil code, particularly in family matters, contrary to the new postwar civil code, and this situation apparently results from the method of selection, age, attitudes, and other qualifications of the conciliators; and (4) there is some reason to suspect that the chōtei proceedings, which should be entirely voluntary, tend to be coercive in the social context within which they operate.

Bearing on the compliance of chōtei practices with the Civil Conciliation Law itself, one study[51] particularly indicates that the actual chōtei

[49] These points were discussed as possible problem areas in a preliminary way in Henderson, "The Pattern and Persistence of Traditional Procedures in Japanese Law" (1955), and at that time the Japanese literature related to these problems was generally rather uncritical. In the intervening years (1955–63), a growing concern about confining the role and improving the performance of chōtei is evident in the periodical literature.

See the following sampling: Sasaki, "Minji chōtei ni okeru [gōi] no kentō," 9 *Kanazawa hōgaku* (nos. 1 and 2) 23–31 (1963); Kawashima Takeyoshi 川島武宜, Nagano Kiyoshi 長野潔, Hasebe Mokichi 長谷部茂吉, Niimura Yoshihiro 新村義廣, and Iijima Sanseki 飯嶋三碩, "Chōtei seido no jitsujō to kekkan," 調停制度の實情と欠陥 (The actual condition and deficiency of the chōtei system), 28 *Hōritsu jihō* 177–95 and 347–65 (1956); Sasaki Yoshio, "Minji chōtei ni okeru hōteki handan to jian no kaimei" *Minji soshō zasshi* (no. 7) 143–76 (1961); Kawashima Takeyoshi, "Shakai kōzō to saiban", *Shisō* (no. 432) 1–17 (1960); Sasaki Yoshio, "Chihō ni okeru minji chōtei" 地方における民事調停 (Civil conciliation in the rural areas), 32 *Hōritsu jihō* 1051–57 (1960); Sasaki Yoshio, "Minji chōtei ni okeru gōi no hōteki seishitsu ni kansuru ichishiron" *Shimadai hōgaku* (no. 7) 31–54 (1962); Endō Makoto 遠藤誠, "Ureubeki wakai chōtei no seikyō" 憂うべき和解調停の盛況 (The lamentable success of conciliation and compromise), 33 *Hōritsu jihō* 496–501 (1961); Koyama Noboru, "Chōteihō chūsaihō", 38 *Hōritsugaku zenshū* 8–10 (1958).

[50] Note that this problem may be cast in terms of number one (above); namely, one interpretation holds that failure to consider the legal positions of the parties is a violation of Article 1 of the Conciliation Law. Although a clear understanding of the parties' positions in law would be desirable at the chōtei proceedings, it would not be a matter of much importance because, in our view, chōtei must be entirely voluntary and auxiliary to the court system. Hence it might be better to allow the parties to move the case to the court for litigation if their legal position is not being protected in chōtei rather than trying to make chōtei more like litigation. Of course our position would force improvement in the litigation process in order to make it more practical, cheaper, and quicker for small claims (see chapter X).

[51] Sasaki, "Minji chōtei ni okeru gōi no hōteki seishitsu ni kansuru ichishiron," *Shimadai hōgaku* (no. 7) 31 (1962).

practices in Shimane prefecture violate some important provisions of the law and leave others largely inoperative. In addition, the annual statistics on chōtei published by the Japanese government tend to confirm these findings with respect to Japan as a whole. Especially important in this regard is the fact that, apparently because of overwork, the judges who are appointed by the law (Article 7 [1]) to act as chairmen of the chōtei committees, and who are presumably also required to meet with the committee at the chōtei sessions (Superior Court Rules 17 and 18), in fact usually attend only the final meeting, or an occasional inspection of the premises in dispute (meeting-on-the-spot).[52] Also, from examining the records of the 431 chōtei cases handled in 1958 by the Matsue Summary Court,[53] it appeared that practically no useful interim reports of the many chōtei sessions held without the judge's presence were made by the committees, and therefore the judge was unable to review the records and lend his expertise in making the legal decisions necessary to a proper operation of some of the important provisions of the law (e.g., Article 13, decision to terminate the chōtei because of the impropriety of the petition; Article 14, decision to terminate because of the impropriety of the agreement reached by the parties; Article 17, decision by the court disposing of the case despite a failure to reach agreement by the parties). The thrust of this conclusion is that, without a judge available, the application of the legal standards required by the statute itself to the subject matter of the dispute is virtually impossible; furthermore, the legal judgment necessary to enable the committee to comply with the chōtei law itself is lacking.

Likewise, concerning the factual development of chōtei cases, it seems that meetings-on-the-spot (Supreme Court Rule 9), factual investigations, and examinations of evidence including third-party witnesses (Supreme Court Rule 12) are used surprisingly seldom in chōtei proceedings throughout the country. The relatively small use made of these various legal provisions is shown statistically on a country-wide basis by chart XVII, confirming the findings based on the review of the case records in Shimane prefecture.

[52] Sasaki, "Minji chōtei ni okeru hōteki handan to jian no kaimei," *Minji sosho zasshi* (no. 7) 149–150 (1961).
[53] *Id.* at 143–76 (1961).

CHART XVII
USE OF LEGAL AND FACTUAL DETERMINATIONS IN CHŌTEI PROCEEDINGS
IN ALL SUMMARY COURTS (1960)

Article 13	Committee cases	493 out of 55,396 cases*	0.9%
	Judge acting alone as conciliator	46 out of 2,292 cases†	2.0%
Article 14	(Matsue Summary Court only)	None out of 431 cases‡	0. %
Article 17	Committee cases	8 out of 55,396 cases §	——
	Judge cases	3 out of 2,292 cases‖	——
Supreme Court Rule 9 (on-the-spot sessions)		3,655 out of 57,688 cases#	6.3%
Supreme Court Rule 12 (taking evidence)		338 out of 57,688 cases**	0.6%

* 1 *Shihō tōkei nempō* 442–43 (1961).

† *Ibid.*

‡ Sasaki, *op. cit. supra* note 52, at 151 (1961). Sasaki checked the local records at the Matsue Summary Court on this point to get these results. Unfortunately, the all-Japan statistics, excellent though they are, do not give this breakdown. Consequently we cannot check this point on a countrywide basis.

§ 1 *Shihō tōkei nempō* 442–43 (1961).

‖ *Ibid.*

Id. 446–47 (1961).

** *Ibid.*

Turning to the substantive standards applied by conciliators in the disposition of cases, some critics argue that Article 1[54] requires a three-step process:[55] determination of the facts, including the examination of third-party witnesses, if necessary; determination of the legal position of the parties; then application of common sense [*jōri*] in attempting to achieve agreement between the parties by mutual concessions. Rather than following the procedure of determining legal and factual issues first, the conciliators apparently often rely on the testimony of the parties only, and without resolving frequent conflicts, proceed immediately and repetitiously to encourage a settlement agreement by mutual concession. Stated another way, the critics feel that rather than using mutual concessions [*gojō*] properly as a method, the conciliators make it the sole purpose of the proceeding.[56]

In Shimane prefecture in 1958,[57] a poll of conciliators (133 questioned,

[54] Civil Conciliation Law (1951), art. 1:
  The purpose of this law is to devise, by mutual concessions of the parties, solutions for disputes concerning civil matters, which are consistent with reason and befitting actual circumstances.

[55] Kawashima *et al.*, "Chōtei seido no jitsujō to kekkan," 28 *Hōritsu jihō* 347–65 (1956). See Kawashima's remarks at 347; cf. Koyama Noboru, "Chōteihō chūsaihō," in 38 *Hōritsugaku zenshū* 8–10 (1958).

[56] Sasaki, "Minji chōtei ni okeru gōi no hōteki seishitsu ni kansuru ichishiron," *Shimadai hōgaku* (no. 7) 41 (1962); and Sasaki, "Minji chōtei ni okeru [gōi] no kentō," 9 *Kanazawa hōgaku* (nos. 1 and 2) 21 (1963) shows the difference in attitude on this point between the parties and the conciliators.

[57] Sasaki, "Minji chōtei ni okeru hōteki handan to jian no kaimei," *Minji soshō zasshi* (no. 7) 156–58 (1961).

73 answered) posed three questions bearing on the importance attached by the conciliators to preliminary factual and legal determinations. The first question inquired as to whether the conciliators thought it necessary to consider the legality of each party's position. Only 28 per cent of those answering thought it was necessary. The second question asked whether a claim for usurious interests should be paid; only 45 percent answered that it definitely need not be paid. The third question asked whether it was necessary to make a factual investigation in cases of conflict of testimony between the parties; only 27 per cent of the conciliators indicated that they thought it necessary.

Coupled with the relatively few factual investigations made, as shown by the national statistics in chart XVII, and the fact that generally the legal expert on the committee, the judge, attends only the final meeting,[58] the foregoing attitudes of the conciliators lend considerable weight to the views of the critics that the chōtei proceedings tend to make mutual concession the goal, rather than aiming at achieving a solution consistent with reason and the circumstances by means of mutual concessions. The evidence also suggests that, in Osaka and Shimane prefectures at least, the chōtei process is rather similar to the standardless settlement negotiations which we reviewed in the case of Nuinosuke during the Tokugawa period (1808).

Several comments made in answering another section of the Shimane poll addressed to parties to chōtei proceedings indicate considerable dissatisfaction on the part of the parties with this particular characteristic of chōtei. For example, one party referred to conciliators as Eight-Sided Beauties *(happō bijin)*,[59] meaning that they smile at all and are true to none. Others refer to chōtei as Okay-Okay *(mā mā)* justice, or Fifty-Fifty *(seppan)* or Please-Please *(dōka dōka)* justice.

Referring to the selection and qualification of conciliators, an analysis of the records of the Shimane Court indicated that, despite the requirement that conciliators' lists be made up annually, actually as a rule the same people served as conciliators year after year. In Shimane, 65 per cent of them were over sixty years old, and the average age was sixty-two; and 69 per cent had more than five years' experience; 70 per cent owned their own houses. Some critics[60] have charged that the elderly conciliators tend

---

[58] However, in many cases there are lawyers who serve as conciliators.

[59] Sasaki, *op. cit. supra* note 57, at 163 (1961).

[60] Kainō, "Mimpō to kaji chōtei," 28 *Hōritsu jihō* 148–153 (1956); but see a spirited objection to Kainō's suggestion that the judges also sometimes participate in the application of the old, instead of the new, Civil Code provisions: Judges Yoshimura Hiroyoshi 吉村弘義 and Horiuchi Setsu 堀内節 , "Kaji chōtei wa mimpō o nashikuzushi ni hakai suru ka" 家事調停は民法をなしくずしに破壊するか (Does family conciliation demolish the civil code bit-by-bit), 9 *Hōritsu no hiroba* (no. 4) 30–37 (1956). Also see Endō Makoto,

to remain, whether consciously or unconsciously, committed to the older family and village traditions which were legally abolished by the amendments in the civil laws after 1945. No doubt, to some degree this is true; and at the same time, since legislation is never wholly efficacious immediately, it is probably inevitable during a certain transition period. This problem is inextricably related to our next topic, the inconsistent use of compulsion in the chōtei process.

Whether compulsion, either in the form of social pressure or judicial power, may be employed in the chōtei process without doing violence to the essence of the system is a problem which had concerned the more thoughtful Japanese scholars[61] even before the establishment of the new constitution. It has been quite properly asserted that chōtei only has merit in a constitutional system to the extent that it is voluntarily used by the parties and not made an exclusive remedy, either legally or as a practical matter.[62] Hence the problem of compulsion really has two aspects: (1) practical compulsion, accruing from the actual setting of the hearing, the social relationship between the parties, the relationship between the parties and the conciliators, and the absence of alternative remedies, as a practical matter, especially after chōtei has been attempted and has failed; and (2) legal compulsion, specifically provided for in the chōtei statutes.

The first type of compulsion in conciliation—that arising from the nature of the hearing, the social relationships of the parties and conciliators, and the lack of practical, alternative remedies—is quite subtle, and a study of it leads to much broader problems, which we will touch upon in chapter

---

"Ureubeki wakai chōtei no seikyō," 33 *Hōritsu jihō* 496, 497 (1961); and Taniguchi Tomohei 谷口知平 , "Kaji chōtei iin no shakai kaisō to shiso" 家事調停委員の社會階層 と思想 (The social class and thought of conciliators in family matters), 30 *Hōritsu jihō* 21–26 and 64 (1958).

With respect, this writer feels that Kainō, *id.*, exaggerates the difficulty in obtaining information about the operation of the chōtei system simply because the hearings are not public. Our experience has been that the judges, lawyers, and parties have always been very cooperative at all times in allowing a student of the system to observe the hearings or review documents for a legitimate scholarly purpose. Also see Taniguchi, *id.* and Sasaki, *op. cit. supra* note 56, for encouraging examples of what can be done to clarify the actual operations of chōtei by polls, tedious review of records, and analysis of excellent statistics published on the subject annually by the Supreme Court.

[61] E.g., Miyake, "Chōteihō," in 12 *Shinhōgaku zenshū* 36–37 (1937); Hozumi Shigetō, "Chōteihō," in 38 *Gendai hōgaku zenshū* 239 (1931); Nakajima Kōdō, "Chōtei jōkō to kore ni kansuru ichi kōsatsu," 12 *Hōritsu jihō* 602–12 (1940); also see Miyazaki Sumio, *Chōteihō no riron to jissai* 51–62 (1942).

[62] Koyama, *Chōteihō, chūsaihō* 8–10 (1958); Kaneko Hajime 兼子一, Yanagawa Masao 柳川真佐夫 , and Kume Ai 久米愛 , "Chōtei utagainaki ni shimo arazu" 調停疑なきにし もあらず (Conciliation is not without problems), *Jurisuto* (no. 20) 26 (Oct. 15, 1952), for the theory that compulsory conciliation was first rationalized as a means of reform, then extended during the war to become a general method of solving disputes. This brief article is an early, candid critique of conciliation under the new Civil Conciliation Law at a time when most of the material was devoted to expressing the uncritical official view.

X. We will confine ourselves here to the sources of this sort of coercion and ways in which it manifests itself in the chōtei hearings. First, some observers feel[63] that the conciliators may be overzealous, to the point of being coercive, in their attempts to obtain a settlement, regardless of the satisfaction of the parties or the legal merits of the terms suggested. Second, there is a feeling that because of the remnants of the Confucianistic family and social system, chōtei may favor the stubborn, the stronger, or the traditionally authoritative party at the expense of the legal rights of the weaker.[64] How such coercion might be accomplished in a chōtei session leads back to the analysis suggested at the outset of the study (chapter I). Conciliation is not only a part of the Japanese traditional approach to civil disputes, but it also may have the conservative effect of transmitting through the results of chōtei proceedings other Tokugawa values of official social and family authority. The tight ties of the family, the more intimate personal relationships between tenant and landlord, master and servant, the close associations in the rural village, the traditional, but more recent, subordination to the Imperial state—all of these things furnish the background for conciliating Japanese disputes.[65] Third, this collectivistic social context could not only provide an atmosphere of compulsion to the hearing, but the coercion might arise from the fact that the conciliators are selected from the prestige strata[66] and are acting as officials; officials are much more authoritative and awe-inspiring to the Japanese than our "public servant." It has been said that the Englishman is proud of the state because it belongs to him, but the pre-war Japanese was proud of the state because he belonged to it. Like any good caricature, the statement portrays a certain truth.

Fourth, once chōtei is commenced, in a practical sense there may be little actual alternative for the parties but to settle on the terms finally offered. This compulsion may result from several sources: the party often does not know that he has a right to terminate the chōtei without reaching a settlement;[67] if he knows the law well, he may feel that the court might

[63] Endō Makoto, "Ureubeki wakai chōtei no seikyō," 33 *Hōritsu jihō* 496, 499 (1961); Kaneko *et al., op. cit. supra* note 62, at 28–29 (1952); compare Sasaki Yoshio, "Minji chōtei ni okeru hōteki handan to jian no kaimei," *Minji soshō zasshi* (no. 7) 162–63 (1961); Kawashima *et al.,* "Chōtei seido no jitsujō to kekkan," 28 *Hōritsu jihō* 177–96 and 347–65 (1956).

[64] Kawashima *et al.,* "Chōtei seido no jitsujō to kekkan," 28 *Hōritsu jihō* 349–50 (1956); Kaneko *et al., op. cit. supra* note 62, at 28 (1952), Kaneko's and Kume's remarks.

[65] Kainō, "Mimpō to kaji chōtei," 28 *Hōritsu jihō* 148–53 (1956).

[66] Taniguchi Tomohei, "Kaji chōtei iin no shakai kaisō to shisō," 30 *Hōritsu jihō* 21–26 (1958); Sasaki, *op. cit. supra* note 63, at 155 (1961); Kawashima *et al., op. cit. supra* note 63, at 188–93 (1956).

[67] Sasaki, *op. cit. supra* note 63, at 163, chart 10 (1961) showing that 31 per cent of the 367 parties answered that they did not know that they could reject a settlement proposal which did not satisfy them. In Osaka the percentage of those who knew their rights was a little,

issue a decision (Article 17) settling the dispute in the terms offered, and that any subsequent lawsuit in the same court would be similarly handled by encouraging such a compromise [*wakai*] anyway; the party may not be able to afford the initial fee required to induce a lawyer to accept a later lawsuit;[68] more often he cannot afford the time and forbearance it would take to litigate under present court conditions.[69]

It is in this sort of context that chōtei may operate to coerce the parties, in a practical sense if not legally, to settle their disputes by chōtei; by the same token, it can operate to preserve traditional ways; or, as some conservatives would say, because of this situation, chōtei is best suited to the Japanese. Yet, there can be no doubt that some aspects of the Japanese tradition raise serious problems of adaptation to the current emphasis on the equality and dignity of the individual under the new constitution. It is this latter problem which makes two recent Supreme Court cases,[70] dealing with the second type of compulsion (legal), very interesting.

The special chōtei statutes in effect until 1951 contained two types of compulsory provisions, now of only historical interest because their most objectionable features were avoided in the new conciliation legislation (Family, 1948; Civil, 1951).[71] Yet they have become the occasion for a significant analysis by the Japanese Supreme Court of the relation-

---

but not much higher. See Sasaki, "Minji chōtei ni okeru [gōi] no kentō," 9 *Kanazawa hōgaku* (nos. 1 and 2) 19 (1963).

[68] By rules of the bar association, it is customary for lawyers to request an advance retainer based on a percentage of the claim.

[69] See the two Supreme Court cases below which were in litigation nine and fourteen years respectively. In fact one of the concurring judges (Kawamura Daisuke, 14 *Saikō saibansho hanreishū* 1669–73 [1960]) bases his opinion of unconstitutionality in part on the fact that it is actually impractical for a party to litigate again after he has gone through the conciliation process and then furthermore contested the validity of that decision in the courts. Also see Kawashima *et al., op. cit. supra* note 63, at 349 (1956), where he refers to the fact that rents especially have increased so much that often by just delaying an evacuation proceeding, the tenant may make a nice profit by staying on at a lower rate, which profit he can usually manage to retain in the ultimate settlement. Similar strategems were very much at work in a chōtei session witnessed by the writer in August, 1962. The owner of land upon which a tenant had built a building under a twenty-year lease alleged, with sound basis in the law, that he was entitled to evacuation of his land which had been leased to the defendant-tenant soon after World War II at a rate several times less than the current rate, but since an evacuation suit would have taken several years for the landowner to conclude, the tenant-houseowner was negotiating for a substantial sum to be paid to him before he would move.

[70] Suzuki v. Ishigaki, 10 *Saikō saibansho hanreishū* 1355–98 (1956); and Nomura v. Yamaki, 14 *Saikō saibansho hanreishū* 1657–1720 (1960).

[71] Cf. Kaneko *et al., op. cit. supra* note 62, at 29 (1952); most pertinent are Kaneko's doubts regarding the compulsory provisions allowing conciliators to assess fines if parties do not attend after receipt of summons. Also *quaere* whether decision by the court (Article 17) and referral to chōtei (Article 20) are really consistent with the voluntary spirit of chōtei in the modern theory.

ship between chōtei and lawsuits under the constitutional provisions related to the right of public trial.

The two types of compulsory provisions in the older law may be called Voidable Committee Decision *(kyōsei chōtei)*[72] and Substitution of Trial for Conciliation *(chōtei ni kawaru saiban)*. The voidable committee decision provisions[73] permitted the chōtei committee to suggest a settlement to the parties in cases where chōtei had failed, and if neither party objected to the committee's settlement within a prescribed period, the settlement became binding like a judgment. On the other hand, in substitution of trial for conciliation,[74] the court, not the committee, ordered a settlement, which it determined to be reasonable in the circumstances and where the chōtei discussions had failed, and this settlement so ordered by the court became binding. The chief differences between the two were that the court, not the committee, ordered the settlement in substitution of trial for conciliation, and the settlement so ordered could not be avoided by a simple protest by a party. It will be noted that the Civil Conciliation Law (1951) has a hybrid provision (Article 17) wherein the court may issue a decision settling a case where chōtei has failed, but a party may void the decision by a simple protest to the court within two weeks.[75]

The two Supreme Court cases cited above considered the constitutionality of the pre-war provisions on substitution of trial for conciliation under the new postwar constitution (1947) as applied to two house-evacuation cases filed originally in 1947 and 1946, and decided in 1956 and 1960. Hence, these two cases were in litigation for nine and fourteen years, respectively, before they were finally decided. In the 1947 case[76] the house-owner sued the tenant in the Nakagawa Summary Court requesting evacuation. The court on its own motion transferred the case to chōtei which failed, and the court then substituted its order in lieu of a chōtei

---

[72] See Miyazaki Sumio, *Chōteihō no riron to jissai* 50–61 (1942), but note that his book written in 1942 used the term Compulsory Conciliation *(kyōsei chōtei)*, whereas we refer to this procedure as "voidable committee decision" because the postwar authors often use his term *(kyōsei chōtei)* to refer to substitution of trial for conciliation.

[73] "Voidable committee decision" provisions were found in the following pre-war laws: Land-Lease House-Lease Conciliation Law, art. 24 (1922); the Tenant Conciliation Law, art. 36 (1924); and the Commercial Conciliation Law, art. 2 (1926). Texts of these laws may be seen in Miyazaki, *op. cit. supra* note 72, at 237–71 (1942).

Note that the Commercial Conciliation Law, arts. 4 and 5, provided that by agreement of both parties the conciliation committee could render an arbitration award in accordance with CCP art. 786–805. See Miyazaki, *Chōteihō no riron to jissai* 60 (1942).

[74] The Temporary Conciliation Law for Monetary Obligations, art. 7 (1), and the Farm Land Reform Law, art. 12 (1) provided for this type of disposition. The latter law provided for voidable committee decisions too. Neither form of compulsion was provided for in the Personal Affairs Conciliation Law or the Mining Industry Conciliation Law. Texts of these laws may be found in Miyazaki, *op. cit. supra* note 72, at 273–95 (1942).

[75] Note that this provision (Article 17) was used in only 11 out of 57,688 cases in 1960.

[76] Suzuki v. Ishigaki, 10 *Saikō saibansho minji hanreishū* 1355–98 (1956).

agreement, ordering the tenant to evacuate. The tenant appealed successively to the Nagoya District Court, Nagoya High Court, and finally the Supreme Court, alleging, among other arguments, that he was deprived of access to the courts, as guaranteed in Article 32 of the constitution, and a public trial (Article 82). In a disappointing decision,[77] fifteen Supreme Court judges upheld the actions of the lower courts, eight to seven,[78] and sustained the order to evacuate based on the old provision for substitution of trial for conciliation.[79]

The second case involved the same legal provisions and similar facts except that the case started in 1946 in the Tokyo District Court, hence

---

[77] For an authoritative analysis of both of these cases, see Shindō Kōji 新堂幸司 , "Kyōsei chōtei o iken to suru kettei ni tsuite" 強制調停を違憲とする決定について (Concerning a decision declaring compulsory conciliation unconstitutional), *Jurisuto* (no. 209) 44–49 (1960); and for critical scholarly opinion on the first case, see Sendai District Court Judge Nakagawa Tsuyoshi 中川毅 , "Kyōsei chōtei no ikensei" 強制調停の違憲性 (Unconstitutionality of compulsory conciliation), 8 *Hanrei taimuzu* (no. 2) 164–67 (1957) citing *Daishinin* decisions; and Nakata Junichi 中田淳一 , "Chōtei ni kawaru saiban no gōkensei" 調停に代る裁判の合憲性 (Constitutionality of substitution of trial for conciliation), 35 *Minshōhō zasshi* (no. 4) 605–18 (1957); for criticism of the second case, see Taniguchi Yasuhei 谷口安平 , "Junzen taru soshō jiken ni tsuki nasareta chōtei ni kawaru saiban no kōryoku" 純然たる訴訟事件につきなされた調停に代る裁判の効力 (The effect of substitution of trial for conciliation which was applied to a case which started as a pure lawsuit), 68 *Hōgaku ronsō* (no. 1) 120–35 (1960).

[78] The fifteen judges were aligned as follows:

Majority:	Minority:
Chief Justice Tanaka, Kōtarō	Justice Mano, Tsuyoshi
Justice Kuriyama, Shigeru	Justice Kotani, Katsushige
Justice Saitō, Yūsuke	Justice Shima, Tamotsu
Justice Kawamura, Matasuke	Justice Fujita, Hachirō
Justice Tanimura, Tadaichirō	Justice Iwamatsu, Saburō
Justice Kobayashi, Shunzō	Justice Irie, Toshirō
Justice Kimura, Zentarō	Justice Ikeda, Katsu
Justice Tarumi, Katsumi	

[79] The legal pattern of the applicable statutes is rather complicated because of the intervening extraordinary wartime statutes (1942), their subsequent partial repeal (1945), the establishment of the new constitution (1947), and the enactment of the new Civil Conciliation Law (1951) repealing the special chōtei laws and also the remainder of the wartime laws relating to conciliations. The Wartime Special Civil Law, art. 19 (2) made the Temporary Conciliation Law for Monetary Obligations, art. 7 (1) providing for Substitution of Trial for Conciliation applicable in conciliation cases under the Land-Lease, House-Lease Law, which was the law under which the original chōtei was conducted in this case. However, Law 46 (1945) after the war, which repealed the Wartime Special Civil Law, specifically left art. 19 (2) still effective when this case was filed in 1947. In fact said art. 19 (2) was repealed by the Civil Conciliation Law (1951), Supplemental art. 4, which amended Law 46 (1945) by deleting art. 19 of the Wartime Special Civil Law from the provisions which had been left still applicable by said Law 46 (1945). The Civil Conciliation Law, Supplementary art. 13, also provided that cases filed before its effective date would be handled by the prior laws. Hence the old provisions for substitution of trial for conciliation were still effective, except for the problem of constitutionality raised by the intervening new constitution, art. 34 and 82 (1947).

involved one less appeal. In 1960 the court reversed itself nine to six[80] and declared the action of the lower courts unconstitutional. For the first time in its history, the new Supreme Court had reversed itself in a civil suit. Also, for the first time it had held lower court action unconstitutional in a civil case.[81] The reversal is explained by the fact that six of the judges on the court which decided the first case had retired and had been replaced by six new judges. Only Kawamura Matasuke changed his view fundamentally (constitutional to unconstitutional), although Judge Shima, by reason of the change in the reasoning of the majority, changed his vote from unconstitutional to constitutional in the second case. Actually, however, his basic reasoning remained essentially unchanged, as he argued in both cases that such lower court judgments were no bar to a later action; hence they did not deprive the parties of access to the courts.

The arguments in the two cases were quite diverse, since a total of twelve opinions were reported: five dissenting opinions besides the majority opinion in the first case; and three concurring and two dissenting opinions, besides the ruling opinion in the second case. In consequence, a full presentation of the judges' reasoning with all of their collateral nuances would be inappropriate for our purposes here, although the arguments furnish considerable insight into the court's methods[82] and philosophy. Suffice it

[80] The judges were aligned this time as follows:

Majority:	Minority:
Justice Fujita, Hachirō	Chief Justice Tanaka, Kōtarō
Justice Irie, Toshirō	Justice Shima, Tamotsu
Justice Shimoiizaka, Masuo*	Justice Saitō, Yūsuke
Justice Okuno, Kenichi*	Justice Tarumi, Katsumi
Justice Takagi, Tsuneshichi*	Justice Takahashi, Kiyoshi*
Justice Kotani, Katsushige (concurring)	Justice Ishizaka, Shūichi*
Justice Ikeda, Katsu (concurring)	
Justice Kawamura, Daisuke* (concurring)	
Justice Kawamura, Matasuke	

The reversal resulted from a change of personnel on the court.

*Note that the six judges marked by asterisks were new judges; also note that two judges changed their opinions: Kawamura Matasuke—constitutional to unconstitutional, and Shima Tamotsu—unconstitutional to constitutional, but Judge Shima still held, as the key point in his opinion, that such a lower court judgment was not a bar to later suit and so it is the fact that the majority changed its opinion which really accounts for the change in his opinion.

[81] *Hanrei jihō* (no. 228) 5 (1960).

[82] For example, the majority opinion in the second case (Nomura v. Yamaki, 14 *Saikō saibansho hanreishū* 1657–1720 [1960]) declares the action of the lower courts unconstitutional, but it does not declare any of the applicable statutes unconstitutional, because it holds that the lower courts misconstrued the statutes. In fact, due to the newness of judicial supremacy (Constitution art. 81), there is considerable scholarly controversy as well as a number of unanswered questions as to the effect of a reversal of a lower court decision based on constitutional grounds, and the holdings of these decisions do not really raise the question of the constitutionality of the statutes. However, the following judges, either in their dissents in the first case (Suzuki v. Ishigaki, 10 *Saikō saibansho hanreishū* 1355–98 [1956]) or in the concurring opinions of the second case, reasoned that the following

to say that the outcome of the second case represents a recognition by the court that substitution of trial for conciliation is not sufficient "access to to the courts" under the new constitutional framework.

The majority reached this conclusion by application of the constitution, Article 32,[83] guaranteeing access to the courts, and Article 82,[84] guaranteeing a public hearing. The court held that, especially where the plaintiff initially files a suit, as he did in this case, it was a denial of public trial guaranteed under Articles 32 and 82 to transfer his case to chōtei

---

statutory provisions were unconstitutional as applied to the facts of the case by the lower court:

First Case:	Dissenter	*Unconstitutional Statute*
	Mano	Temporary Conciliation Law for Monetary Obligations, art. 7 (1).
	Kotani	,,
	Shima	,,
	Iwamatsu	,,
	Ikeda	Wartime Special Civil Law, art. 19 (2).
Second Case:	Concurrers	*Unconstitutional Statute*
	Kotani	Temporary Conciliation Law for Monetary Obligations, art. 7 (1).
	Ikeda	Wartime Special Civil Law, art. 19 (2).

(Note that by the time of the second case, Mano and Iwamatsu had retired, and Shima based his opinion this time on a legal argument that the original decision substituted for chōtei was not *res judicata*.)

[83] Japanese Constitution, art. 32 (1947): "No person shall be denied the right of access to the courts."

[84] Japanese Constitution, art. 82 (1947):

Trials shall be conducted and judgment declared publicly. Where a court unanimously determines publicity to be dangerous to public order or morals, a trial may be conducted privately, but trials of political offenses, offenses involving the press or cases wherein the rights of people as guaranteed in Chapter III of this Constitution are in question shall always be conducted publicly.

American courts have considered analogous constitutional problems concerned with conciliation, arbitration, and abbreviated procedures of small claims courts. Compare Klein v. Hutton, 49 N.D. 248, 191 N.W. 485–90, 167 A.L.R. 831n (1922), holding the North Dakota conciliation statute constitutional (John H. Wigmore submitted a brief on behalf of the American Judicature Society); and Flour City Fuel and Transfer Co. v. Young, 150 Minn. 452, 185 N.W. 934 (1921), upholding constitutionality of a Minnesota statute establishing a conciliation court but holding unconstitutional a provision thereof requiring the losing party to post a bond to pay judgment, as a condition to removal to the municipal court from conciliation; note 34 *Col. L. R.* 934, 945–46 (1934). On compulsory arbitration, see Application of Smith, 381 Pa. 223, 112 A.2d 625, appeal dismissed sub. nom. Smith v. Wissler, 350 U.S. 858 (1955), upholding constitutionality of jury trial, but holding against unreasonable conditions for appeal from award; and Talhelm v. Buggy, 68 Dauph. 310, 9 D. & C. 2d 482 (Pa. C. P. 1955), upholding constitutionality of Pennsylvania Compulsory Arbitration Statute, establishing appointive boards of arbitration comprised of attorneys, against charges of violation of Pennsylvania Constitution, art. V, sec. 15 providing that "all judges required to be learned in the law...shall be elected"; cf. McClure v. Boyle, 141 N.E.2d 229 (Ohio C. P. Trumbull Co. 1957) dismissing an action and holding that an award under the Pennsylvania Compulsory Arbitration Statute was not such a "judgment" as was entitled to protection under the full faith and credit clause of art. IV of the United States Constitution.

and then to substitute the court's decision after chōtei had failed to produce agreement. Fortunately, this view prevailed ultimately over the position taken by some of the dissenters (and the majority in the first case) to the effect that the court's substitution of its decision was sufficient access to the courts within the meaning of Article 32, apparently simply because the decision was rendered by a court. Some of these judges further reasoned that it is within the province of the legislature to determine by law whether such a "trial" must be public and, as was the case here, if the law does not require a public trial, it is not a violation of Article 82 to conduct a closed hearing. Also, happily, the court rejected an impractical minority view voiced by some of the judges[85] in both cases to the effect that substituting the decision for chōtei was not *res judicata*, or a bar to a later suit. These judges therefore reasoned that since the actions of the lower courts were not judgments barring later suit, the tenants, who were ordered to evacuate, were not deprived of their constitutional rights of access to the courts because they could still sue on the merits despite the prior court order.

These two Supreme Court cases were concerned with disputes which carried over under the provisions of the older chōtei laws, which had been repealed by the Civil Conciliation Law (1951). Yet they are nevertheless significant cases because, along with the recent criticisms of the actual operation of the chōtei system, they raise the important question of the proper role of chōtei in a modern legal order and of the relationship of chōtei to the rule-of-law as embodied in the new Japanese constitution.[86] In a sense the new statutory chōtei represents progress in Japanese legal development, because it has brought a portion of the total conciliation in Japan, which hitherto had been largely an extralegal, social phenomenon, into the realm of the law and the courts. Yet chōtei is not a proper substitute for a legal system enforceable in the courts, and in the final chapter we will consider this problem of properly accommodating the chōtei system within the modern legal framework.

[85] The judges who argued that the decision substituted for chōtei by the court of first instance was not *res judicata* were Kawamura Daisuke (concurring) 14 *Saikō saibansho hanreishū* 1669–73 and Ishizaka and Shima (dissenting) 14 *id*. 1673 and Tarumi (dissenting) 14 *id*. 1675 (1960). Compare on this point Suekawa Hiroshi *et al.*, "Chōtei ni kawaru saiban no gōkensei o megutte" (Centering around the constitutionality of substitution of trial for conciliation), 35 *Minshōhō zasshi* (no. 5) 528–54 (1957), and especially the remarks of Taniguchi at 545.

[86] Note that the pre-1947 Japanese Supreme Court (*Daishinin*) had reviewed decisions based on the laws providing for substitution of trial for conciliation: 24 *Daishinin minji hanreishū* 大審院民事判例集 (Collection of civil cases of the Supreme Court [pre-1947]) 91 (March 9, 1945), construing the Temporary Law for Conciliation of Monetary Obligations, art. 7; 23 *Daishinin minji hanreishū* 444 (Aug. 10, 1944), construing the same law. Cf. 12 *Saikō saibansho hanreishū* 381–413 (March 5, 1958).

CHAPTER X

Perspective and Appraisal

OUR TERMINAL reflections on the merits and meaning of Japanese conciliation practices inevitably lead into collateral fields where some of the comparisons suggested and problems raised can at this point only be noted for further study. We can say this much, however, at the outset of our appraisal. Voluntary chōtei of the sort which Japan has been developing since 1951 has considerable merit so long as it can be confined to the role of an optional, auxiliary procedure to complement the adjudicatory system. On the other hand both the historical and the theoretical analyses which follow indicate that to the extent that they become exclusive or coercive remedies for the disputants, either by statute, practice, or lack of alternatives, conciliatory practices fall short of the goals of the modern rule-of-law. In this regard, we make some reservations later about the extensive use of court Compromise *(wakai)*.

HISTORICAL SYNOPSIS

Returning to some of the questions raised at the beginning of this study, our historical survey of the Japanese civil dispute-settlement process from Tokugawa to modern times leaves little doubt of the continuity and predominance of conciliation. In both traditional and modern Japan, conciliation of one sort or another has been and still is effective in settling the vast majority of disputes arising in the gradually changing social context. The point to emphasize here is that Japanese conciliation itself, as might be expected, has undergone some significant changes, both formally and functionally. Especially notable are the changes which have occurred in the relationship between conciliation and adjudication as the positive-law order has evolved and strengthened in moving through three stages: from the Tokugawa multi-status society to a society of dual-status (governed and governor), and now in the postwar period, to a single-status society under a genuine rule-of-law (individual citizenship) guaranteed by the 1947 constitution.[1]

---

[1] For clarity, note that "status," of course, refers to the roles of law in the respective societies. See chapter I, note 31 for our usage of the term, *rule-of-law*. Briefly, "rule-of-law" as used here is an expression of political values. It is the legal dimension of popular (therefore limited) government.

In historical perspective, we have been able to observe these significant functional changes taking place in the form of an accommodation between the didactic conciliatory practices which originated in the pre-Tokugawa villages on the one hand and the gradually evolving, centralized system of positive-law adjudication, which had its origins with the Tokugawa Shogunate, but which has continued to develop more rapidly, of course, throughout modern times under the imported codes and Meiji constitution. Four stages particularly seem to epitomize this accommodation of conciliation within the positive-law order.

The first, primitive conciliation, which we have called didactic conciliation (see chapter I) to avoid confusing it with later voluntary forms, had its origins in the villages of Japan, before there was any Shogunate positive law of consequence to the private transactions of the villagers; consequently, those civil disputes which were not resolved peremptorily by family status authorities were resolved rather exclusively by village conciliators. Second, as a Tokugawa law developed, we find a two-stage dispute-resolution process, wherein didactic village conciliation persisted as the first step. But a rudimentary system of Shogunate adjudication was added, in which didactic conciliation techniques were adopted as the core of its procedures also, particularly in handling the numerous cases spawned by rising commercialism. As we noted earlier, during these first two stages there may have been less conciliation than the nature of the process might indicate. The villages gradually developed their "courts" which enforced their "law" even though the courts were not well labeled,[2] and when there was conciliation, one suspects that the "conciliation" principle was not that it is better to agree, but rather, "You had better agree!"—a principle more like adjudication. Nevertheless, the disputants often did yield to the pressures and instructions of the conciliators and agree to settle rather than risk violence.

Third, after the enforcement of the Japanese Code of Civil Procedure (1891), we enter a phase of ambiguity, wherein the positive-law courts and codes presumed to cover nearly all private transactions and civil disputes arising therefrom, but where, in fact, most disputes continued to be either conciliated locally and informally by traditional methods subsisting in social practice beneath the shallow, actual reach of the new code law, or conciliated within the adjudicatory system by efforts of the judges employing code compromise techniques (e.g. CCP 136) or, increasingly after 1922,

---

[2] See Radin, "A Restatement of Hohfeld," 51 *Harv. L. Rev.* 1142–64, 1145 (1938) and Hoebel, *The Law of Primitive Man* 19–28 (1954) for descriptions of what we have called "anthropological adjudication" (chapter III), which more nearly describes the main stream of Tokugawa dispute settlement as described in this study (chapters IV through VI) than conciliation, if that term implies free agreement, first to conciliate or secondly to settle.

by use of the new statutory chōtei procedures, thereafter incorporated into the system of adjudication itself.

Fourth, a very different legal and practical adjustment between chōtei and adjudication is now in process as required by the new constitutional order dating from 1947. This final phase has seen the traditional family and village relationships legally transformed by the new individualism of the 1947 constitution and the land reform laws; also, official action has been subjected to new standards of judicial review, legally at least. To accomplish this transition in reality as well as on the law books, of course, requires time and profound social readjustments, one of which involves a re-evaluation of the conciliation practices to make them consistent with a rule-of-law.

The current statistics on litigation indicate perhaps that a proper adjustment between modern, voluntary conciliation and adjudication has not yet been reached. Inasmuch as conciliation predated adjudication in Japan, it is likely that the role of adjudication will increase as the Japanese social practices become gradually rationalized under centralized codes enforceable in efficient courts; the functions of conciliation might decline accordingly. But, the induction of chōtei into the legal system, where its voluntary character is protected, amplifies the social value of its role which will then presumably at some point become balanced with adjudication. The trend in favor of lawsuits over statutory chōtei cases, which has continued since 1948 (but at a rather slow rate since 1956) is worth watching in the future. It might be that this trend would increase, if the efficiency of the litigation process were improved.

Thus conciliation itself is being limited and redefined to do new jobs under new circumstances. It is in fact becoming an optional, auxiliary procedure within the system of adjudication for the amicable settlement of that vast bulk of disputes in any society which should not go to formal judgment. The generalized chōtei statutes of 1948 (Domestic Affairs) and 1951 (Civil) have initially formulated such an auxiliary role for conciliation, and the recent scholarly criticism and Supreme Court cases testing the constitutionality of pre-war didactic (compulsory and therefore exclusive) chōtei imply a proper concern now for making the actual chōtei practices consistent with the new role as legally defined. It may well be that the compromise procedure will also require re-evaluation in the near future.

The essence of this new legal formulation is that the voluntary character of chōtei is protected by the positive law. Qualitatively, chōtei must be voluntary; in a modern legal order compulsory chōtei is not only an inconsistency in terms, but a denial of the constitutional right of public trial. Such a qualitative limitation implies important quantitative restrictions as well, because it means that as a remedial device chōtei is optional and therefore not the exclusive remedy in any given case. Many cases can and will be handled initially as lawsuits, and others will ultimately be referred to litigation in the courts at the option of the parties, if conciliation proves unsatisfactory. The primacy of the positive law of contract which guarantees the voluntary character of chōtei agreements implies a practicable, alternative remedy in the form of adjudication. These are the basic differences between modern and Tokugawa conciliation.

APPRAISAL

Any evaluation of conciliation must take into account its historical types and uses. For example, conciliation of nonjusticiable disputes occurring outside of a common legal order must be judged by different criteria than didactic conciliation between parties within a nascent or authoritarian regime and by still different criteria than voluntary conciliation in a state which has achieved, to some degree, a rule-of-law. At this point, we are concerned only with a theory of voluntary conciliation which is consistent with modern Japanese constitutionalism and a rule-of-law. The need for clear thinking on this point is aggravated because Japanese traditional conciliation has always been highly valued in Japan, and it is still frequently said, especially by officials and conciliators, that conciliation is a preferred method of dispute settlement and somehow peculiarly appropriate to the Japanese personality, tradition, or philosophy. Often one wonders whether such comments are not based upon an inadvertent failure to distinguish the traditional didactic conciliation with all of its subtle coercions from the new constitutional conception of voluntary conciliation. Since 1948 there has been a clear legal break with the past regarding the role of conciliation which must be clearly understood.

On the theoretical level, F. S. C. Northrop has given much recent attention to the philosophical meaning of conciliation (in his terms "mediation"). He has been much concerned with the problems of conciliation as a voluntary and exclusive method of dispute settlement, and we owe much to his pioneering thoughts on the subject. Particularly convincing is his insistence that a dispute-settlement method implies basic epistemological and ethical notions. In understanding "mediation," it is most helpful to have the underlying assumptions, which are required to justify the process, clearly articulated. However, the comprehensiveness of Northrop's task and the scope of his erudition is such that he should be read directly.[3] No

---

[3] The fullest discussion of Northrop's "mediational approval theory of law" (i.e. conciliation as an exclusive remedy) is Northrop, "The Mediational Approval Theory of Law in American Legal Realism," 44 *Va. L. Rev.* 347–63 (1958). Also see Northrop, "The Epistemology of Legal Judgments," 58 *N. W. L. Rev.* 732–49 (1964); Northrop, *The Meet-*

adequate restatement of his theory is practicable here. Suffice it to say that his construct, the "mediational approval theory of law," is a system based on a radically empirical epistemology, an approval ethic, and a psychological "man-to-man-ness," all of which is synthesized into a thoroughly subjective system wherein both facts and values are personal, not demonstrable or social, and even the voluntary agreement necessary to solve a particular dispute by mediation is achieved "emotively" by man-to-man-ness.[4]

Northrop's "mediational approval theory of law" is, if we understand it, a theory of dispute settlement which he feels is widely used in Asia and which is both voluntary and exclusive. Contrariwise, our conclusion based on western constitutional theory and Japanese conciliation practice is emphatically to the effect that voluntary conciliation can only occur in practice when it is a nonexclusive auxiliary to a system of adjudication and supported by a law of contract.[5] These differences raise five questions which require further study, perhaps, but which can be discussed preliminarily here. First, of course, as Northrop carefully articulates, radical empiricism is quite a different theory of knowledge than that upon which modern science is based, and we proceed here upon the specific assumption that the dualistic theory of science[6] is more useful—without overlooking the fact that "there is radically empirical immediacy" and that human fallibility counsels us to remember that even theories of knowledge are only hypotheses.

Second, the approval theory of ethics, despite its ideal attractiveness, is highly antisocial without agreements produced by "man-to-man-ness," which one hesitates to posit ontologically because of copious contrary data of warring and feuding.

Third, Northrop makes a special use of the term *law*. We suppose that

---

ing of East and West 374–404 (1945); Northrop, "A Comparative Philosophy of Comparative Law," 45 *Cornell L. Q.* 617–58 (1959–60); Northrop, *The Complexity of Legal and Ethical Experience* 204–15 (1959); and Northrop, *Philosophical Anthropology and Practical Politics* 115–68 (1960).

[4] Northrop, "The Mediational Approval Theory of Law in American Realism," 44 *Va. L. Rev.* 357–59 (1958); also *Jen* (Confucius), *chit* consciousness (*Hindu*) or Nirvana consciousness (Buddhist) perform this heavy duty for Northrop.

[5] It is difficult to see how Northrop, "A Comparative Philosophy of Comparative Law," 45 *Cornell L. Q.* 617–58, 618 (1959–60) has added a third "major species of law" to Maine's law-of-status and law-of-contract except in the utopian anarchic sense (see note 7). Because of its nature as an agreement, freely negotiated, the mediational theory can only find a *legal* basis in the law-of-contract theory, as is true of any other individual freedom, guaranteed by *law*, as opposed to other solutions (see chapter I).

[6] For example, see Einstein, *The World as I See It* 60 (1934); Conant, *Modern Science and Modern Man* 103–41 (1952); Northrop, *The Meeting of East and West* 291–310 and 436–78 (1946); Northrop, "A Comparative Philosophy of Comparative Law," 45 *Cornell L. Q.* 617 –58 at 643–57 (1959–60).

the "mediational approval theory of law" is only "legal" in the same natural-law sense that some forms of utopian anarchy[7] are legalistic (i.e., everyone so ideally understands and complies with the rules of society— in turn based on unanimously agreed values—that no enforcement, be- yond discussion, is necessary).

Fourth, as opposed to Northrop's Asian philosophy, the Asian data (Japanese, Philippine, Tibetan, and Chinese)[8] certainly indicate that in some Asian communal practice conciliation without the support of an enforceable law of contract is not voluntary. Such communal conciliation as has been reported to date seems usually to be didactic and an expression of authority and power in the specific social context rather than voluntary, as required by Northrop's approval ethics. Of course, disputants in these communities do eventually "agree" to do what they come to see that they will have to do. Such Asian conciliation has the virtue of a degree of patience with the defendant, but it is scarcely voluntary.

Finally, we would suggest that, to the extent that Northrop implies (and this point seems to be only implicit) that conciliation is peculiarly Asian or oriental, his theory is much too limited. Prestate conciliation and didactic conciliation are apparently phenomena encountered among the American Indians, the Africans, and even early Anglo-Saxons. In his- torical perspective, we suspect that didactic conciliation, rather than being oriental, is simply primitive in the sense that it is developmentally prior to adjudication, although conciliation of another type may later coexist usefully within a litigation process.

Northrop also notes that in fact the mediational-approval theory of law

[7] For such an approach to this problem in the theory of anarchism (Godwin, Proudhon, Bakunin, Kropotkin, and Bertrand Russell), see convenient summaries in Gray, *The Socialist Tradition,* 114–35, 230–56, and 352–83 (1946). We might add that Northrop's "mediational approval theory of law" in leaving concretization of the "law" (see Kelsen, *General Theory of Law and State* 131–38 [1945]) to each set of disputants is almost an inverse correlate of the early, equally formal, legal theory of Kelsen (also Stammler) leaving concretization to one despot on an *ad hoc* basis; that is, pure despotism can represent an order of law if there exists in the despotic state a written or unwritten basic norm to the effect that legal relations of the subjects are to be determined exclusively by the concrete decisions of the despot in each individual case. See Bodenheimer, "Reflections on the Rule of Law," 8 *Utah L. Rev.* 1–11, 2 (1962), citing Kelsen, *Allgemeine Staatstlehre* 335–36 (1925), and also Stammler, "Recht und Willkür," in 1 *Rechtsphilosophische Abhandlungen und Vorträge* 111 (1925).

[8] Our study of the Japanese villages indicate that they relied more on what we have called anthropological adjudication or on didactic, as distinguished from voluntary, con- ciliation. Also, it seems most unlikely that any Asian villages, to which Northrop refers (44 *Va. L. Rev.* 360), ever relied on his "mediational approval theory of law"; see also Barton, *Ifugao Law* (1919); and Michael, "The Role of Law in Traditional, Nationalist and Communist China," *China Quarterly* 124–68 (Jan.-March 1962) for analysis of Philip- pine and Chinese village adjudication respectively. Also see Ekvall, "Mi sTong: The Tibetan Custom of Life Indemnity," 4 *Sociologus* (no. 2) 136–45 (1954) for information on Tibetan mediation.

is only a theory of dispute settlement and that it has never been employed successfully in Asia or anywhere else as a system of "law" for channeling the activity of an extensive area or complex society. Modern society, of course, requires principles of law—some mere signal rules and others of more moral content—to order territorially extensive, complex, industrial activities and supply the modicum of predictability underlying the division of labor and trade implicit in industrial society.

This channeling function of legal rules is not only necessary to any legal system, separate and apart from its dispute-resolution role, but historically it seems that channeling is also related to and reliant upon dispute resolution. Complex society requires that the law courts (1) enforce and vindicate the channeling rules, and (2) refine and amplify them by decisions in novel cases which serve as precedents for future action. Of course, the latter judges' function, which Llewellyn has called the "molecular law-making power,"[9] is a pronounced feature of Anglo-American law, but it has its counterpart to a varying and generally increasing degree, in many of the civil-law countries, as well as in primitive societies.

Without efficient courts to perform such functions effectively, the excessive use of conciliation stunts the growth and refinement of the body of rules necessary to sustain complex community life; it dulls the citizens' sense of right, essential to the vindication of the law. It may also allow old rules and social prejudices, which new legislation has sought to abolish, to influence the outcome of disputes; or it may allow a new regime to ignore the law in favor of its new policy, as happened in Japan in the 1930's. In other words, conciliation is neither conservative nor progressive in principle; it is simply unprincipled. It may favor the powerful over the weak, in the name of bargaining; it ordinarily forces plaintiffs to discount their claims; it may operate to compromise large-scale, group interests which might better be handled by forthright reform legislation. In short, conciliation is only an adjunct to, not a substitute for, a legal order; and if relied upon excessively, it is not merely nonlegal—it has antilegal results, as shown by the Japanese wartime writings on chōtei (chapter IX). It takes a legal framework to protect the voluntary character of conciliation; and if it is not voluntary, conciliation will likely become in practice simply a standardless use of force.

The above analysis points to the criteria for a proper relationship between conciliation and adjudication. Since conciliated solutions are only personally satisfactory and not socially meaningful—except in a do-as-you-please sense—it is clear enough that only those disputes whose effects are limited to the disputants themselves can properly be settled by conciliation. In a law-of-contract society, the scope and theory of contract

[9] Llewellyn, *Jurisprudence-Realism in Theory and Practice* 516 (1962).

itself can be adapted both to define the limits and to provide the framework to preserve the free bargaining positions of the parties, which is the essence of conciliation. This scope may be coextensive with the range of contractual compromise and novation. By analogy the principles for protection of contractual parties against fraud, duress, illegality, and mistake may also be useful to avoid the dangers of compulsion. But most important, it is necessary that if the parties so desire, they have the right to their day in court. Conciliation must be truly auxiliary to a court system where the party can take his rights, as he sees them, and get them measured by legal standards[10] with a maximum of efficiency and dispatch. As such an auxiliary, it can be very useful to mitigate the frequent excesses of adversary, all-or-nothing litigation.

What then are some of the types of disputes which could be properly handled by voluntary conciliation? The general criterion would be those cases which involve only issues existential and particular to the disputants. Most appropriate are cases that can be freely conciliated to produce an agreement without a loss of legal right, including cases where conciliation may educate the parties at an early date to understand and accept their legal obligation.

Without presuming to be exhaustive, five situations readily come to mind where voluntary conciliation will produce quick and inexpensive results, probably more difficult to achieve by litigation. First, in many cases unsophisticated persons will become involved in a dispute based on ignorance of their legal position. Upon thinking the matter through in the course of conciliation, they may be quite willing to accede to the requirements of the law, once it is understood. Second, disputes often arise because one party has possession of the subject matter of the dispute or the upper hand in some other respect and stubbornly refuses, therefore, to recognize the legal right of the weaker party in the *de facto* situation; but being confronted before others with the impropriety of his position, he may willingly recognize all or part of the other person's right. Third, in cases similar to the second situation above, but in which the parties are relatives, partners, or have other relationships requiring close future associations, conciliation is particularly valuable if it can obtain recognition of the rightful claims of the weaker without a lawsuit. The all-or-nothing result of a judgment and execution, however correct, may be no solution at all to broader problems of mutual coexistence imposed by labor relations, family or even business relationships, from which rather minor misunderstandings may arise and become exaggerated in a lawsuit. Fourth, there is the opposite situation where the stronger party in fact has the right as well, but the

---

[10] See Vanderbilt, *Minimum Standards of Judicial Administration* xxxiii (1949) for the importance of this point.

weaker party simply cannot perform. Conciliation may produce a compository result wherein both parties will get some relief, whereas a lawsuit prosecuted to judgment and compulsory execution would yield little or nothing, minus fees and expenses. Fifth, in cases where one party has the right, but to enforce it is manifestly unfair, conciliation is flexible enough to produce an equitable result agreeable to both parties. These five types of disputes have an element in common: namely, the factual and legal positions of the parties become clear to them during the process. Even in cases where the facts remain cloudy, free conciliation may provide a voluntary and congenial atmosphere for bargaining over the value of the claim, which both parties know (whether they admit it or not) is not 100 per cent sound for either of them. When the applicable legal principles are conflicting, however, it may be desirable for proper channeling to litigate and clarify the rule for both the instant case and future conduct.

In all of the above examples, it may be possible to reach a satisfactory result with less expenditure of time, money, and adrenalin than in a lawsuit, and no doubt such cases encompass the vast bulk of lawsuits filed. As we have seen, in Japan only 37 per cent of the cases filed go to judgment or other court disposition, and probably less than a third of the lawsuits filed ordinarily go to trial in the United States (e.g., New York Supreme Court, 29 per cent).[11] Furthermore, the result and the manner of reaching that result may be more acceptable to the disputants than if they become enmeshed from the beginning in the technicalities of a lawsuit, requiring the intervention of lawyers. Much more flexible adjustments of interests, including possible commitments for future conduct, are also attainable by a conciliation agreement, whereas a judgment is usually of relatively fixed form. Also, the disputants with continuing associations may feel more satisfied emotionally with an agreed result than if the decision takes the form of total vanquishment of one by the other in a judicial pronouncement.

NEW PROBLEMS AND POTENTIALS FOR CHŌTEI

As a voluntary, auxiliary procedure, legally constituted and judicially supervised, Japanese chōtei today is quite a different institution from the traditional didactic conciliation, which blends into anthropological adjudication as discussed in chapter III. Likewise its potentials and practical problems are not the same. As we have seen, one of the chief differences in the environment of modern Japanese chōtei arises from the rather advanced legal order of which it is now a part. This new legal order seeks

[11] Zeisel, Kalven, and Buchholz, *Delay in the Court* 11 (1959). See also Virtue, *Survey of Metropolitan Courts Final Report* 233 (1962); and for the American lawyer's role in settlement, see Sindell, *Let's Talk Settlement by Joseph and David Sindell* (1963).

to guarantee certain rights, enforceable in the regular court system against anyone, including officials, who violates them. Two of these important rights guaranteed in Japan are the right to conciliate (settle disputes by private agreement) and the right of access to the courts; or stated another way, the right not to conciliate any more than one chooses. These rights are stated clearly enough in the law: Article 32 of the constitution provides that no person shall be denied the right of access to the courts; the Conciliation Law of 1951, Article 1, provides for optional conciliation, and Articles 14 and 19 make it possible for a party to refuse to make further concessions and to institute a lawsuit; or, of course, he can go to court in the first place without any conciliatory efforts at all. We have noted in chapter I that such an option is necessary to render conciliation voluntary. Hence, this is an important accomplishment in Japanese legal history, but we cannot satisfy ourselves at this point with the simple legalities of the situation.

The practicality of a lawsuit as an alternative: We also need to know if there is in fact a realistic alternative remedy in the Japanese courts, and if so, how practicable is it, in case a party decides he does not want to conciliate, informally or otherwise. Perhaps conciliation is prevalent (chapter VIII) simply because the courts are cumbersome, unfair, expensive, or too slow to be useful to the citizens, or because the citizens know that further conciliation is about all they will get in the court anyway. In other words, the existence of a court system and a right of access to it does not supply the alternative remedy, which is required to render conciliation voluntary, unless the court system can handle all of the cases presented to it fairly and within the practical limits of the parties' time and money. This question introduces the whole problem of current judicial administration and trial procedure, which can only be touched upon briefly here.

Certainly there is no serious question about the integrity and competence of Japanese courts. Considering Japanese income levels, the costs of litigation may be somewhat high, but probably the expense of Japanese litigation as such is not a major problem. In this regard, recent proposals[12] to charge the loser with the court costs and winner's attorney fees may have some merits in avoiding plaintiffs' nuisance suits or deliberate and expensive prolongation by defendants.[13] On the other hand, even though the volume of Japanese litigation per capita is extremely light by our standards (see chapter VIII), court congestion and delay is a serious prob-

---

[12] See Chief Justice Tanaka Kōtarō's greeting in *Minji saibankan kaidōyōroku* 民事裁判官会同要録 (Essential records of the conference of judges in civil matters) in 78 *Minji saiban shiryō* (Materials on civil adjudication) 7–9 (1960).

[13] See Zeisel *et al., op. cit. supra* note 11, at 292–94 (1959) for a similar system said to work well in Austria.

lem in Japan,[14] although just how serious it is comparatively[15] is difficult to measure. Faced with serious court congestion, the question becomes then, how much delay is equivalent, practically speaking, to denial of access to the courts? When does delay amount to coercive conciliation or private settlements—either out of court or by the courts? Certainly delay also weakens evidence, favors defendants,[16] causes hardships to litigants generally, and worst of all, corrodes the reputation of the courts and discourages reliance upon them. At some point the aphorism sometimes attributed to William Gladstone becomes true: "Justice delayed is justice denied."

Delay in court and the settlement ratio as a cure: Not limited to Japan, delay in court is a ubiquitous,[17] timeless,[18] and complex problem with an extensive literature,[19] and our interest in it here is rather limited. We are concerned with it in Japan only as a problem factor in maintaining a proper relationship between voluntary conciliation and adjudication. It will therefore suffice to note as general background that court congestion is best cured by better procedural rules and more judges. These measures, however, requiring budgetary (hence political) support, are generally difficult to obtain from legislatures. Judges are too few and too dignified

[14] For examples of concern over this problem in Japan, see articles in the symposium entitled "Soshō no sokushin to kōsei na saiban," 30 *Hōritsu jihō* 4–51 (1958); and Saikō saibansho jimu sōkyoku, *Minji saibankan kaidōyōroku* in 78 *Minji saiban shiryō* (1960).

[15] For an example of one method of comparison of United States and Japanese delay in 1953, which we suspect only tells a small part of the story, see Saikō saibansho jimu sōkyoku, "Shōwa nijūhachi-nendo minji jiken no gaikyō" 昭和二十八年度民事々件の概況 (The general condition of civil cases for the year 1953), 6 *Hōsō jihō* 1618–47, 1634 (1954).

[16] See Vanderbilt, *The Challenge of Law Reform* 77 (1955).

[17] See Zeisel *et al.*, *Delay in the Court* xxiii, note 6 (1959), quoting the *Autobiography of Goethe* (1749–1832) to the effect that in the Wetzlar court, where he practiced law for a while, "Twenty thousand cases had piled up, sixty could by disposed of every year, while twice as many were added." Also see Judge Ulysses S. Schwartz's references to literary comment from several countries on court delay (English: *Hamlet*, Gilbert and Sullivan, Dickens' *Bleak House;* French: Moliere; Russian: Chekhov) in Gray v. Gray, 6 Ill. App. 2d 571, 578–79, 128 N.E. 2d 602, 606 (1955).

[18] See Nims, "New York's Hundred Years of Struggle for Better Civil Justice," 25 *N.Y.S.B. Bull.* 83 (1953).

[19] For useful recent studies on court congestion in Japan and the United States, respectively, see the symposium of articles, "Shihō seido no tōmen suru mondai" 司法制度の当面する問題 (Problems confronting the judicial system), *Jurisuto* (no. 265) 10–168 (1963); and "Soshō no sokushin to kōsei na saiban" 訴訟の促進と公正な裁判 (Expediting lawsuits and a fair trial), 30 *Hōritsu jihō* 1248–93 (1958); Zeisel *et al.*, *Delay in the Court* (1959); and articles in the symposium entitled "Lagging Justice" in 328 *The Annals of the Am. Acad. of Pol. and Soc. Science* 1–163 (1960); and for voluminous other sources, see Klein (compiler), *Judicial Administration and the Legal Profession; A Bibliography* (1963); "Selected Bibliography," in Zeisel *et al.*, *Delay in the Court* 297–303 (1959); and "Selected Annotated Bibliographies on Judicial Selection and Court Administration," 45 *J. Am. Jud. Soc'y.* (no. 8) 17–28 (1962).

to become an effective pressure group, and so, lacking popular support, court reform is usually long overdue before relief can be legislated. Perhaps it is a melancholy truth that a populace gets no better legal system than it deserves. Nevertheless, when antiquated procedures and shortages of judges[20] are allowed to continue causing a backlog of cases and consequent pressures on the court, the only other cure, save perhaps to work the judges even harder and more efficiently,[21] is to reduce the number of cases for the court by increasing the settlement ratio.

The judge's settlement role—Japanese compromise and American pretrial: We have seen that the Japanese judge's most direct settlement efforts after a suit is filed are by using his discretionary compromise procedures at any stage of the trial. But he also participates on the chōtei committee to settle suits before they are filed as lawsuits. On the other hand, American judges tend to use their pretrial procedures,[22] available in most courts, although of course pretrial has a dual purpose—settlement and trial preparation. Because it is thought that these different approaches in the United States and Japan may be mutually instructive, parallel references will be made hereafter to the experience in the United States.

In a congested court, the relationship between conciliatory (settlement) efforts and adjudication becomes rather convoluted because prompt and practical alternative adjudication is necessary to render conciliation voluntary; and conciliatory efforts are needed by the congested courts to reduce the cases to be adjudicated. In this sort of tail-chasing lies considerable danger for the constitutional right of access to the courts. Inadvert-

[20] See Kaneko Hajime, "Sosho chien to shihō seisaku.' 訴訟遅延と司法政策 (Delay of litigation and judicial policy), 30 *Hōritsu jihō* 1248–50, 1250 (1958). But perhaps Japan needs more lawyers even worse than it needs more judges, because, as mentioned in chapter VIII, in 60.4 per cent of the cases in the district courts and 89.2 per cent of the cases in the summary courts of Japan in 1962, one or both of the parties appeared without counsel. It is hardly necessary to elaborate as to the effect of this fact upon the work of the judge. Also it would seem to require an inquisitorial rather than umpire role for the judge. So, it is quite academic to speak of adjusting Japanese civil procedure in favor of a more adversary approach or more party presentation to relieve the overworked judges, until this sort of a condition is corrected. It would be necessary first to build up an adequate bar and then require litigants to use lawyers, before any procedural changes could be made to relieve the judge of the heavy burden he now has to shoulder in these cases where the party is not represented by a lawyer. See Azegami Eiji 畔上英治, "Minji soshō o miru kakudo" 民事訴訟をみる角度 (An angle from which to view civil suits), 30 *Hōritsu jihō* 1263–66, 1263 (1958) for a description of the difficulty caused to the judge by failure of the parties to hire lawyers. Also see generally Henderson, "The Role of Lawyers in U.S.-Japanese Business Transactions," 38 *Wash. L. Rev.* 1-21 (1963).

[21] Zeisel *et al., Delay in the Court* 5 (1959).

[22] See generally Van Alstyne and Grossman, *California Pretrial and Settlement Procedures* 167–209 (1963); and Virtue, *Survey of Metropolitan Courts Final Report* 244–52 (1962); and Nims, *Pre-Trial* (1950) for a description of United States pretrial system; and Fisher, "Judicial Mediation: How it Works through Pretrial," 10 *U. Chi. L. Rev.* 453, 457 (1943); cf. Randall, "Conciliation as a Function of the Judge," 18 *Ken. L. Rev.* 330–40 (1929–30).

ently, didactic conciliation in court may become the alternative to "voluntary" conciliation out of court.

It is this problem of the relationship between court congestion and the settlement ratio which brings into sharp relief the further question of the proper role of the judge in settling cases during trial, and here we are talking primarily about Japanese compromise, not chōtei. In our thinking, the judge's primary role is of course to decide cases in accordance with the law and on the evidence presented (or elicited, in Japan, where the adversary system is not so well developed). Thus the judge's conciliatory or settlement role is subsidiary at best, and inconsistent at worst, with his judicial duty.

With a burdensome backlog of cases and with the best of intentions, the judge as conciliator may prematurely take a position based on hearsay, fragmentary evidence, or a hunch; or he may without realizing it intimidate unsophisticated parties by informal remarks which convince them that, however strong they may think their case is, it is hopeless in the particular judge's court. Of course it would be a rare judge who would knowingly transform his role as a judge to that of a fixer or a bully. But, we are especially concerned with how his settlement efforts look to the parties. Legally the parties have a right to a free option to settle or litigate.

This specific problem of post-filing judicial pressure to settle lawsuits seems to be currently viewed with more concern in the United States than in Japan. For example, Chief Justice Earl Warren, addressing himself to this general problem in the United States, said:

> These statistics are a record of delay piled upon delay in the federal courts. But, serious as they may be, they are no accurate measure of the extent to which our administrative weaknesses have caused injustice. They do not reflect the hardship and suffering caused to unfortunate victims of such delays, *nor the inadequate settlements which individuals are frequently forced to accept on that account.* Neither do these figures include what are probably the worst and most numerous cases of all: those instances in which citizens with causes that cry for justice under law have turned from our court system in despair and have sought ways of working out their problems without resort to the courts at all.[23] (emphasis added)

Similar views have been voiced by Chief Justice Warren elsewhere,[24] as well as by Justice William J. Brennan, Jr.,[25] Judge Arthur T. Vander-

[23] Warren, "Delay and Congestion in the Federal Courts," 42 *J. Am. Jud. Soc'y.* (no. 1) 9 (1958).

[24] Warren, "The Problem of Delay: A Task for Bench and Bar Alike," 44 *A.B.A.J.* 1043–46 and 1069 (1958).

[25] Brennan, *Proceedings of the Attorney-General's Conference on Court Congestion and Delay in Litigation* 87 (1956).

bilt,[26] and Judge Bernard Botein,[27] to name only a few. Their point is, of course, that not all cases should be settled by whatever means, for we have already seen the effect on the law of excessive settlement bargaining. We can conclude, perhaps, that if litigation is not a positive good, it is, at least in some cases, a necessary evil to serve as a vehicle of the right-consciousness of the citizenry.

On the other hand, for perspective we must bear in mind that, despite these recent expressions of concern in the United States about the judge's overuse of settlement devices, historically there has been in the United States, as in Japan, an overwhelming policy in the law to the effect that the law favors amicable settlement. Indeed, the proposition is generally treated as self-evident, and therefore it is not usually supported by reasoning in the cases;[28] and its origins can reach back as far as the book of

---

[26] Vanderbilt, *The Challenge of Law Reform* 63 (1955); and Vanderbilt, 65 *Time* 17 (Feb. 21, 1955).

[27] Botein, "Our Courts Face the Future," 139 *New York Law Journal* (no. 15) 4 (Jan. 22, 1958).

[28] See, for example, Brown v. Guarantee Insurance Company, 155 Cal. App. 2d 191, 319 P.2d 69 at 79 (1958), "And it is fundamental that the law favors settlements"; Wahl v. Barnum, 116 N.Y. 87, 22 N.E. 280 at 282 (1889), "The law regards with favor, and seeks to uphold, settlements of pending or threatened litigations..."; Handley v. Mortland, 54 Wn.2d 489 at 496, 342 P.2d 612 at 616 (1959), "The law favors amicable settlements of disputes, and is inclined to clothe them with finality..."; Sanders v. Lawn Mutual Insurance Company, 194 Pa. Super. 475, 168 A.2d 758 at 761 (1961), "The law favors the amicable settlement of controversies and it is the duty of the courts to encourage rather than to discourage parties from resorting to compromise as a mode of adjusting conflicting claims..."; Empire Industries Inc. v. Northern Assurance Company, 342 Mich. 425, 70 N.W.2d 769 at 770 (1955), "Compromise settlements are favored by the law."

It may be noted here, however, that some state courts have given reasons to buttress the seemingly axiomatically accepted legal proposition that the law favors settlements. At least four reasons have been advanced. First, settlements reconcile contending parties. The law which is constituted to maintain peace and order, therefore favors any medium designed to promote and justify peace. See, for example, Tatum v. Carter, 270 Ala. 445, 119 So. 2d 223 at 225 (1960).

Second, "In view of the present and increasing volume of litigated actions practical necessity requires that settlements be effected in all cases where permissible and which are fairly susceptible to disposal in that manner," Bartlett v. Traveler's Ins. Co., 117 Conn. 147, 167 A. 180 at 182 (1933); for otherwise, the resultant congestion in the courts of law would materially impede the disposition of cases and thereby throttle judicial dispensation.

Third, the "injured party obtains acceptable compensation without the delay, expense, inconvenience, anxiety, and uncertainty of result attendant upon the pursuit of litigation; the party primarily liable is relieved of like annoyances..."; Bartlett v. Travelers' Ins. Co., 117 Conn. 147, 167 A. 180 at 183 (1933).

Fourth, "It is to the interest of the State that there should be an end to litigation, settlements not only terminate litigation, but also prevent litigation therefore the law favors settlements." "Courts exist to furnish remedies where they cannot be obtained by peaceable means," In re Thomas, 85 Conn. 50 at 54, 81 A.972 at 973 (1911).

Genesis.[29] Lawyers of almost universal prestige, such as Gandhi[30] and Lincoln,[31] have also made the strongest pleas for avoidance of litigation by compromise. This is as it should be. Clearly the injustice with which we are concerned here and to which Chief Justice Warren refers is not caused by private settlements as such, but rather by the heavy judicial reliance upon them and the judges' excessive efforts to produce them after suit has been filed, because the courts are too slow and crowded. The problem in Japan, as elsewhere, is to find a criterion with which to draw the line between adjudication and judicial, private-settlement efforts to achieve the maximum of good from both.

In considering criteria to untangle the bench's dual role as judge and settlement catalyst, two principles suggest themselves from the best American practice. First, the judge should refrain from active settlement efforts after trial begins. Of course, this suggests a problem for Japanese practice because the trial starts soon after filing and continues intermittently. Second, if the judge's settlement role is to be limited to pretrial, then the same judge should not later perform the trial function. This latter principle holds true even though in the United States pretrial has two purposes—to prepare the case for trial, and to attempt settlement. Considering pretrial as a procedure for trial preparation, of course, there is an argument for the efficiency of having the same judge hear the case later. However, experience, especially in the larger metropolitan courts of the United States, seems to demonstrate that using different judges for the trial and pretrial functions is generally feasible in the preparatory work,[32] and it is certainly preferred for the settlement discussions.

---

[29] E.g., Jenkins v. Fields *et al.*, 240 N.C. 776, 83 N.E.2d 908–911 (1954) citing the Bible, Gen. 13:8–9, for one of the earliest recorded compromises, between Abram and Lot. Also see Matt. 5:9: "Blessed are the peacemakers: for they shall be called the children of God."

[30] Gandhi, tr. Desai, *Autobiography* 167–68 (1948); cf. Corbett, *My India* 39–45 (1952).

[31] Abraham Lincoln as quoted in 3 *Martindale-Hubbell* 123 A (1962) as follows:
Discourage litigation. Persuade your neighbors to compromise whenever you can. Point out to them how the nominal winner is often a real loser—in fees, expenses and waste of time. As a peacemaker, the lawyer has a superior opportunity of being a good man. Never stir up litigation. A worse man can scarcely be found than one who does this. Who can be more nearly a fiend than he who habitually overhauls the register of deeds in search of defects in titles, whereupon to stir up strife and put money in his pocket? A moral tone ought to be enforced in the profession which would drive such men out of it.
Also, as quoted in the frontispiece of Frank, *Courts on Trial* (1950), Learned Hand said: "I must say that, as a litigant, I should dread a law suit beyond almost anything else short of sickness and death." See also Nims, "The Cost of Justice: A New Approach," 39 *A.B. A.J.* 455–58 (June 1953).

[32] Van Alstyne and Grossman, *California Pretrial and Settlement Procedure* 193 (1963); and Kincaid, *A Study of Pre-Trial Usage in Nine Areas of the United States* (unpublished report, 1955). Judge Kincaid studied pretrial, largely in state court operations, in Denver,

If it is sound principle to confine the judge's settlement activity to the pretrial phase, and then also to assign the trial and pretrial work to different judges, we find that Japanese chōtei conforms to the standard rather well, whereas compromise raises serious questions. At his discretion the judge can try to compromise the lawsuit at any stage of the proceeding (CCP 136); and since the trial proceeds by a series of intermittent hearings from the time of filing until judgment, the case is continuously at trial. The judge can therefore use his considerable influence at any time to obtain a settlement.

The Japanese literature reviewed in this study does not, however, reflect dissatisfaction with the compromise procedures as they operate in Japan,[33] which may indicate that the judicial exercise of discretion under CCP 136 is generally satisfactory.[34] Moreover, the Japanese continuous trial aided by the judge's compromise power should make it possible to settle those cases that normally can and will be settled without trial at a date earlier than settlement would occur in an American court with a backlog, which would cause cases to lie dormant for months and then finally get settled when the trial date arrives. The Japanese judge's inquisitorial role, the lack of broad discovery procedures permitting an early fixing of the facts by the *lawyers*, the Japanese Preparatory Procedure *(jumbi tetsuzuki)*,[35] and the entire mode of the Japanese intermittent trial

---

Chicago, Washington D.C., Trenton, New York, Brooklyn, Philadelphia, Cleveland, and Detroit as preparation for the California compulsory pretrial instituted in 1958, and he found that in five of these areas the trial and pretrial work was kept separate quite satisfactorily. Also see generally, Nims, *Pre-Trial* (1950); and Comment, "California Pretrial in Action," 49 *Calif. L. Rev.* 909–30 (1961), among the voluminous writings on pretrial generally.

[33] We have only investigated this practical aspect in a preliminary fashion. Actual operations, as distinguished from dryly legal analysis, under the compromise procedure, of CCP 136 have apparently not been extensively studied in Japan either. Perhaps the most detailed comment can be found in Iwamatsu Saburo and Kaneko Hajime (ed.) *Hōritsu jitsumu kōza, Minji soshō-hen, (dai-san-kan [dai-isshin tetsuzuki, 2])* 法律實務講座民事訴訟編第三巻第一審手続 (Lectures in practical aspects of law; Compilation on civil suits, Vol. 3; [Procedure of first instance, part 2]) 99–168, 139 and 167 (1959).

[34] Apparently the German code emphasizes the judge's role in settlement discussion even more strongly than the Japanese code. See German ZPO 349, directing single-judge courts to try to settle the case. In ZPO 296 the collegiate court is authorized, but not directed, to try to settle at any stage of the proceedings, which is similar to Japanese CCP 136. See Toussaint, "Conciliation Proceedings in the Federal Republic of Germany, Switzerland, Austria, Scandinavia, England and the United States," 10 *Int'l. Soc. Sci. Bull.* 616–28 (1958).

[35] Actually, the ordinary Japanese pretrial is somewhat similar *in function* to some of the pretrial practice in the United States. Whether it is used or not is discretionary with the court. See Supreme Court Rules of Civil Procedure, Articles 15–25, but also see Kozeki Toshimasa 古関敏正 , "Shinkenbu no setchi" 新件部の設置 (Establishment of the new case section), 11 *Hōsō jihō* 1202–39 (1959), for an interesting account of an experiment conducted in the Tokyo District Court. Unfortunately, the experiment was discontinued.

are enough different from the practice in the United States that we can merely suggest that in view of the foregoing analysis, which we suspect is generally sound, the compromise practices may raise serious questions of judicial propriety[36] under a rule-of-law.

Chōtei as a pretrial settlement device: It is precisely because of the difficulty of establishing proper standards for judicial behavior in the settlement process, especially during trial under the pressures of congested courts, that the Japanese experience with chōtei is especially interesting. Provided that the functioning of the system is true to its current legal conception, chōtei solves the problem of what cases should be settled and when, by furnishing a congenial environment prior to suit and leaving the settlement to the preferences of the parties. Chōtei is not "pretrial" in the American sense because it does not concern itself with simplifying the case for a possible trial later; but it does solve the dilemma of the double role for the judge by keeping settlement activity voluntary and adjudication separate. Analytically, one would suppose that with such procedures available in Japan, those cases that do get to court as suits are sufficiently litigious to suggest very sparing use of the compromise procedure during trial.

As mentioned briefly in chapter IX, Norway has also apparently found a similar answer to the settlement problem in its traditional conciliation system, which varies in detail[37] from Japanese chōtei, but in general

---

[36] See Kaplan, von Mehren, and Schaefer, "Phases of German Civil Procedure," 71 *Harv. L. Rev.* 1193–1268 and 1443–72, 1223 (1958) describing the similar German practice: The intensity and candor of the court's drive toward settlement will astonish an American observer. In few cases does settlement go unmentioned and it is the judge who generally initiates the discussion. Frequently the suggestion will come at the commencement of oral-argument and may even precede that event;...Especially when it comes at a later point, it may be accomplished by a speech by the judge which spares neither side. If the judge meets resistance or hesitation, he may dictate an outline of his proposed settlement into the minutes and give the parties time to consider. Cf. Klizke v. Hern, 242 Wis. 456, 8 N.W.2d 400, 401–2 (1943) (dictum); Livermore v. Bainbridge, 44 How. Pr. 357 (49 N.Y. 125), *aff'd*, 14 Abb. Pr. (n.s.) 227 (56 N.Y. 72) (1873); Allen v. Allen 132 Kan. 468, 295 Pac. 705 (1931); Rosenfield v. Vosper, 45 Cal. App. 2d 365, 114 P.2d 29 (1941); Livant v. Adams, 17 App. Div. 2d 784, 232 N.Y.S. 2d 641 (1962).

[37] For example, in contrast to Japanese practice, in Norway all civil cases, with minor exceptions, must go before elective conciliation commissions as a prerequisite to suit, and also attorneys are not allowed to appear for or with the parties and generally neither judges or lawyers are allowed to serve on the commission. Royal Norwegian Ministry of Justice, *Administration of Justice in Norway* 28–31 (1957). Also see Orfield, *The Growth of Scandinavian Law* 185–86 (1953); Grevstad, "Norway's Conciliation Tribunals," 2 *J. Am. Jud. Soc.y.* 5–18 (1918). This is a reprint from the *Atlantic Monthly* 671 (1893).

design, function,[38] and long history (since 1795),[39] it is strikingly similar. North Dakota (through numerous immigrants) and Denmark[40] have shared the Norwegian tradition, and they have both used similar conciliation systems; however, their systems were repealed in 1943 (North Dakota)[41] and 1952 (Denmark).[42]

In several other European countries[43]—France, Italy, Germany, Austria, Switzerland, Belgium, Spain, and perhaps others—conciliation systems have been instituted within the framework of the courts and the codes of civil procedure. Most of these systems are traceable to the French experiments with conciliation dating from the French Revolution. Some of them make prior attempts at conciliation a prerequisite to a lawsuit; others make conciliation optional with the parties or the judge either before filing a suit or after suit has been instituted. A detailed study of these systems would be required before confident comparisons could be made with either Japanese chōtei or compromise procedures. It seems, however, that most of them differ substantially from Japanese chōtei in that the conciliatory effort is made the responsibility of the judge acting alone, without the participation of laymen that we find in the Japanese and Norwegian conciliation. For the same reasons they have an over-all resemblance to Japanese compromise procedures. Germany adopted a preliminary conciliation system as a prerequisite to suit in the *Amtsgericht* (regular courts of first instance) in 1924, but it proved unpopular and was repealed in 1950.[44] France passed a new law in 1949, which did away "with the so-called '*grande conciliation*' which the *juge de paix* was forced to

[38] The heavy reliance on conciliation in Norway is shown by the 1961 statistics kindly furnished by letter from Professor of Law Torstein Echkoff of the University of Oslo:

	Conciliation Council	District Court	Circuit Court	Supreme Court	Total
Percentage	73.8	23.1	2.4	0.7	100%
Absolute Numbers	28,144	8,785	927	256	38,112

For Norwegian judicial statistics for the years 1955 to 1960, see Statistisk Sentralbyra, *Sivilrettsstatistikk 1960* designated *Norges Offisielle Statistisk A 34.*

[39] Orfield, *op. cit. supra* note 37, at 185 (1953).

[40] Reginald H. Smith, "The Danish Conciliation System," 11 *J. of Am. Jud. Soc'y.* 85–93 (1927); Ostenfeld, "Danish Courts of Conciliation," 9 *A.B.A.J.* 747–48 (1923); Teisen, "The Danish Judicial Code," 65 *U. Pa. L. Rev.* 543–70, 560 (1916).

[41] *Supplement to the 1913 Compiled Laws of N.D. (annotated 1913–1925)* section 9192 a (1)–9192 a (15); Klein v. Hutton, 49 N.D. 248, 191 N.W. 485–490, 167 A.L.R. 831 (1922) upholding constitutionality. The repealing statute was: 1943 *Session Laws*, chapter 228; also see discussion of the following: Anonymous, "Act to Provide for Conciliation," 2 *J. Am. Jud. Soc'y.* 151–57 (1918); Shafer, "North Dakota's Conciliation Laws," 9 9 *A.B.A.J.* 748–49 (1923). Shafer states: "...I think that in actual experience in our state the results have not justified, or at least have not come up to, the hopes and expectations of the authors of the measure" (p. 749).

[42] Danish conciliation commissions were abolished by Law No. 220, June 20, 1952, but the judge is still empowered to conciliate at first instance.

[43] Biglia and Spinosa, "The Function of Conciliation in Civil Procedure," 10 *Int'l Soc. Sci. Bull.* 604–16 (1958); and Toussaint, *op. cit. supra* note 34, at 616 (1958).

attempt in respect of all matters which fell within the competence of the *tribunal civil* and left intact the *'petite conciliation'* which provides for obligatory conciliation proceedings in all other cases."[45] In the United States some jurisdictions have interesting analogous systems, particularly in the field of domestic relations;[46] it is clear, however, that the trend in the United States is in the direction of more reliance on the settlement potential of lawyers' negotiations and the multipurpose American pretrial conference.[47] Indeed, in both England and the United States, the role of the lawyer in settlement negotiations and the right-consciousness of the people are both too well developed to leave much room for extensive institutionalized court conciliation.

In conclusion, it is worth reminding ourselves again that court congestion and the resultant problem, which it poses for voluntary conciliation

[44] Kaplan *et al.*, "Phases of German Civil Procedure," 71 *Harv. L. Rev.* 1223–24, note 123 (1958) for citations to the repealing statute and Rosenberg, *Lehrbuch des Deutschen Zivilprozessrechts* sec. 112, at 487–94 (4th ed. 1949) for an account of the conciliation phase of the German proceedings and its failure in practice.

[45] Biglia and Spinosa, *op. cit. supra* note 43, at 612–13 (1958).

[46] E.g., see Calif. CCP sec. 1730–72. For a description of the California Conciliation Court and its work, see Burke, "Conciliation Court," in *Family Law for California Lawyers*, ed. Stumpf *et al.*, 337–56 (1956), where Michigan, Wisconsin, and New York County are also said to have conciliation procedures, and also the Japanese procedure is noted.

It is interesting to find that before the Civil War, six states, including New York and California, inserted provisions into their constitutions empowering their legislatures to establish tribunals of conciliation. See Reginald H. Smith, "The Place of Conciliation in the Administration of Justice," 9 *A.B.A.J.* 746–47 (1923). Also the American Judicature Society devoted considerable space in writings promoting conciliation as a judicial method in 1918 and again in 1927. See 2 *J. Am. Jud. Soc'y.* (no. 1) 3–29 (1918), 2 *id.* (no. 4) 151–58, and 11 *id.* (no. 3) 85 (1927). However, the use of conciliation in the United States has been largely associated with the small claims court movement, and conciliation in this sense is really more in the nature of informal adjudication. See, for the history to 1939, Cayton, "Small Claims and Conciliation Courts," 205 *Annals of the Am. Acad. of Pol. and Soc. Sci.* 57, 58 (1939); and see Institute of Judicial Administration, *Small Claims Courts in the United States* (no. 3–U6) 1–48 (1955), and *1959 Supplement* (no. 7–U 57) 1–19 (1959), with many citations to literature to 1955 and 1959, respectively. Extensive literature may be found in Northrop, "Small Claims Courts and Conciliation Tribunals: A Bibliography," 33 *Law Lib. J.* 39–50 (1940). Also see reports of recent experiments, Grinnell, "Congestion, Conciliation, Arbitration and the Berkshire Experiment," 38 *Mass. L. Q.* 38 (April 1953); Institute of Judicial Administration, *Compulsory Arbitration and Court Congestion; the Pennsylvania Compulsory Arbitration Statute—a Supplementary Report—1959* (1959).

[47] See Chief Justice Earl Warren's strong recommendation that all federal judges use pretrial under Federal Rule 16. 42 *J. Am. Jud. Soc'y.* 11 (1958). Also see Kincaid, *op. cit. supra* note 32, at 9 (1955) where he finds that the courts of Cook County, Illinois, and the Supreme Court in New York make the settlement discussion the chief purpose of pretrial; and Phillips, "Breaking the Judicial Log Jam: Connecticut's Blitz on Court Congestion," 45 *A.B.A.J.* 268–71 (1959) where the author describes week-long, special pretrial drives in Connecticut with primary emphasis on settlement; Thode, "The Case for the Pretrial Conference in Texas Re-examined," 41 *Tex. L. Rev.* 545–66 (1963); and Van Alstyne and Grossman, *California Pretrial and Settlement Procedures* 21 (1963), pointing out the settlement emphasis in the new California rules. The American lawyer's settlement role is well told in Sindell, *Let's Talk Settlement* 13–18 (1963).

and the judiciary are but symptoms of two underlying deficiencies: too few judges[48] and inadequate trial procedures. These latter problems are quite beyond our scope here, but enough has been said already, we trust, to indicate the high relevance of their solution to the achievement of a conciliation system which is actually voluntary. As described in chapter IX, there are other stubborn practical problems in the functioning of chōtei; but be that as it may, chōtei has come a long way, and it is a fitting symbol of the inventive and adaptive genius of its authors that they have been able to guide it to a posture of real utility and example in the solution of universal judicial problems arising from an industrial environment so different from the traditional setting of Japanese conciliatory practices.

[48] See Nibu Yurito 仁分百合人, "Minji soshō ga nagaku kakarisugiru koto to sono taisaku" 民事訴訟が長くかかりすぎることとその対策 (Countermeasures against delays in civil litigation), *Jurisuto* (no. 265) 18–24, 19 (1963) for a chart showing the increasing burden on Japanese judges from 1936 to 1960. Note that the approximate number of trial judges of general civil jurisdiction in the United States in 1961, excluding justices of the peace, was: state 3,751 (Supreme Courts, 337; Intermediate Appellate [exist in only 14 states] 286; major trial, 3,128) and federal about 300. American Judicature Society, "State Federal Judicial Salary Summaries," 45 *J. Am. Jud. Soc'y.* (no. 10) 255 (for state statistics) and 234 (for federal) (1962). In 1964 Japan had 2,014 judges, including Assistant Judges *(hanjiho)*. These figures were supplied by Judge Toji Tao of the Legal Training and Research Institute. Since Japan has much less ordinary litigation (probably not more than 10 per cent as much per capita) and half as much population as the United States, superficial comparison might lead one to assume that Japan, with 2,014 judges to roughly 4,050 for the United States has enough judges, but such a picture is distorted because in the United States, like England, there are several times as many "amateur judges" (i.e., justices of the peace, etc.) as there are professional, full-time judges, whereas Japan has almost entirely professional career judges. Also collegiality, the retrying of fact questions on appeal, the heavy load of administrative work other than "ordinary litigation" and the high number of parties appearing without lawyers, among other differences, burden the judge with responsibilities quite different than those of the United States judge. Also the justices of the peace in the United States should, perhaps, be added to the United States total, since in most states they probably have a role comparable to the Japanese summary court judge.

Appendices

APPENDIX I

A. *List of Tokugawa Shōguns*

Shōgun	Tenure	Shōgun	Tenure
1. Ieyasu 家康	1603–05	9. Ieshige 家重	1745–60
2. Hidetada 秀忠	1605–23	10. Ieharu 家治	1760–86
3. Iemitsu 家光	1623–51	11. Ienari (Hitotsubashi) 家齊	1786–1837
4. Ietsuna 家綱	1651–80	12. Ieyoshi 家慶	1837–53
5. Tsunayoshi 綱吉	1680–1709	13. Iesada 家定	1853–58
6. Ienobu (Kōfu) 家宣	1709–12	14. Iemochi (Kii) 家茂	1858–66
7. Ietsugu 家継	1712–16	15. Yoshinobu (Mito) 慶喜	1866–68
8. Yoshimune (Kii) 吉宗	1716–45		

B. *Chronology of Japanese legal history*

(Periodization of Japanese legal history is not entirely standardized but the following conforms with the general political
divisions)

Yamato Period 大和	—to 702	Muromachi Period 室町	—1333–1467
Nara Period 奈良	—702–810	Sengoku Period 戰國	—1467–1573
Heian Period 平安	—810–1185	Azuchi-Momoyama Period 安土—桃山	—1573–1603
Kamakura Period 鎌倉	—1185–1333	Tokugawa Period 徳川	—1603–1868

The era names during the Tokugawa and their dates in the Christian
era are:

Keichō	慶長	—1596–1614	Shōhō	正保	—1644–47
Genna	元和	—1615–23	Keian	慶安	—1648–51
Kan'ei	寛永	—1624–43	Jōō	承應	—1652–54

Meireki	明暦	—1655–57	Meiwa	明和	—1764–71
Manji	萬治	—1658–60	An'ei	安永	—1772–80
Kambun	寛文	—1661–72	Temmei	天明	—1781–88
Empō	延寶	—1673–80	Kansei	寛政	—1789–1800
Tenna	天和	—1681–83	Kyōwa	享和	—1801–3
Jōkyō	貞享	—1684–87	Bunka	文化	—1804–17
Genroku	元祿	—1688–1703	Bunsei	文政	—1818–29
Hōei	寶永	—1704–10	Tempō	天保	—1830–43
Shōtoku	正徳	—1711–15	Kōka	弘化	—1844–47
Kyōhō	享保	—1716–35	Kaei	嘉永	—1848–53
Gembun	元文	—1736–40	Ansei	安政	—1854–59
Kampō	寛保	—1741–43	Man'en	萬延	—1860
Enkyō	延享	—1744–47	Bunkyū	文久	—1861–63
Kan'en	寛延	—1748–50	Genji	元治	—1864
Hōreki	寶暦	—1751–63	Keiō	慶應	—1865–67

After the Meiji restoration

Meiji	明治	—1868–1911
Taishō	大正	—1912–25
Shōwa	昭和	—1926———

C. Table of Japanese measures and their English equivalents

Tokugawa money units:

Gold (*kin* 金):
$$4 \ shu \ 朱 = 1 \ bu \ 分$$
$$4 \ bu \ 分 = 1 \ ryō \ 兩$$

Silver (*gin* 銀):
$$1 \ kan \ 貫 = 1{,}000 \ momme \ 夂$$
$$1 \ coin \ (ichimai \ 枚) = 47 \ momme$$

Copper (*zeni* 錢):
$$1 \ kan \ 貫 = 1{,}000 \ mon \ 文$$

Because of the frequent recoinage and debasement of money in the Edo period, gold, silver, and copper were usually exchanged by weight. In 1609 the rate was set at 1 *ryō* (gold) = 50 *momme* (silver) = 4 *kamme* (copper). Later the rate fluctuated but was roughly:

$$1 \ ryō = 50 \ to \ 80 \ momme = 4–7 \ kamme.$$

Length:

	1 *bu*	分 =	0.12 inches
10 *bu*	分 = 1 *sun*	寸 =	1.2 inches
10 *sun*	寸 = 1 *shaku*	尺 =	.994 feet

6 *shaku* 尺	= 1 *ken*	間 =	1.99 yards
60 *ken* 間	= 1 *chō*	町 =	119.00 yards
36 *chō* 町	= 1 *ri*	里 =	2.44 miles

Area:

1 sq. *ken* 間	= 1 *tsubo*	坪 or *bu* 分 =	3.95 sq. yards
30 *bu* 分	= 1 *se*	畝	=	119 sq. yards
10 *se* 畝	= 1 *tan*	反	=	0.245 acres
10 *tan* 反	= 1 *chō*	町	=	2.45 acres

Volume:

	1 *shaku* 勺	= 0.0318 pints	
10 *shaku* 勺	= 1 *gō*	合 = 0.318 pints	
10 *gō* 合	= 1 *shō*	升 = 3.18 pints	
10 *shō* 升	= 1 *to*	斗 = 3.97 gallons = 4.795 U.S. gals.	
4 *to* 斗	= 1 *hyō*	俵 = 1.99 bushels	
10 *to* 斗	= 1 *koku*	石 = 4.96 bushels = 5.12 U.S. bushels	
2½ *hyō* 俵	= 1 *koku*	石	

Weight:

	1 *momme*	=	匁	0.132 oz. av.
160 *momme*	=	1 *kin*	= 斤	1.322 lbs. av.
1,000 *momme*	=	1 *kan*	= 貫	8.267 lbs. av.

APPENDIX II
GLOSSARY

In the following list of Japanese terms, three types of material are included in the definitions. In the first place, for those terms which have recurred in this study with some frequency, an English "equivalent" has been devised for convenience of expression and to avoid overuse of romanized Japanese. In the list the equivalent is capitalized and follows the romanization of the Japanese term and its characters thus: *Rōjū* 老中 Senior Council. Not all of the terms listed have occurred in the text often enough to require a formal equivalent.

Second, in some cases where the equivalent does not correspond precisely to a literal translation of the characters of the term or where no equivalent has been used, the literal translation, when it appeared that it would add insight into the origin or meaning of the institution, has been included in parenthesis.

Third, besides the equivalent, and occasionally literal translations, both of which are often inadequate to express the function of the referent, we

have often included such collateral explanations and information as time
and space permitted. Thus a term with all three types of material will
appear as follows:

Wakadoshiyori	若年寄	Junior Council (young elders); four *hatamoto* who supervised the other *hatamoto* and assisted the Senior Council *(rōjū)*.
1. Aitai naisai	相對内濟	Mutual conciliation.
2. Aitai sumashirei	相對濟令	Mutual Settlement Decrees; decree ordering that debts be settled mutually without lawsuits.
3. Ama	尼	Buddhist nun.
4. Asagamishimo	麻上下	Formal type of linen outer garment for court wear.
5. Ashigaru	足輕	Light foot; low rank of warrior; usually with menial battle duties rather than actual fighting.
6. Ashō	亞相	Chinese equivalent of Dainagon 大納言, a high councilor.
7. Atoshiki sōron	跡式相論	Dispute involving the succession to property.
8. Atsukai	扱	Conciliation (handle).
9. Atsukainin	扱人	Conciliator.
10. Azukarikin	預金	Money Deposited; if interest was charged on the principal, it was the basis for a money suit; if no interest was charged, it was a main suit.
11. Azukarisho	預所	Entrusted Land; land of the Shogunate assigned to a nearby daimyō or Shogunate official for collection of taxes, general administration, and adjudication.
12. Azukarisho kakari	預所掛	Officer in Charge of Entrusted Lands; the official in the finance commission with the duty to supervise all entrusted lands and the accounting from the officials of entrusted lands.
13. Azukari yakunin	預役人	Officials of Entrusted Lands; a nearby daimyō or Shogunate commissioner given the duty of managing additional Shogunate lands.

14. Baishin	陪臣	(Second attendant). The term was used for vassals of vassals; usually refers to daimyō vassals vis-à-vis the Shōgun.
15. Bakuchi	博奕	Gambling.
16. Basho jukudan	場所熟談	Earnest Negotiations on the Spot; usually meaning attempts to settle land disputes at the disputed territory.
17. Basho jukudan ukeshōmon	場所熟談 請證文	A document guaranteeing the terms of settlement on the spot.
18. Bugyō	奉行	Commissioners; the term used for the most important administrative and judicial officials in the Tokugawa Shogunate.
19. Bukan	武鑑	Daimyō Directory; a list of the daimyō, their ranks, titles, *koku*, and chief retainers, etc.; compiled privately for sale in Edo.
20. Buke	武家	Warrior House; a house or family with warrior status.
21. Buke densō	武家傳奏	Liaison Officers to the Warriors; one of the pivotal officials between the court-noble status group and the Shogunate. They were court nobles appointed by the Shogunate and responsible to the Kyoto Deputy Governor *(shoshidai)*.
22. Buke kakari no shusso	武家掛之 出訴	Petitions brought against a warrior.
23. Buke no tōryō	武家の棟梁	(Main rafter in the roof of warrior houses). The term meant feudal supremacy; the highest position in the feudal order; a Kamakura term which does not seem to have been used in the Tokugawa period.
24. *Buke Shohatto*	武家諸法度	A group of regulations imposed upon the daimyō by the Shogunate. It was repromulgated at each succession to the Shogunate and included some of the most basic prin-

		ciples upon which Tokugawa power was based.
25. Bunkoku	分國	The many small feudal domains presided over by local warlords just before the Tokugawa period.
26. Bushi	武士	Warrior; a general term including all members of the warrior status group.
27. Chidai	地代	Land rent.
28. Chigyō daka	知行高	The total assessed rice capacity for a fief. Sometimes *chigyō* meant a bannerman's fief as opposed to *ryōchi* 領地 or *hanryō* 藩領 for daimyō.
29. Chigyō kyūchi	知行給知	When a *chigyō* was used with *kyūchi*, it meant a *hatamoto* fief, and *kyūchi* meant a *gokenin*'s stipend.
30. Chigyōsho	知行所	Usually a *hatamoto*'s domain.
31. Chōgai	帳外	Outside the Registry; meant a person who was not registered on a piece of land in question. Another meaning referred to a case handled out of order on the court docket.
32. Chōnai	帳内	Inside the Registry; a person registered on the land in question or the land of the "court."
33. Chōnin	町人	Townsmen; including both the artisans and merchants.
34. Chōri kogashira	長吏小頭	An inferior official of the outcasts below the Eta Danzaemon.
35. Chōsho	調書	Conciliation Agreement; the document drawn up by the conciliator embodying the settlement agreed upon by the parties. Protocol; in chōtei, it means the formal agreed settlement filed with the court and given the force of a judgment.
36. Chōtei	調停	Conciliation; modern conciliation corresponding roughly to *atsukai* when used to indicate procedure, and corresponding to Tokugawa

		naisai when used to indicate the result reached.
37. Chōtei ni kawaru saiban	調停に代る裁判	Substitution of Trial for Conciliation.
38. Chū	忠	Loyalty to Master; one of the Confucian ethical concepts; proper relationship with a master; accentuated in Tokugawa Confucian thought.
39. Chūgen	仲間	Menials; the lowest ranking warriors.
40. Chūsai	仲裁	Arbitration; Code of Civil Procedure Articles 786–805.
41. Chūtsuihō	中追放	Medium Banishment; the middle type of banishment; one of the standard Tokugawa penalties provided in the *Osadamegaki*.
42. Daikan	代官	Deputy; some forty officers in charge of the Shōgun's domains *(goryō)*; each usually had about fifty thousand *koku* under him.
43. Daikansho	代官所	A deputy's administrative territory.
44. Daimyō	大名	(Great name). A feudal lord with ten thousand *koku* of assessed rice productive capacity in the Tokugawa period.
45. Daishin-in	大審院	The Great Chamber of Decisions; the highest court in the Japanese judicial hierarchy after 1875 to 1948.
46. Deiri	出入	Dispute; broader than *kuji* or *soshō*; usually, but not always, a civil dispute.
47. Deiri atsukai	出入扱	Handling by adversary procedure.
48. Deirimono	出入物	Adversary Proceedings; a case brought by a private petitioner as opposed to a case prosecuted by officials; usually but not always civil cases.
49. Deirisuji	出入筋	Adversary Procedure; procedure based on private petition.
50. Dōchū bugyō	道中奉行	Highway Commission; composed of

one great inspector and one finance commissioner from the fiscal section; had judicial powers over cases arising on the five highways.

51. Dōjōke　　　　　堂上家　　Imperial court nobles with ranks high enough to include privileges to go to the emperor's court; analogous to Audience *(omemie)* in the Shōgun's court.

52. Dōri　　　　　　道理　　　Reason; in the decision of cases it meant a standard of justice, all things considered; a sort of practical natural law.

53. Dōshin　　　　　同心　　　Police; a sort of marshal or sheriff of the town commission.

54. Edo-barai　　　　江戸拂ひ　Deportation from the Confines of Edo; actually the culprit was expelled from one of the four gates of the city which in later times were well within the actual urban area.

55. Edo machi bugyō　江戸町奉行　Edo Town Commission; two officials of bannerman rank (north and south) who handled the administration of Edo and regulated the townsmen's activity.

56. Edo machi bugyō　江戸町奉行　A conference chamber suit with
　　hatsuhan hyōjō　初判評定　initial endorsement by the town
　　kuji　　　　　　公事　　　commissioner on duty for the month.

57. Enkiridera　　　　縁切寺　　Divorce Temples; two temples with traditional jurisdiction to grant divorce to wives fleeing to the temple compound.

58. Enza　　　　　　縁座　　　Vicarious Liability of Relatives; liability for the criminal acts of their superior relatives.

59. Eta　　　　　　　穢多　　　Outcasts (much contamination), a hereditary, pariah status group whose occupations were considered unclean from the standpoint of Buddhism and Shintoism (leather tanners, butchers, undertakers, etc.).

60. Fuda sashi　　　　札差　　　(Sign displayer). Authorized rice

		brokers in Edo who financed the warriors by buying rice futures from them.
61. Fudai daimyō	譜代大名	Hereditary Daimyō; used to indicate daimyō recognizing Tokugawa overlordship before Sekigahara; hence the most loyal group of daimyō under the Tokugawa Shogunate.
62. Furegashira	觸頭	Announcement Chief; the temple which had the duty of relaying orders from the Shogunate to other temples of the same sect and endorsing petitions from the temples to the Shogunate.
63. Fuyu funyū	不輸不入	Immunity from tax and entry held by Medieval Manors *(shōen)* against Imperial officials.
64. Gekokujō	下剋上	Social upheaval wherein the lowly get power and position; descriptive of the social condition of the Sengoku period (1467–1573).
65. Genin	外人	Outsiders; others.
66. Gimmi	吟味	Inquisition; usually referring to criminal hearings or investigations, but also sometimes used to indicate the hearing in a civil type of trials by our standards.
67. Gimmimono	吟味物	A Criminal Matter; a case handled by official inquisition instead of adversary procedure.
68. Gimmimono shirabeyaku	吟味物 調役	The trial-investigating officers of the temple and shrine commission.
69. Gimmi suji	吟味筋	Inquisitorial procedure.
70. Gisō	議奏	Imperial Council; five members.
71. Gō	郷	A geographic subdivision in early Imperial administration; roughly equivalent to a village; abolished by Toyotomi Hideyoshi.
72. Gobugyōsama	御奉行様	Commissioners.
73. Gofunai	御府内	Inside the Capital; the jurisdiction of the town commissioners. In later

		years Edo actually extended far beyond the territory defined as *gofunai*.
74. Gojō	互譲	Mutual Concession.
75. Gokaidō	五街道	Five Highways; the main traffic arteries to and from Edo: Tōkaidō; Nakasendō; Nikkōdō; Kōshūkaidō; Ōshūkaidō.
76. Gokenin	御家人	Housemen; Shogunate vassals below the rank of *hatamoto*; numbered some seventeen thousand in the early eighteenth century; during the Kamakura period it meant all direct vassals of the Shogunate.
77. Gokumon	獄門	A type of capital punishment (prison gate); the third highest penalty in the Tokugawa penal system, consisted of decapitation and display of the severed head on a stand at Shinagawa or Asakusa.
78. Goningumi	五人組	Five-Man Group; all commoners (in general householders with property) were required to organize with their neighbors, usually into groups of five contiguous houses; in the rural areas a person need not hold property to be included in a five-man group.
79. Goningumichō	五人組帳	Five-Man Group Registry; a registry of persons in a village broken down into their five-man group; the Preface *(maegaki)* included important Shogunate regulations for the village.
80. Gorikai	御利解	A term referring to the practice of authoritative persuasion by the judge in order to induce a party to accept a private settlement.
81. Gorin gojō	五倫五常	In general, the Confucian ethical code; might be translated *(gojō)*: 1. humanity, 2. justice, 3. politeness, 4. wisdom, 5. fidelity; the Five Relationships *(gorin)*: 1. master

		and servant, 2. father and son, 3. husband and wife, 4. brothers (older and younger), 5. friends.
82. Goryō	御料	The Shōgun's direct domains; popularly referred to as *tenryō* 天領.
83. Gosanke	御三家	Three Houses; Tokugawa branch families at Owari, Kii, and Mito, originally established for Ieyasu's younger sons.
84. Gosankyō	御三卿	Three Lords; Tokugawa houses established for two of Yoshimune's sons and one of Ieshige's sons; Tayasu 田安, Hitotsubashi 一橋, Shimizu 清水.
85. Gosekke	五攝家	Five Families of Succession; Konoe 近衛; Nijō 二条; Ichijō 一条; Kujō 九条; Takatsukasa 鷹司.
86. Gōshi	郷士	Village Warrior; local gentry; engaged in farming in peace and fighting during wartime.
87. Goshuinchi	御朱印地	Land donated to a temple or shrine certified by a document bearing the Shōgun's red seal.
88. Gōso	強訴	A forceful petition or demonstration by farmers, usually against their overlord; gathering at the front of an official's mansion and making demands.
89. Gotairō	五大老	Five Great Elders; a council set up by Hideyoshi and as a top policy council to rule after Hideyoshi's death.
90. Gotōke	御當家	The Incumbent House; usually used to refer to the Tokugawa house.
91. Goyōbeya	御用部屋	A workroom near the Shōgun's quarters, where his chief advisers worked.
92. Gozen saiban	御前裁判	Trials before the Shōgun himself (see *ojiki saiban*).
93. Gun	郡	District; a subdivision of a Province *(kuni)* containing several Villages *(mura)*.

94. Gundai   郡代   District Deputy; a local official similar to a *daikan* but administering more land of the Shogunate; usually administering over one hundred thousand *koku*.

95. Gyakuzai   逆罪   Crime against Confucian superiors, such as patricide.

96. Hadan todoke   破談届   Notice of Failure in Negotiations; notice to the court of the failure of talks aimed at private settlement of a dispute during trial.

97. Haiken issatsu   拝見一札   Receipt of Service; a receipt given to the plaintiff by the defendant and his local officials certifying that they had received the endorsed complaint.

98. Hairyō daka   拝領高   A grant of rice from the Shogunate.

99. Hajimete no kujiai   初而公事合   First Hearing; same as *Shotaiketsu*, the initial hearing in a civil trial; it was formal, with the commissioners themselves in attendance.

100. Hakama   袴   A sort of trousers worn as formal dress by men.

101. Hampō   藩法   Domain Law; legal codes of the daimyō; or, more generally, all law operative in a daimyō domain.

102. Han   藩   Domain; fief; used to indicate a daimyō's domain.

103. Hanketsu   判決   Judgment; a modern term for a court decision on the merits.

104. Happō bijin   八方美人   Eight-Sided-Beauty; a person who smiles at all but is true to none.

105. Hariso   張訴   Posted Petition; a petition posted on the door of an office or building to register a complaint to officials or against officials; usually a desperate measure to gain recognition of a grievance.

106. Haritsuke   磔   Crucifixion; second highest penalty in the Tokugawa system.

107. Hatakata mononari   畑方物成   Tax on Dry Fields; originally pay-

		able in kind, but later converted to money payment.
108. Hatamoto	旗本	Bannermen; Shogunate vassals with audience privilege, but under ten thousand *koku;* they filled most of the official positions in the Shogunate.
109. Hatsuhan	初判	Initial Endorsement; had jurisdictional significance because the various commissions of Edo and Kyoto had specific power to endorse certain petitions depending on the specific areas and types of fiefs.
110. Heinin	平人	Commoners; as opposed to a warrior, religious person, court noble, or outcast; farmers and townsmen.
111. Hentōgaki	返答書	Answer; the defendant's response to the petition of the plaintiff in Adversary Procedure *(deirisuji)*.
112. Higiri	日限 or 日切	Day Certain; a date fixed in the future by a judgment in a main suit; required full payment by the date set.
113. Hikiai	引合	Interrelated.
114. Hikiai mono	引合物	A suit involving parties or witness from different fiefs.
115. Hikiai nin	引合人	A person (such as a witness) from an outside jurisdiction who was involved in a trial.
116. Hikimawashi no ue gokumon	引廻しの上獄門	Leading about in Public, then Decapitation with Exposure of the Head; a type of penalty.
117. Hinin	非人	Nonhuman; usually beggars; but since the *hinin* were organized and licensed, they constituted a status group.
118. Hinin gashira	非人頭	Chief of the Nonhumans; a position in Edo subordinate to the Eta Danzaemon in Shogunate law.
119. Hinin oshioki	非人御仕置	Autonomy of the *hinin* (it sometimes meant the Outcasts, too) to

execute their own members once
the Shogunate imposed a penalty
on them.

120.	Hinobe negai	日延願	Request for Continuance; usually requested in order to negotiate for a private settlement.
121.	Hito goroshi	人殺	Homicide (kill a person).
122.	Hito kadowakashi	人勾引	Induce a person to run away; abduct; also included kidnaping.
123.	Hitonushi	人主	Man Owner; a person who guarantees the character and performance of a servant to the *hitoyado* which in turn guarantees him to a master.
124.	Hitotsugaki	一書	(One writing). The divisions in Tokugawa legal documents marked off by the numeral one at the beginning of each separate item.
125.	Hitoyado	人宿	Men's Hall; a sort of hiring hall; establishments which guaranteed the character of a workman to be hired by another and also took the responsibility to repay advanced wages if the workman absconded.
126.	Hitsuke	火附	Arson. Arson was extremely dangerous in Edo because of the inflammable character of the buildings and the layout of the city; hence it was punished severely.
127.	Hitsuke aratame	火附改	Arson Inspector; officers in Edo with limited criminal jurisdiction to apprehend arsonists, etc.; later the office was abolished.
128.	Ho	保	A kind of rural subdivision in pre-Tokugawa administration; the reorganization of the Sengoku period outmoded the old subdivisions *(Shō gō ho ri)* and Hideyoshi abolished them.
129.	Hodomura	ほどむら	A kind of paper.
130.	Hōjitsugen	法實現	Realizing the Law; a term of Miyazaki Sumio. Law here means

		a transcendental goal or standard; probably the purpose of the Japanese militarists in 1942.
131. Hōki	放棄	Abandonment of a claim by the plaintiff (modern).
132. Hōkōnin	奉公人	Servant; usually a domestic servant, but sometimes the lesser vassals of a warrior were called *hōkōnin*, especially if they were retained temporarily.
133. Hōkōnin ukejō	奉公人請状	Workman's Guaranty; a document from the *hitoyado* to the master guaranteeing a servant at the time the servant was retained.
134. Hombyakushō	本百姓	Main Farmer; a land-owning farmer as distinguished from a tenant farmer.
135. Hommeyasu sashidashi	本目安 差出	Submission of the Actual Petition; the petition revised in accordance with instructions received at the *meyasu tadashi*.
136. Honji	本寺	Main Temple; the main temple in a given sect; had jurisdiction to settle certain disputes among its branch temples and was responsible for them to the Shogunate; must endorse petitions from its personnel to the Shogunate.
137. Honjo bugyō	本所奉行	Honjo Commissioner; a third town commissioner established in Edo in 1702, abolished in 1719.
138. Honke	本家	Main House; also meant the patron (court noble) of a *shōen* in the Kamakura period.
139. Honkuji	本公事	Main Suit; suits for property or for money lent with security without interest; given better court protection than *kanekuji*.
140. Honnen no sei	本然の性	Essential Nature; Principle *(ri)* as manifested in a given object.
141. Honzan	本山	(Main Mount). Same as *honji*, main temple.

142. Hosanin	補佐人	Assistant or advisor in modern legal proceedings, not necessarily a lawyer.
143. Hosoku iken	補足意見	Concurring opinion.
144. Hōtei	法廷	Court.
145. Hyakushō	百姓	Farmers.
146. Hyakushōdai	百姓代	Farmers' Representative; usually a wealthy member of the village who acted as overseer of the administration for the farmers; he was one of the *murayakunin* along with the *nanushi* and *kumigashira*.
147. Hyōgi	評議	A conference of the conference chamber.
148. Hyōjō kuji	評定公事	A Conference Suit; case requiring the conference chamber's decision; they were handled preliminarily by one of the three commissions depending on the jurisdiction of the parties.
149. Hyōjōsho	評定所	Conference Chamber; the highest Shogunate court, composed of the three Edo commissions (eight commissioners); and on formal days, one senior councillor; also *metsuke* and *ometsuke* attended.
150. Hyōjōsho harigamichō	評定所帳紙帳	Record of posted notices of the conference chamber; valuable source of material on *Hyōjōsho* practice; a compilation of regulations for judiciary officials posted in the *Hyōjōsho*.
151. Hyōjōsho ichiza	評定所一座	Full Bench of the Conference Chamber.
152. Hyōjōsho ichiza hyōketsu	評定所一座評決	Conference Decision of the Full Bench of the Conference Chamber; legal opinions on important matters referred to the conference chamber.
153. Hyōjōsho taiketsu	評定所對決	Conference Chamber Confrontation; the first hearing in cases before the conference chamber.
154. Hyōjōsho tomeyaku	評定所留役	Conference Chamber Recording

		Officers; underlings in charge of examinations and hearings in the conference chamber.
155. Hyōjōuke	評定請	Conference Receipt; an appearance the day before trial to confirm the time and availability or readiness for trial of the parties.
156. Ie	家	House; the typical unit of family organization; broader than the western family, including family name, property, residence, and persons.
157. Ieatoshiki	家跡式	Succession to a House.
158. Ienushi	家主	Houseowner; houseowners had certain responsibilities for their tenants' debts and conduct.
159. Iiwatashi	言渡	Order or instruction from an officer.
160. Iken	違憲	Unconstitutionality.
161. Ingū	院宮	Certain high temples patronized by Imperial relatives; usually an Imperial relative became the chief priest.
162. Inkyo	隱居	(Concealed living). A legal institution involving retirement from the house leadership, with certain property rights.
163. Iriai	入會	Commons (enter jointly); the lands near a village in which the villagers have joint rights to use the grass and wood and other natural growth.
164. Iriairon	入會論	Disputes over the Use of Commons; villagers had rights to gather the products of certain uncultivated lands appurtenant to the village; there were often disputes over the extent of the right or the boundaries of the commons.
165. Isshū hōgi	一宗法義	Doctrine of a Buddhist sect; in disputes involving questions of doctrine of a single religious sect, the officials of the sect had summary jurisdiction.

166. Itoma no jō	暇の狀	(Leisure paper). A euphemism for a divorce paper.
167. Jibun shioki	自分仕置	A term indicating the autonomy of local lords to administer justice.
168. Jidan	示談	Informal Conciliation; negotiation to settle a dispute.
169. Jikata	地方	Land Officials; section of the deputy's office in charge of land, cultivation, and taxes.
170. Jikata oyakusho	地方御役所	Office of Local Affairs.
171. Jiki tadashi	直糺	Trial by the commissioner himself.
172. Jikyōron	地境論	Boundary Disputes; lawsuits to determine the boundaries of villages, fields, or fiefs.
173. Jingikan	神祇官	A Ministry of Shinto in the *ritsuryō* system (702).
174. Jinji soshō tetsuzukihō	人事訴訟 手續法	Procedural Law for Personal Affairs (1939).
175. Jinushi	地主	Land Owner.
176. Jinya	陣屋	Deputy's Office.
177. Jisha bugyō	寺社奉行	Temple and Shrine Commission; four hereditary daimyō. The highest of the three commissions with important initial endorsement power over diversity cases, from private fiefs outside the Kantō and all types from the Shoshidai.
178. Jisha bugyō hatsuhan hyōjō kuji	寺社奉行 初判評定 公事	A Conference Suit Initially Endorsed by the Temple and Shrine Commission.
179. Jisha hikiaimono	寺社引合もの	Interrelated Matters with Temples and Shrines; suits involving a temple and shrine or its personnel and persons of another status group.
180. Jisharyō	寺社領	Temple or Shrine Fiefs.
181. Jisha yaku	寺社役	Temple and Shrine Officers; underlings in the temple and shrine commission, who handled disputes as examiners and judges in the preliminary and intermediate stages; they correspond to the *tomeyaku* in

		the finance commission, and their title was changed later.
182. Jitō	地頭	Land Lord; feudal lords below daimyō in their capacity as governor of a fief; the Shogunate's tax collector assigned to the *shōen* in the Kamakura period.
183. Jitō sage	地頭下げ	Reference to the Land Lord; requirement that the overlords try to settle the case after it was filed in the Shogunate court in land disputes.
184. Jōdai	城代	A Castle Deputy; a representative of the Shōgun in charge of a major castle, such as Nijō in Kyoto or Osaka Castle or Sumpu.
185. Jodoshū hatto	浄土宗法度	An early code used by the Shogunate for regulation of the Jōdo Buddhist sect.
186. Jōkamachi	城下町	Castle Town; the seat of daimyō governments; the town surrounding a daimyō castle in his domain.
187. Jōmenhō	定兒法	A method of tax assessment based on the average yield in the past.
188. Jōri	常理	Common Reason.
189. Jōshu	城主	Castle Lords; daimyō with castles in their domains.
190. Jumbi tetsuzuki	準備手續	Preparatory procedure.
191. Jumpū bizoku	淳風美俗	Virtuous Ways and Beautiful Traditions; a standard term to refer to the "Japanese" way.
192. Kabunakama	株仲間	Guild (stock association). Type of commercial organization sanctioned by Yoshimune. It was the counterpart of the medieval *za* destroyed by Hideyoshi; abolished by Mizuno Tadakuni in 1842 but re-established in 1851.
193. Kachi	徒士	Vassal without the privilege to ride a horse; a foot warrior; above the *ashigaru*, whose duties were more menial than military.

194. Kagoso   駕籠訴   Palanquin Petition; running and thrusting a petition into the palanquin of passing official, a desperate measure to gain recognition for a suppressed grievance.

195. Kahō   家法   House Law; the law of the various military houses.

196. Kaikyū   階級   Social class, as opposed to *mibun*, legally defined status.

197. Kajichi   家質   House Mortgage.

198. Kakekomiso   駈込訴   (Running in to complain). Rushing into an office without permission to thrust a petition upon the officials.

199. Kakiire shōmon   書入證文   Mortgage Deed.

200. Kakubutsu chichi   格物致知   Unify knowledge of various things; the epistemological aspect of Chu Hsi's philosophy which required examination of the objects outside the observer as a source of knowledge.

201. Kakushi baijo   隱賣女   A secret prostitute; an unlicensed prostitute.

202. Kamon   家門   House Families; lesser Tokugawa branch families of daimyō rank.

203. Kampaku   關白   Chief Minister (connected with all government affairs and explains them to the emperor); the top official in the old Imperial court who managed all matters of governance and kept the emperor informed.

204. Kanebi   金日   Money Dates; two dates when the conference chamber devoted itself to money suits.

205. Kanekuji   金公事   Money Suit; civil suits for money but for interest without security; special procedure was used for these cases; in general the protection given in the court for *kanekuji* was very weak and the procedure dilatory.

206. Kanhasshū   關八州   Eight Kantō Provinces: Musashi 武蔵, Sagami 相模, Kōzuke 上野,

		Shimotsuke 下野, Hitachi 常陸, Shimōsa 下總, Kazusa 上總, Awa 安房.
207. Kanhasshū no hoka	關八州之外	Outside-the-Eight-Kantō-Provinces; indicates the area over which the temple and shrine commission had authority of initial endorsement of petitions in diversity cases.
208. Kanjō bugyō	勘定奉行	Finance Commission; four bannermen, divided into two sections, judicial and fiscal. The two judicial commissioners had important powers of initial endorsement over diversity cases from the Shogunate lands and private fiefs in the *Kanhasshū*.
209. Kanjō bugyō hatsuhan hyōjō kuji	勘定奉行 初判評定 公事	Finance Commission Initial Endorsement Conference Suit; suits involving diversity of jurisdiction between private fiefs in the *Kantō* were handled this way.
210. Kanjō bugyō kakari nanuka mono	勘定奉行 掛り七日 もの	A Seven Day Matter with the Finance Commission in Charge; a type of money case involving parties within five *ri* (twelve and one half miles) of Edo. It was endorsed to require private negotiations within six days, and if settlement were not reached, to require appearance in the finance commission for trial on the seventh day after endorsement.
211. Kanjō bugyō ryōhan no nai-yoriai kuji	勘定奉行 兩判之内 寄合公事	An Inner-session Suit Endorsed by both of the Finance Commissioners.
212. Kanjō gashira	勘定頭	Finance Officer; an early predecessor of the finance commission.
213. Kanjō gimmi kumigashira	勘定吟味 組頭	Chief Investigator of the Finance Commission; chief in charge of auditing the fiscal operations.
214. Kanjō kumigashira	勘定組頭	A chief of clerks in the Finance Commission.
215. Kanjōsho	勘定所	Finance Office (building).

216. Kankai	勸解	Encouraging Settlement; the term for the conciliation procedure from 1875–91.
217. Kankai kakari	勸解掛	Official for Encouraging Settlement; an early Meiji term.
218. Kantō	關東	The area surrounding Edo or present day Tōkyō (see *Kanhasshū*).
219. Karisumashi	假濟	Provisional Settlement; a settlement in land and water cases which was effective for a temporary period after which the result was reviewed for fairness before it was made finally binding.
220. Karō	家老	House Elder; usual title of the top advisors to a daimyō.
221. Karyō	過料	Penal fine.
222. Kashin	家臣	House Vassal; retainer of a feudal lord.
223. Kashira	頭	Chief; leader.
224. Katanagari-rei	刀狩令	Hideyoshi's Sword Hunt.
225. Kata sumikuchi	片濟口	Unilateral Settlement Agreement; an agreement to settle a dispute, which is sealed by the plaintiff only.
226. Katoku kuji	家督公事	Suit Over House Control.
227. Kattekata	勝手方	Fiscal Officers; the two finance commissioners who handled Shogunate fiscal collections, disbursements, and accounting.
228. Kemi	毛見	A survey of a crop by sampling it to determine prospective yield and tax assessment.
229. Keshiin	消印	Canceling the Endorsements; after a settlement or judgment the plaintiff took the complaint (answer and judgment attached) to the commissioners who had endorsed the suit and had them cancel their endorsement, signifying completion of the suit.
230. Kettei	決定	Ruling (on a legal point in modern usage).
231. Ki	氣	Natural Existence; one of the parts

		of Chu Hsi's ontological dualism; the contaminating element in his ethics.
232. Kienrei	棄捐令	Discard Decrees; decrees extinguishing debts as of a certain time.
233. Kihanryoku	既判力	*Res judicata.*
234. Kinchūgata gojōmoku	禁中方 御條目	Regulations for the Imperial court; the basic rules imposed by the Shogunate on the Imperial court and court nobles in 1615.
235. Kingin deiri	金銀出入	Disputes Over Money; (gold and silver).
236. Kinri goryō	禁裡御料	The Imperial Estate.
237. Kinri sentō goryō	禁裏仙洞御料	The estate of the retired emperor.
238. Kinri tsuki	禁裡付	Attached to the Imperial court; Shogunate officers on duty at the Imperial court.
239. Kinsei	近世	Recent Era; usually *kinsei* means the Tokugawa period, but Ishii Ryōsuke uses it to refer to the period 1468–1858. It is rendered "recent era" to indicate the relatively deep concept of history in Japan.
240. Kirigane	切金	Limited Payments; installations fixed by a judgment in a money suit requiring the defendant to repay the plaintiff in a fixed number of installments on fixed days in the future.
241. Kirisute gomen	切捨御免	Cut down and throw aside without further ado; privilege of warriors to use their swords to obtain proper respect from commoners.
242. Kisai jiken	既濟事件	Concluded cases.
243. Kishitsu no sei	氣質の性	Existent Nature; the Natural Existence *(ki)* as manifested in an object; except for sages, it means impurities, ethically.
244. Kishōmon	起請文	Religious Oath; a document sealed under supernatural oath.

245. Kō   講   A kind of mutual financing or insurance.

246. Kō   考   Filial piety; loyalty to the family.

247. Kōfu kimban   甲府勤番   The Shogunate deputy in charge of defense at Kōfu City.

248. Kōgi   公儀   Public; referred to Shogunate concern or interest as opposed to less worthy private matters.

249. Kōgi e kakari   公儀へ懸り   Serious matter affecting the Shogunate.
     sōrō omoki shina 候重き品

250. Kōhei   公平   Equity.

251. Kōjōsho   口上書   Record of Testimony Given; same as *kuchigaki* except *kōjōsho* was used if one or both parties were privileged persons.

252. Kōke   高家   High Houses; several houses of special rank and function in the Tokugawa Shogunate; their rank was based on geneological prestige from prior periods and they held important jobs connected with protocol and ceremony.

253. Kokudaka   石高   Assessed Rice Capacity [of a feudal lord's domain].

254. Kokugaku   國學   Classical Nationalism; philosophy of such men as Motoori Norinaga, who emphasized Japanese culture over the Chinese, which resulted in political emphasis on the Imperial cause in preference to the Shogunate.

255. Kokumin kyōdōtai 國民協同體   Citizen's Cooperative Structure (Miyazaki Sumio).

256. Kokushi   國司   Provincial governors of the prefeudal period under the Imperial court at Kyoto; in the Kamakura period they retained civil power, but the *Shugo* appointed by the Kamakura Shogunate had military power.

257. Kokushu   國主   Lords of Provinces; in general, the

larger outside daimyō; nearly all had over two hundred thousand *koku.*

258. Komedaka	込高	Incidental rice taxes to cover spillage, transport, etc.
259. Kosakunin	小作人	Tenant Farmer (small cultivator).
260. Koshikake	腰掛	Waiting Room; the waiting room for litigants and witnesses in the Edo courts.
261. Koshu	戸主	Househead (door owner); a post-Meiji term.
262. Kōtai yoriai	交替寄合	About thirty bannermen with duties of alternate annual attendance at Edo and their fief. They were treated like daimyō but did not have ten thousand *koku.*
263. Kōwaka sarugaku	幸若猿楽	An ancient type of drama, from which Nō plays originated.
264. Kuchigaki	口書	Recorded Testimony; the record prepared by underlings and certified by the parties, after attempts at private settlement had failed; upon this record the commissioner rendered his decision; it included comment by the underling (*tomeyaku,* etc.), as well as his analysis of the facts.
265. Kuchigaki kakunin	口書確認	Confirmation of the Recorded Testimony.
266. Kuge	公家	Court Noble (public house); a general term for all Imperial court nobles. In the Tokugawa period they lived in Kyoto on meager estates and cultivated the arts under strict Shogunate regulation. Konoe with about two thousand *koku* was the richest house.
267. Kugyō	公卿	Top ranking court nobles; above third rank (*sammi* 三位) or in the office of Sangi 参議 or above.
268. Kuji	公事	Suit; sometimes distinguished from Dispute *(deiri)* as a case of first in-

		stance instead of a case referred from below to a higher office.
269. Kuji	口事	Dispute; these characters for dispute were changed to *kuji* 公事 in the Sengoku period.
270. Kuji atsukai	公事扱	Handling as a petitioner's suit.
271. Kuji jōchō	公事上聴	Practice wherein the Shōgun observed, usually secretly, the trials of the conference chamber without participating in the decision.
272. Kujikata	公事方	Judicial Officers; the two finance commissioners who handled disputes from the Shogunate domains and private fiefs in the *Kanhasshū* and participated in the conference chamber.
273. Kujikata osadamegaki	公事方 御定書	Written Decisions for Lawsuits; the nearest thing to a code achieved by the Tokugawa regime; completed under Yoshimune, eighth Shōgun (1742).
274. Kujimei	公事銘	Suit Title; various types of claims had fixed titles in the Tokugawa practice, and these fixed types of claims were divided into categories, the handling of which was different; hence the importance of an accurate title.
275. Kujishi	公事師	Suit Solicitor; a sort of shyster lawyer whose activities were prohibited; must be distinguished from the legitimate *kujiyado*.
276. Kujiyado	公事宿	Suit Inn; licensed inns in Edo where out-of-town parties were required to stay while engaged in a lawsuit; the suit-inn proprietor served as a legal advisor.
277. Kumiaihō	組合法	Association Law; autonomous regulations for various trade associations.
278. Kumigashira	組頭 or 與頭	Group Chief; the number-two officer in most villages of the Toku-

		gawa period. He assisted the headman and sometimes acted on his behalf.
279. Kumigashira	組頭	Company Chiefs; the officers in charge of the companies of housemen in the Shogunate military organization.
280. Kumi-naoshi	組直	Revision of a legal opinion by order of the senior council.
281. Kuni	國	Province; the historical subdivisions recognized at least as early as the Taihō Code, 702 A.D., some sixty-six in all Japan, depending on the period.
282. Kunimochi	國持	A daimyō holding a whole province; same as *kokushu*.
283. Kuniyaku	國役	Labor levy on Edo townsmen; fifteen days of labor per man per year, later converted to money payments.
284. Kura yashiki	倉屋敷	Storage Residence; an establishment maintained usually in Osaka by the various daimyō to handle their rice and convert it to money.
285. Kyōgi rikon	協議離婚	Divorce by Agreement.
286. Kyōke hikiaimono	京家引合もの	Interrelated Matters of Kyoto Houses; suits between court nobles and members of other status groups.
287. Kyōsei chōtei	強制調停	Compulsory Conciliation.
288. Kyōsei itchi	教政一致	Instruction and administration are synonymous; the Confucian theory that officials are completely wise and that their duty is to instruct the populace through law.
289. Kyōto shoshidai	京都所司代	Kyoto Deputy Governor; the Shogunate representative in Kyoto, charged with regulating and controlling the activities of the Imperial family and court nobles as well as the city of Kyoto and the four outlying provinces of Ōmi, Yamato, Yamashiro, and Tamba.

290. Machibure   町觸   Town Proclamations; regulations issued by the town commission, but usually approved by the senior council.

291. Machi doshiyori   町年寄   Town Elders; three families in Edo, Taru 樽, Tate 館, and Kitamura 喜多村, who stood between the *machibugyō* and the headmen of the various subdivisions (*machi* 町) of Edo.

292. Machi yakunin   町役人   Town Officials; the headman, monthly officer, five-man-group chief and house owner were called collectively *machi yakunin* in any given case.

293. Machi yoriai   町寄合   Town Meeting; assembling of townsmen to discuss their administrative problems and make rules and decisions.

294. Maemae yori no rei   從前々之例   Prior Precedent.

295. Matsuji   末寺   Branch Temple; a lesser temple over which another temple *(honji)* has supervisory power.

296. Meirei   命令   Order.

297. Metsuke   目付   Inspector (eye attacher); the officers responsible to the junior council and with the duties of policing the bannermen, announcing regulations to them, and attending the conference chamber meeting.

298. Meue no mono   目上の者   A person of superior status or station who must be respected as such by the observer.

299. Meyasu tadashi   目安糺   Examination of the Petition; a preliminary step to determine defects in the petition and have them corrected, if possible; if the petition were without faults, it was endorsed for service on the defendant.

300. Mibun   身分   Status; legally defined social position.

301. Mibun shihai   身分支配   Status Group Officials; each status

		group in Tokugawa law had its own organization and officials of limited power over internal affairs.
302. Mikasazuki	三笠附	Kind of gambling based on completing a poem.
303. Mikudari-han	三行半	(Three and a half lines). A document of divorce given to a wife by a husband at his will signifying his permission for her to leave and remarry.
304. Misai jiken	未済事件	Pending cases.
305. Mittsū	密通	A broad term including adultery, seduction, and fornication.
306. Mizunomi byakushō	水呑百姓	(Water drinking farmer). A tenant farmer, low-ranking farmers in the villages.
307. Monzeki	門跡	A high-ranking temple patronized by court nobles as well as the Imperial family; somewhat less prestige than the *Ingū*.
308. Mōshitate sho	申立書	Formal Proposal or Application.
309. Mōshiwatashi	申渡	Instruction; order.
310. Mōsō	盲僧	An ordinary blind man not necessarily a member of the Blind Guild (Tōdō).
311. Mujin	無盡	Mutual Finance.
312. Mujinkin	無盡金	Mutual Finance Funds; money collected from numerous members of the association and then used by certain members selected in various ways for enterprises; the principal was to be returned for use by others later.
313. Mujō	無城	Castleless Lord; daimyō without castles; ranked lower than *kokushu* and *jōshu*.
314. Mura	村	Village; an area of land as well as a group of houses.
315. Muragime	村極め	Village Rule; one name for regulations established autonomously by villages for their own observance.
316. Mura hachibu	村八分	(Village eight parts). A penalty

imposed by villages on their members, which amounted to ostracism in eight out of ten important village affairs.

317. Murakuji 村公事 Village Suit; a suit by one village against another conducted by the *mura yakunin* (village officials).

318. Mura yoriai 村寄合 Village Meeting; all members of a village met occasionally to elect officers or review the administration and establish rules.

319. Mushuku 無宿 No Residence; a person not registered any place; or a person of unknown registry.

320. Myōji 苗字 Family name; in general only privileged persons (warriors, bonzes court nobles, etc.) had family names in the Edo period.

321. Myōrei ritsu 名例律 First chapter of the Criminal Prohibitions *(ritsu)* of the *Yōrō ritsu* (718 A.D.).

322. Naisai 内済 Private Settlement; a settlement mutually agreed upon by the parties; the Shogunate court sought such private settlement in nearly all civil proceedings.

323. Naisai ihen deiri 内済違變出入 Dispute over Breach of a Private Settlement; a suit arising from disagreement over what had been settled, or failure to comply with the terms of the agreement.

324. Naisai seiritsu 内済成立 Establishment of a Private Settlement.

325. Naishō nite 内證にて Handling in Private; private settlement of a dispute.
torimochi 取持

326. Naiyoriai 内寄合 Inner-session; a council meeting of all members of a commission; certain types of lawsuits were handled by *naiyoriai* meetings, others by *tegiri* or the conference chamber as a matter of jurisdiction.

327. Nakamagoto 仲間事 Mutual Affairs; a special category

of intimate personal relationships which the Shogunate courts would not undertake to adjust by lawsuit; they were left to the private negotiation and settlement of the parties themselves.

328. Nakama okite 仲間掟 Association Rules; regulations for trade guilds and merchant associations established by themselves for their own internal regulation.

329. Nanitozo ojihi o motte 何卒御慈悲を以て Please by Your Gracious Benevolence; the form for beginning a specific request for action by the court in a petition.

330. Nanukamono 七日物 Seven Day Matter; a civil suit which was endorsed on the back with a seven-day period for private negotiations for settlement and orders to appear in court thereafter, should negotiations fail; this sort of endorsement was used for money suits where the parties were within five *ri* of Edo.

331. Nanushi 名主 Headman (possessor of a name); chief of towns or villages in the Edo period; entitled *shōya* 庄屋 in some areas.

332. Negai sage 願下げ Withdrawal; where the plaintiff voluntarily withdraws a petition filed in a Shogunate court without either receiving a decision or registering a private settlement.

333. Nimbetsuchō 人別帳 Registry of Classified Persons; a registry of person kept by the local officials in charge of the land upon which the person resided.

334. Nindaku 認諾 Acknowledgment of the claims by the defendant; a modern legal term.

335. Ofuregaki 御觸書 Proclamation; decrees issued for general promulgation to the populace as opposed to *kakitsuke* 書付 decrees (usually from one official to

another) and *tasshi* 達, order (a specific order to a person, usually an official).

336. Ohizamoto   お膝下   (Under the Shōgun's knees). Edo; the seat of the Shogunate.

337. Oie sōdō   御家騒動   House Disturbance; disputes over the succession or control of a daimyō house.

338. Oioi gimmi   追々吟味   Successive Hearings; after the first hearing in a civil suit, detailed investigations and hearings were conducted by the clerks or *tomeyaku*.

339. Ojiki saiban   御直裁判   Direct Trial Before the Shōgun; after Ietsuna this practice was discontinued.

340. Omemie   御目見   Audience Privilege; for all of the Shogunate vassals with *Hatamoto* rank or above.

341. Ōmetsuke   大目付   Great Inspectors (great eye attacher); four or five bannermen—the "eyes" of the senior council with duties of policing the daimyō and attending court sessions.

342. Ometsuke   御目付   Inspectors (eye attacher); ten bannermen—the "eyes" of the *wakadoshiyori* (see *metsuke*); they policed the bannermen and attended certain court sessions.

343. Ōnaiyoriai   大内寄合   Great Inner-session; meeting of both the fiscal and judicial sections of the finance commission.

344. Ōnawa kyūchi   大繩給知   Great Rope Grant; referred to the surveying practice of measuring in favor of the taxpayer; the measure was a rope.

345. Ongoku bugyō   遠國奉行   Commissioners of Distant Provinces; the officials of the Shogunate situated in strategic ports, roads, and defense points to enable the Shogunate to maintain its supervision over the whole country's defense and administration; see chart

		VI (p. 83) in the text for their location.
346. Ongoku kingin deiri	遠國金銀出入	Money Disputes from Distant Provinces; a special title for suits between Osaka merchants, primarily, and persons from the outlying areas of Kyūshū, Shikoku, and Chūgoku and handled by the *Ongokuyaku*.
347. Ongokuyaku	遠國役	Distant Province Officers; three officers in the Osaka Town Commission charged with handled money suits between Osaka persons and other parties from Kyūshū, Chūgoku, or Shikoku.
348. Ongoku yakunin	遠國役人	Officials of Distant Provinces; a broad term including a Shogunate commissioner outside Edo and the Kyoto Deputy Governor and Osaka Castle Deputy.
349. Ōnin no ran	應仁の亂	The dispute of the Ōnin period (1467–77); a dispute over succession between the adoptive and real sons of the Muromachi Shōgun. The dispute touched off more than a century of political chaos and struggle for power terminating in the Tokugawa Shogunate.
350. Ōrusui	大留守居	Great Attendant During Absence; the Shōgun's deputy at the castle while he was away. The position seems to have become less important as the Shogunate became stabilized in power.
351. Osa byakushō	長百姓	Chief Farmer; another title for the position of Group Chief *(kumigashira)*.
352. Osadamegaki	御定書	Written Decisions; the compilation in two books (*jōkan* 上巻 and *gekan* 下巻), by Yoshimune and his officials in 1742.
353. Osaka jōdai	大坂城代	Osaka Castle Deputy; in charge of

Osaka Castle and the defense of
western Japan; with special power
over the commerce and trade of
Osaka and the four provinces of
Harima, Izumi, Settsu, and Kawa-
chi.

354. Oshikomi 押込 (Pushed in). A penalty imposed on
warriors only; required them to
stay at home and not appear in
public.

355. Oshirasudome 御白州留 Detainment in Court; a type of
penalty; to make parties accede to
the wishes of the judge without
formal judgment.

356. Osobashū 御側衆 Side Advisers; five to eight personal
assistants to the Shōgun. Among
other duties they took turns staying
at the castle at night to take care of
personal arrangements for the Shōgun; sometimes a strong personality
from this group had considerable
influence on policy.

357. Osorenagara 乍恐 With Humble Apologies; the form
for beginning a petition in the Edo
courts.

358. Osso 越訴 Transcendent petitions; petitions
brought over the heads of subordinate officers.

359. Otōchi 御當地 (This place). A popular name for
Edo.

360. Ōyake 公 Public; the state; the community;
the term in Confucian thought has
a moral connotation as opposed to
private (*watakushi* 私).

361. Oyako kuji 親子公事 Suits involving Parent and Child;
one of the suits against Confucian
relationships and hence usually un-
acceptable in Shogunate courts.

362. Oyakuryō daka 御役料高 A salary attached to an office instead of a house or man.

363. Ōyoriai 大寄合 Great Meeting; extraordinary ses-

sions of the conference chamber attended by all of the senior councillors.

364. Rakuchaku	落着	Decision in a criminal case as opposed to Judgment *(saikyo)* in a civil case.
365. Rangaku	蘭學	Dutch Learning; the study by Japanese of western subjects introduced by the Dutch at Nagasaki.
366. Rempan shōmon kore aru shoukeoi tokuyō wariai uketori sōrō sadame	連判證文 之有諸請 負徳用割合 請取候定	Agreement Dividing the Profits from a Joint Enterprise; one of the four types of relationships which were known as *nakamagoto* and concerning which petitions were not acceptable in Shogunate courts.
367. Renza	連座	Vicarious liability of officials or others for the criminal acts of their subordinates and associates.
368. Ri	理	Principle; a sort of natural-law principle; one of the parts of Chu Hsi's ontological dualism.
369. Ribetsujō	離別狀	Divorce paper granted at will by a husband to an unwanted wife; (a separation paper); same as *itoma no jō* (leisure paper) or *sarijō* (parting paper).
370. Ritsu	律	Criminal Prohibitions; the criminal law of the *ritsuryō* codes adopted under Chinese (Tan'g) influence in the early eighth century.
371. Rōjū	老中	Senior Council; a group composed of four or five hereditary daimyō, who supervised the whole administration, made policy, and served as a court of last resort in law suits during the Tokugawa period.
372. Rōnin	浪(牢)人	Wandering men; masterless warriors. Because of confiscation of numerous daimyō domains under Iemitsu, the displaced retainers *(rōnin)* became a major problem.

373. Rōnindai 牢人台 Level in court where *rōnin* sat during trial.

374. Ronsho 論所 Land and Water Disputes; a broad term including disputes involving land and water; since they were important to Shogunate finance, they were afforded the maximum procedural protection in the Shogunate Courts.

375. Rusui 留守居 Deputy During Absence; each daimyō had a *rusui* who remained in charge of his Edo establishment while he was in his fief; many daimyō also had *rusui* at warehouses in Osaka to handle their rice.

376. Ruzai 流罪 Exile on an island (equivalent to *entō* 遠島).

377. Ryō 令 Administrative Regulations; the administrative provisions of the *ritsuryō* codes adopted under Chinese (Tan'g) influence (702 A.D.).

378. Ryō 兩 Tokugawa monetary unit in gold.

379. Ryōchi deiri 領地出入 Disputes over Fiefs.

380. Ryōshu 領主 Daimyō in their capacity as governor of a fief; daimyō fiefs were referred to as *ryō* 領 as opposed to the *hatamoto chigyō* or *gokenin kyūchi*.

381. Sadame 定 Decision or Regulation.

382. Saibanjō no wakai 裁判上の和解 Compromise during Trial; as distinguished from compromises apart from trial (Civil Code 695–96) and before trial (Civil Procedure 356).

383. Saikyo 裁許 Judgment; the decision of a Shogunate judge in a civil case.

384. Saikyo kobami 裁許拒み Refuse a Judgment; the act of repudiating the decision of a deputy and seeking review in the finance commission.

385. Saikyo mōshi-watashi 裁許申渡 Announcement of Judgment; usually done formally by the full bench in the conference chamber or commissions concerned.

386. Saikyo uke shōmon 裁許請證文 Acknowledgment of Judgment.

387. Sanbugyō 三奉行 Three Commissions; temple and shrine, Edo town and finance commissions, but the Edo town commission seldom functioned as a commission in the sense of a council.

388. Sankin kōtai 參觀交代 Alternate Annual Attendance; daimyō alternating annual service between Edo and the domains; a practice established in the early Tokugawa period to control the daimyō; it became one of the keys to Tokugawa power and a stimulus to trade and commerce.

389. Sashibi 差日 Date of Appearance; the date set for hearing in a Tokugawa court.

390. Sashibi izen tsukitodoke 差日以前着届 Report to Court Before the Date of Appearance; parties were required to report three or four days (depending on the court) before trial.

391. Sashibi taiketsu 差日對決 Trial on Appearance Date.

392. Sashidashi 差出 Notice.

393. Sashidashi negai 差出願 Request to Submit the Complaint; an application to the plaintiff's overlord to get the overlord to seal the complaint to a Shogunate court.

394. Sashigami 差紙 Summons; a paper requiring court attendance of a party or witness.

395. Sashizoenin 差添人 Accompanying Petitioner; the plaintiff's town or village official, whose seal of approval was always a precondition to filing a suit in a court above the village level.

396. Sashizu 差圖 Instruction; an answer to a legal question (*toiawase* 問合) put to the senior council by other Shogunate officials.

397. Sato *(ri)* 里 A small village or subdivision in the pre-Tokugawa local administrative organization.

398. Seikyō itchi 政教一致 Unity of Administration and Instruction; the idea that adminis-

trators taught official truth, that lawsuits resulted primarily from ignorance.

399. Seii taishōgun   征夷大將軍 Generalissimo-for-Conquering-the-Barbarians; the chief military position in the Imperial court organization of Kyōto after Minamoto no Yoritomo. At first a temporary office. The first incumbent was Sakanoue no Tamuramaro 坂上田村麿 at the beginning of the Heian period.

400. Seisai   制裁 Village Adjudication; generally it means punishment by lynching or other group action.

401. Sendō tsuki   仙洞附 Officials attached to the retired emperor.

402. Sengi   詮議 Criminal Investigation or Hearing.

403. Sengoku   戰國 Warring Provinces.

404. Sentō goryō   仙洞御料 Lands and stipends for a retired emperor.

405. Seppuku   切腹 Self disembowelment with a sword; instead of decapitating warriors for infamous crimes, they were ordered to commit suicide in this fashion; hence a substitute for capital punishment, but it was also a symbol of honor; a way to cleanse one's name after personal dishonor or mistake; same as *harakiri*.

406. Sesshō   攝政 Imperial Regent; served as the deputy for the emperor in case of minority or incompetence.

407. Setchūgaku   折衷學 Eclectic School of Confucianism.

408. Shakumeiken   釈明權 Authority to clarify; the judge's authority to seek affirmatively to clarify the facts and the legal issues (modern).

409. Sharitsu   赦律 Law of Pardon; a law passed in 1862 important to the history of Tokugawa criminal law.

410. Shibai kidosen   芝居木戸錢 Gate Receipts in a Joint Theatrical

		Venture; admission fees to the theatre; classed as *nakamagoto*, hence not litigable.
411. Shichichi	質地	Mortgaged Land.
412. Shihai	支配	Jurisdiction; *shihai* sometimes meant personal power of command over individuals, as well as jurisdiction in the territorial sense.
413. Shihai chigai	支配違い	Diversity of Jurisdictions; diversity based on territorial jurisdiction; where one party was from the land of one officer and the other from the land of another officer; was also sometimes used to indicate inter-status suits.
414. Shihō shoshi	司法書士	Judicial Scrivener.
415. Shihōken	司法權	Judicial power.
416. Shiki	職	General term for interests in land during the Kamakura period.
417. Shikijitsu	式日	Formal Days; three sessions of the conference chamber per month which were attended by a senior councillor.
418. Shikikin	敷金	Money for Security; money deposited with the lessor of a house by the lessee to guarantee the payment of rent; and it was returned when the quarters were vacated by the lessee without damage or default.
419. Shikimoku	式目	Formal Provisions; the typical term for written law in the Kamakura period.
420. Shikitari	仕來	Prior customs and precedents.
421. Shimmon seishi	神文誓詞	A religious oath; like a *kishōmon* oath.
422. Shimo yashiki	下屋敷	Lower Mansion; one of the mansions of a daimyō in Edo; most daimyō had three (upper, middle, and lower).
423. Shindai kagiri	身代限り	Compulsory Execution on the defendant's property to satisfy a judgment.

424. Shinkan	神官	Shinto officials.
425. Shinkyū	審級	Modern term for the systems of court appeals.
426. Shi nō kō shō	士農工商	Social hierarchy in Tokugawa thought: warrior, farmer, artisan, merchant; sometimes called *shimin* 四民.
427. Shinshakai no seigikan	新社會の 正義觀	Sense of Justice in the New Society; Yasuda's term; similar to the Nazi idea of "healthy instincts of the people"; see Friedmann, *Legal Theory* (1949), p. 260.
428. Shioki	仕置	Administration (in a broad sense); more specifically, imposition and execution of penalties.
429. Shirasu	白州	Court (white gravel); actually only the lowest level where commoners were seated in the usual Tokugawa courtroom. This level was covered with fine white pebbles.
430. Shiryō	私領	Private Domain; referred to daimyō and bannerman fiefs as opposed to the Shogunate lands *(goryō)*.
431. Shitadori	下どり	The level in court where lesser warriors sat.
432. Shita ni te atsukawan	下にて あつかわん	Handle it on the lower level; to settle a dispute privately without making a public fuss about it or appealing to the higher authorities.
433. Shita ukenin	下請人	Underguarantor; a person who guaranteed a servant to a *hitoyado*, which in turn guaranteed the servant's character and performance to a master.
434. Shizai	死罪	Death penalty by decapitation.
435. Shobutsu uriwatashi shōmon nite kinsu kari sōrō rui	諸物賣渡 證文に而 金子借候類	Type of Money Loan in a Document of Commodity Transfer; where the seller shows that he has advanced the price of the goods sold in the document of transfer.
436. Shōen	庄園	A manor or estate patronized by a court noble in the Heian period. It

		had tax immunity and was, therefore, important in the beginning of feudal decentralization in Japan.
437. Shō gō ho ri	庄郷保里	System of local subdivision in early Japanese history.
438. Shokken	職權	Authority of the court; often used to mean by authority of the court on its own motion (modern).
439. Shokō	諸侯	Various Lords; referred to the daimyō.
440. Shokunin	職人	Artisans such as carpenters, weavers, and other craftsmen or laborers; they were distinguished from merchants *(shōnin)*, but both *shokunin* and *shōnin* were called townsmen, *chōnin.*
441. Shōmyō	小名	(Small name). A Lord with under one hundred thousand *koku* of assessed rice capacity in the Azuchi-Momoyama period (1575–98). The term fell into disuse in the early Tokugawa period, when all feudal lords with over ten thousand *koku* were designated daimyō.
442. Shōnin	商人	Merchants; sometimes called *akindo* (same Chinese characters); according to later feudal ideas, the merchant was a sort of necessary parasite. Although there were some feudal lords who favored recognizing the legitimacy of the merchant's role in Tokugawa society, they did not prevail.
443. Shōnin	證人	Guarantor; this term means witness in modern practice.
444. Shoshidai	所司代	Deputy Governor; the representative of the Shogunate in Kyoto; regulated the Imperial court, nobles, and the city of Kyoto and outlying provinces of Ōmi, Yamashiro, Yamato, and Tamba.
445. Shoshi hatto	諸士法度	Various Rules for Lesser Warriors;

a code for bannermen announced to them in 1623 and 1663; after 1683 the *Buke Shohatto* was used for bannermen as well as daimyō.

446. Shōsū iken   少數意見   Minority Opinion.

447. Shotaiketsu   初對決   First Confrontation; the first hearing in a civil suit; it was conducted by the commissioners themselves; later ones were by underlings, until judgment at least.

448. Shōya   庄屋   Headman; a term equivalent to *nanushi;* which term was used depended on the locality.

449. Shugo   守護   Protector; the provincial military governor representing the Kamakura Shogunate; the civil power was exercised by Imperial court officials, called *kokushi* 國司. In the Muromachi period the *shugo* assumed most of the civil as well as military power.

450. Shuinjō   朱印狀   Document bearing the red seal of the Shōgun; usually used to grant land to shrines and temples.

451. Shujin suji ni   主人筋に   Disputes Between a Feudal Lord
     aikakari sōrō   相掛候   and His Retainer; a suit involving
     deiri   出入   feudal status; hence not acceptable in Shogunate courts as a rule; the lord had power to decide it.

452. Shujū soshō   主從訴訟   Petitions involving Superiors and Inferiors; hence usually left to the discretion of the superior and not acceptable in the Shogunate courts.

453. Shukun   主君   Overlord; the superior in a feudal or Confucian relationship.

454. Shūmon aratame   宗門改   Temple Inspection Registry; a
     chō   帳   registry to certify the adherence to a Buddhist sect; required to prevent Christianity.

455. Shushigaku   朱子學   Orthodox Confucianism; Japanese version of Chu Hsi's (Sung) philosophy, propounded by Fujiwara

			Seika and the Hayashi family among others in the Tokugawa period.
456.	Shusshi chōji	出仕停止	Suspension from official duty; a type of penalty in the ancient Imperial court practice.
457.	Sojō tadashi	訴狀正し	Examination of the Complaints; *sojō* was used instead of *meyasu* (in the finance commission) to signify the complaint in a lawsuit in the temple and shrine commission.
458.	Sojō uragaki	訴狀裏書	Endorsement on the Back of the Complaint (see *uragaki*).
459.	Sompō	村法	Village Law; regulations passed by the villagers for their own observance.
460.	Sōni	僧尼	Buddhist bonzes and nuns; Buddhist clergy.
461.	Soroban	算盤	Abacus; a device for arithmetical calculations.
462.	Sōroku	總録	General Chief of the Blind Guild in Edo.
463.	Soshō	訴訟	Petition; sometimes used to indicate an *ex parte* matter as opposed to an adversary matter *(deiri mono)*.
464.	Sosho	訴所	Registry; place where papers were filed and reports made to the finance commission concerning a suit.
465.	Soshō chien	訴訟遅延	Delay of Litigation.
466.	Sōyoriai	總寄合	General Sessions.
467.	Suiron	水論	Water Disputes; lawsuits over water rights; such suits were numerous and important because of irrigation of rice, the basis of Shogunate finance.
468.	Suji	筋	Channels; used to signify proper administrative channels.
469.	Suji chigai	筋違い	Out of Channels; a petition brought to the wrong court or brought over the heads of inferior officers without their consent.
470.	Sumikuchi	濟口聞届	Pronouncement of the Settlement

kikitodoke

Agreement; in order to bind the parties and make the agreement enforceable as a judgment, it had to be read to the parties and accepted by them in court.

471. Sumikuchi shōmon 濟口證文

Deed of Private Settlement; the written terms of the agreement reached in a dispute by private negotiation; it was sealed by the parties, pronounced in court, and enforceable thereafter as a judgment.

472. Tachiai 立合

Ordinary Session (stand together); three sessions of the conference chamber per month. The senior councillor did not attend; the other three meetings per month when the senior councillor did not attend were *shikijitsu*.

473. Tadashigaki 但書

Proviso; qualifying provision in Tokugawa written laws.

474. Taidan ihen deiri 對談違變出入

Breach of Agreement Dispute.

475. Taihō 大法

Great Law; referred to "natural law," which came to include custom as well as principles of orthodox Confucianism in the Tokugawa period.

476. Taihō ritsuryō 大寶律令

Taihō code (702 A.D.) Chinese type regulations modeled after those of the Tan'g dynasty in China; included a public-land system in a complex, graded, civil bureaucracy.

477. Taika no kaishin 大化改新

Reforms of 636 inaugurating a public-land system, etc., modeled after the Tan'g system.

478. Tairō 大老

Great Elder; a position filled irregularly, from the daimyō houses of Ii 井伊, Sakai 酒井, or Hotta 堀田 when the Shōgun was a minor or incompetent. There were seven in all, five Ii's, one Hotta, and one Sakai.

479. Takumi goto	巧事	Fraud (clever thing); deceit.
480. Tanachingin	店賃金	House Rent.
481. Tanaukenin	店請人	A person who guaranteed to the lessor the reliability of the lessee of a house.
482. Tanauke shōmon	店請證文	(House receipt document). A document from a guarantor to a house owner guaranteeing the reliability of a lessee.
483. Tanin	他人	Other Person.
484. Tashihai	他支配	Another Jurisdiction.
485. Tasū iken	多數意見	Majority Opinion.
486. Tatami	疊	Straw Mats.
487. Tegiri	手限	Summary Jurisdiction (within hand's reach); power of an official; usually officials were limited to a certain grade of penalty they could impose without requesting approval from superiors; hence *tegiri* meant the limit of penalty a given official could impose in criminal trials.
488. Tejō	手錠	Handcuffing; used as a penalty and also imposed during trial.
489. Tenkan	添簡	An Accompanying Letter; the letter sent with a petitioner by his overlord to certify approval of the petition to a Shogunate court.
490. Tenryō	天領	(Heavenly domain). Popular term for the Shogunate domain.
491. Tenshi	添使	Attendant Messenger; the representative of the plaintiff's daimyō who accompanied the plaintiff to court in order to express the daimyō's approval of the petition to the Shogunate court; same as *Tenkan* except that daimyō always sent a messenger instead of a letter.
492. Tenshi sashidashi	添使差出	Submission by the Attendant Messenger; approval of a petition and its submission to the Shogunate by the daimyō under whom the plaintiff resides.

493. Terauke	寺請	Temple certificate showing adherence to a Buddhist sect; therefore non-Christian.
494. Toiawase	問合せ	Asking Advice; an inquiry to the Shogunate senior council from a daimyō concerning a legal question.
495. Tokorobarai	所拂ひ	Banishment from one's native place.
496. Tomeyaku	留役	Recording Officers; important underlings in the conference chamber and finance commission, who acted as judges in the preliminary preparation of cases and intermediate hearings.
497. Tomeyaku tadashi	留役糺	Hearing before the Recording Officer.
498. Tonya	問屋	(Order house). Wholesale house.
499. Torimochinin	取持人	Conciliator; a person who handles a matter; a conciliator in a dispute.
500. Torinoki mujin	取退無盡	Mutual Financing without duty to repay the money withdrawn; a kind of gambling which was prohibited by the Shogunate as a perversion of the purpose of mutual financing devices.
501. Torisage	取下	Withdrawal of a claim (modern).
502. Tōshu	當主	Househead; he had considerable power over both property and personal matters for the whole house; the position normally fell to the eldest son.
503. Tozama	外様	Outside Lords; used to indicate daimyō who only recognized Tokugawa overlordship after Sekigahara (1600); and formally by oath (1611).
504. Tsūjō soshō	通常訴訟	Ordinary Lawsuit; or adversary suits (modern).
505. Tsukefuda	附札	Endorsement attached; a memorandum upon which the senior council or conference chamber wrote their answer to legal ques-

tions put to them from subordinate officials.

506. Tsukiban	月番	Monthly Officer; system used in the magistracies and other councils of rotating routine duty monthly among the members.
507. Tsukigyōji	月行事	Monthly Administrator; an assistant to the *nanushi* in the Edo towns.
508. Tsumami	つまみ	Summary; an outline of a case prepared to brief the commission.
509. Ukagai	伺	A request by subordinate officials to the senior council for approval of a proposed penalty to be imposed in a specific criminal case; usually the term *toiawase* 問合 was used for similar requests regarding civil cases.
510. Uragaki	裏書	Endorsement on the Back; the endorsement on the back of a civil petition by a Shogunate court signifying acceptance of the petition and ordering the defendant to appear.
511. Uragaki haikensho	裏書拝見書	Receipt of Service of the Endorsement; a certificate from the defendant acknowledging presentment of a petition sealed on the back by the commissioners.
512. Uragaki kafu	裏書下附	Granting the Endorsement.
513. Uragaki keshi	裏書消	Cancellation of the Endorsement.
514. Uragaki sōtatsu	裏書送達	Serving the Endorsement; the plaintiff had the duty to serve the endorsed complaint on the defendant in civil suits of the Tokugawa period.
515. Urikake	賣掛	Sale on credit.
516. Uriwatashi shōmon	賣渡證文	Deed of Sale and Conveyance.
517. Uwadori	上どり	Level of the court where the warriors and other privileged persons sat.
518. Wakadoshiyori	若年寄	Junior Council (young elders); four

		bannermen who supervised the other *hatamoto* and assisted the *rōjū*.
519. Wakai	和解	Compromise; a modern term derived from the codes and adopted from the German practice; it has contractual meaning in the Civil Code, Articles 695–96; procedural meaning in the Code of Civil Procedure, Articles 136 and 356.
520. Watakushi	私	Private; has an immoral or unworthy connotation in Confucian thought.
521. Wayo	和與	Conciliation; a term used in the Kamakura practice.
522. Yado azuke	宿預	(The custody of persons). Entrusted to a suit inn by the court.
523. Yakusho	役所	Deputy's Office.
524. Yojin	餘人	Other persons; apparently not considered good usage in the Tokugawa courts, since Nuinosuke (p. 141) was told to use *tanin* instead.
525. Yokoku	餘國	Other Provinces.
526. Yōmeigaku	陽明學	Sometimes referred to as the Ming philosophy; propagated in the Tokugawa period by Nakae Tōju, Kumazawa Banzan, and others.
527. Yoriaiba	寄合場	Older name for the conference chamber.
528. Yoriki	與力	Aides in the town commission; their function was largely police work, but in the early period they seem to have had some part in trials and investigation.
529. Yōshi	養子	Adopted Son; adoption was very common in the Tokugawa period in order to preserve the "house," name and property.
530. Yūjo agedaikin	遊女揚代金	Money Claims by Managers of Pleasure Women; one of the types of claims treated as *nakamagoto;*

		hence petitions concerning such claims were not acceptable in Shogunate courts.
531. Yūshi	猶子	Adoptive son; usually used to indicate adoption of a son in court noble families.
532. Za	座	A sort of guild in the pre-Tokugawa period; some of them continued in the Edo period, but the word for guild in the Edo period was usually *kabunakama* 株仲間.
533. Zahō	座法	Guild Law; regulations passed by guilds to regulate their internal affairs.
534. Zatō	座頭	A member of the Blind Guild (*tōdō* 當道).
535. Zeni	錢	A copper coin.

APPENDIX III

CIVIL CONCILIATION* LAW
(Effective October 1, 1951)
Law No. 222
CHAPTER I. GENERAL PROVISIONS

Article 1. (The purpose of this law.)

The purpose of this law is to devise, by mutual concessions of the parties, solutions for disputes concerning civil matters, which are consistent with reason and befitting actual circumstances.

Article 2. (Conciliation case.)

When a dispute arises concerning a civil matter, a party may make a proposal for conciliation to the court.

Article 3. (Jurisdiction.)

Conciliation cases, except for instances which have special provisions, will be under the jurisdiction of the summary court which has jurisdiction over the domicile, residence, place of work, or office of the defendant, or the district court or summary court which has been designated by mutual agreement of the parties.

Article 4. (Transfer, etc.)

Section 1. In a situation where a court receives a proposal concerning a case not within its jurisdiction, it will transfer it to the district court, family court, or summary court which has jurisdiction over the case. However, when recognized as especially necessary in order to dispose of the case, regardless of the rules of territorial jurisdiction, all or part of the case may be transferred to the jurisdiction of another court, or the court can dispose of it itself.

Section 2. Even in a case where a court receives a proposal concerning a case within its jurisdiction, when it is recognized as proper in order to dispose of the case, the court can transfer all or part of the case to a court of another jurisdiction, in spite of the rules of territorial jurisdiction.

Article 5. (Agencies of conciliation.)

Section 1. The court conducts conciliation by means of a conciliation committee. However, when it is considered appropriate the judge alone may conduct the conciliation.

Section 2. The court, when there is a proposal from the parties, will conduct conciliation by means of a conciliation committee, in spite of the proviso to the previous section.

Article 6. (Organization of the conciliation committee.)

The conciliation committee is composed of one conciliation chairman and two or more conciliation members.

Article 7. (Conciliation chairman, conciliation members.)

Section 1. The conciliation chairmen will be designated by the district court from among the judges.

Section 2. The conciliation chairman will designate the conciliation members for each case from among the following persons:

1. Persons nominated beforehand each year by the district court;
2. Persons designated by mutual agreement of the parties.

Section 3. The conciliation chairman, when he considers it necessary in order to dispose of the case, may designate persons as conciliation members other than those listed in the previous section.

Article 8. (Conciliation assistants.)

The conciliation committee may ask the opinion of the parties and have persons who are recognized as appropriate assist with the conciliation.

Article 9. (Travel expenses, daily fees and lodging money.)

Travel expenses, daily fees and lodging money as provided by the Supreme Court will be paid to the conciliation members and the persons who assist with conciliation in accordance with the provisions of the preceding article.

Article 10. (Fees.)

Section 1. In order to make a proposal for conciliation, a fee will be paid.

Section 2. The Supreme Court will determine the amount of the fee of the previous section, within limits not to exceed one hundred *yen* for each ten thousand *yen* of the amount in the matter to be conciliated.

Section 3. When the amount in the matter to be conciliated cannot be calculated, that amount will be regarded as fifty thousand *yen*.

Article 11. (Participation of interested parties.)

Section 1. Persons interested in the result of the conciliation may obtain permission of the conciliation committee and participate in the conciliation procedure.

Section 2. The conciliation committee, when it is recognized as appropriate, may require persons who are interested in the result of the conciliation to participate in the conciliation procedure.

Article 12. (Preconciliation measures.)

Section 1. When it is recognized as especially necessary for purposes of conciliation, the conciliation committee on the proposal of a party may, as a preconciliation measure, forbid the defendant or others related to the case to make changes in the present situation or to dispose of property or order them to refrain from conduct which would render it impossible or extremely difficult to accomplish the objective of the conciliation.

Section 2. The measures of the previous section will not entail power of execution.

Article 13. (Cases which are not to be conciliated.)

The conciliation committee, when it recognizes that from the nature of the case it is not proper to conciliate, or when it recognizes that a party has made a proposal for conciliation unreasonably and with an improper purpose, may terminate the case as a matter not to be conciliated.

Article 14. (Failure of conciliation.)

When the committee recognizes that there is no expectation of reaching an agreement between the parties, or when it recognizes that the agreement reached is inappropriate, and when the court does not render a decision under Article 17, the conciliation committee may have the case terminated as a matter wherein conciliation [settlement] was not accomplished.

Article 15. (Applicability to conciliation by the judge.)

The provisions of Article 8, Article 9, and Articles 11 through the preceding article will be applied *mutatis mutandis* to the conciliation conducted by the judge only.

Article 16. (Establishment of agreement and its effectiveness.)

When agreement is reached between the parties in the conciliation and it is recorded in the conciliation report, it will be considered an accomplished settlement, and the record will have the same effectiveness as a compromise during trial.

Article 17. (Decision instead of settlement.)

When it is recognized as appropriate in cases where there is no expectation that settlement will be accomplished by the conciliation committee, the court, after hearing the opinions of the conciliation committee members and considering the matter equitably from the standpoint of both parties and reviewing all of the circumstances, may, of its own authority, render a decision necessary to settle the case, within limits not inconsistent with the purport of the parties' proposals. In this decision, payment of money, transfer of goods, and other dispositions of property may be ordered.

Article 18. (Proposal of protest.)

Section 1. The parties or interested persons may make a proposal of protest against the decision of the previous article. The period therefor will be two weeks from the day the notice of decision was received by the parties.

Section 2. When there is a proposal of protest within the period stated in the preceding section, the decision of the same section will lose its effectiveness.

Section 3. When there is no proposal of protest within the period stated in section 1, the decision of the same section will have the same effectiveness as a compromise during trial.

Article 19. (Filing of suits in case settlement is not accomplished, etc.)

When the case is concluded according to the provisions of Article 14 (including cases in which it is applied *mutatis mutandis* under Article 15) or when the decision loses effectiveness in accordance with the provisions of section 2 of the previous article, and when within two weeks from the date of notice to that effect the applicant files a suit on the claim which was the object of the conciliation, the filing of the suit will be regarded to have been instituted at the time of the proposal for conciliation.

Article 20. (Conciliation of court receiving suit.)

Section 1. The court receiving a suit may, of its own authority, when it recognizes it as proper and after transferring the case to conciliation, have the court with jurisdiction handle it or handle it itself. However, cases where the issues and evidence in the case have been settled and there is no agreement among the parties are not within this provision.

Section 2. In cases transferred to conciliation in accordance with the previous section and when settlement has been accomplished or a decision has been confirmed under Article 17, the suit will be regarded as withdrawn.

Section 3. When the court receiving suit handles the case itself through conciliation in accordance with the provisions of Section 1, the court receiving the suit will designate the conciliation chairman from among its judges, in spite of the provisions of Article 7, section 1.

Article 21. (Immediate appeal.)

Against decisions in conciliation procedures, an immediate appeal may be made in accordance with regulations determined by the Supreme Court. The period will be two weeks.

Article 22. (Application *mutatis mutandis* of the Law of Procedure for Non-contentious Matters.)

Excluding situations for which there are special rules, Book I [Articles 1–33] of the Law of Procedure for Non-contentious Matters (1898, Law No. 14), will be applied *mutatis mutandis* concerning conciliation, so long as it [said law] is not contrary to the nature [of conciliation]. However, this provision does not extend to Article 15 of the same law.

Article 23. (Matters not determined by this law.)

Besides the matters determined in this law, other points necessary to conciliation will be determined by the Supreme Court.

CHAPTER II. SPECIAL PROVISIONS
Part 1. Conciliation Concerning Residential Land and Buildings

Article 24. (Residential land and building conciliation cases; jurisdiction.)

Conciliation cases concerning disputes over the lease or other use of residential land and/or buildings will be under the jurisdiction of the summary court which has jurisdiction over the residential land or location of the building in dispute or under the jurisdiction of the district court having jurisdiction over the place if so determined by agreement of the parties.

Part 2. Conciliation of Agricultural Affairs

Article 25. (Conciliation cases in agricultural affairs.)

In cases concerning disputes over the lease or other use of agricultural land or land incidental to agricultural operations, or buildings or other facilities used in agricultural enterprises (hereafter called "Agricultural land, etc.") the provisions of this part will govern, in addition to the matters determined by the preceding chapter.

Article 26. (Jurisdiction.)

Conciliation of the cases of the preceding article will be under the jurisdiction of the district court with jurisdiction over the location of the agricultural land, etc., in dispute, or under the jurisdiction of the summary court with jurisdiction over the location if so determined by agreement of the parties.

Article 27. (Statement of opinions by the tenancy officers, etc.)

Tenancy officers [central government] or tenant supervisors [prefectural] may appear on the date [of conciliation] or at another date and state their opinions to the conciliation committee.

Article 28. (Hearing the opinions of the tenancy officers, etc.)

The conciliation committee must hear the opinion of the tenancy officer or tenant supervisor when it is attempting to conciliate.

Article 29. (Application *mutatis mutandis* to conciliation by the judge.)

The provisions of the preceding two articles will be applied *mutatis mutandis* when the judge alone conducts conciliation.

Article 30. (Application *mutatis mutandis* to the transferrals, etc.)

The provisions in Article 28 will be applied *mutatis mutandis* when the court transfers a case or attempts to dispose of the case itself in accordance with the proviso to Article 4, section 1 or section 2, or when the court attempts to decide the case under Article 17.

Part 3. Conciliation of Commercial Affairs

Article 31. (Conciliation cases in commercial affairs; terms of conciliation determined by the conciliation committee.)

Section 1. Concerning conciliation cases related to disputes over commercial affairs, the conciliation committee, when there is no expectation of reaching an agreement between the parties or when the agreement reached is not recognized as appropriate and when there is an agreement between the parties in writing to the effect that they will comply with such terms as the conciliation committee determines, may, upon application, determine appropriate conciliation terms in order to settle the case.

Section 2. When the conciliation terms of the preceding article are recorded as a conciliation report, it will be regarded as a completed settlement and the report will have the same effectiveness as a compromise during trial.

Part 4. Conciliation of Mine Damages

Article 32. (Cases for conciliation of mine damages; jurisdiction.)

Conciliation cases concerning disputes over compensation for mine damages as provided in the Mining Industry Law (1950, Law No. 289) will be under the jurisdiction of the district court which has jurisdiction over the place where damage occurred.

Article 33. (Application *mutatis mutandis* of the provision concerning conciliation of agricultural affairs, etc.)

The provisions of Articles 27 through 31 will be applied *mutatis mutandis* to the conciliation cases of the preceding article. In such cases the tenancy officers or tenant supervisors in Articles 27 and 28 will be changed to read "the Chief of the Bureau of Commerce and Industry."

CHAPTER III. PENAL PROVISIONS

Article 34. (Punishment for nonappearance.)

If a person related to the case fails to appear without a justifiable reason upon receiving a summons from the court or conciliation committee, the court will impose a fine of three thousand *yen* or less.

Article 35. (Punishment for violation of measures.)

If the parties or participants fail to comply with the measures taken under the provisions of Article 12 (including situations where Article 15 is applicable *mutatis mutandis*) without justifiable reason, the court will impose a fine of five thousand *yen* or less.

Article 36. (Decisions imposing fines.)

Section 1. A decision imposing a fine of the preceding two articles will be executed by order of the judge. This order will have the same effectiveness as a notarized obligation [with power of execution].

Section 2. The execution of a decision imposing a fine will comply with the provisions of the law and ordinances concerning civil procedure. However, service of the decision is not necessary before it is executed.

Section 3. The provisions in Article 207 and Article 208, section 2 of the Law of Procedure for Non-contentious Matters concerning public procurators are not applicable to the decisions imposing fines under section 1.

Article 37. (Crime of revealing conference secrets.)

When a conciliation committee member or a former committee member reveals, without justifiable reason, the progress in the conferences or the opinion of the conciliation committee chairman or of a conciliation committee member or the division of the members on the issue, he will be punished with a fine of five thousand *yen* or less.

Article 38. (Crime for revealing the secrets of other persons.)

When a conciliation committee member or a former committee member, without justifiable reason, reveals the secrets of other persons which he has been able to learn through handling them in his official capacity, he will be punished with penal servitude of six months or less or a fine of ten thousand *yen* or less.

(Supplementary rules are not included in this translation.)

Bibliography

Contents

BIBLIOGRAPHICAL NOTE

This bibliography is divided into two parts: Japanese and western language sources. The Japanese language sources are, however, further divided into Tokugawa and modern sections, because the scholars, journals, books, and even libraries concerned with Tokugawa and modern materials are usually different. The coverage of the materials listed herein is limited generally to works cited in this study, although a few additional works which have been consulted but not cited have also been included. Brief notes have been provided at the beginning of the various sections of the bibliography to call attention to the items which have been most useful in this study. Also occasional comments have been added to the individual materials where it seemed appropriate.

Although there is no beginner's guide in English covering the modern Japanese legal literature, the handbook recently printed in Japanese for use of its students by the Shihō kenshūjo, *Hōrei hanrei gakusetsu no chōsa ni tsuite* (1962), is a useful guide for beginners. For an introduction to Tokugawa legal materials in English, see Dan F. Henderson, "Japanese Legal History of the Tokugawa Period: Scholars and Sources," University of Michigan, Center of Japanese Studies, *Occasional Papers* (no. 7) 100–21 (1957). In addition to the younger historians mentioned in that article (Hiramatsu, Otake, and Maeda), at least two other legal scholars have contributed significant works on the Tokugawa period since the article was published. Hayashi Tōichi has written a book on the Owari domain, and Harafuji Hitoshi has completed articles on the law of obligations.

A word about Japanese libraries may be useful. For modern legal sources, the Saikō Saibansho Toshokan 最高裁判所図書館 (Supreme Court Library) is perhaps the most convenient, for besides a rather complete holding of current Japanese materials, it also has selected western legal periodicals and indices. The *Hōritsu tosho mokuroku* (1950) and *Ippan tosho mokuroku* (1953) and supplements published by the Supreme Court, not only have all of the usual bibliographical data needed on the items listed therein, but also have author indices in alphabetical order and *rōmaji* headings.

The Hōmu Toshokan 法務図書館 (Ministry of Justice Library) is perhaps the most complete collection of both older and current legal sources in Japan. It is also quite convenient to use. Its older catalogues, however, are not as adequate as those of the Supreme Court. For the usual tools of the practicing lawyer, the libraries of the Tokyo Bar Association and the First Tokyo Bar Association are convenient. The Kokuritsu Kokkai Toshokan Miyakezaka Bunshitsu Hōritsu Seiji-bu 國立國會図書館三宅坂

分室法律政治部 (National Diet Library, Miyakezaka Branch, Law and Politics Section) is useful for postwar government records.

For Tokugawa sources the collections at the Ministry of Justice Library, Naikaku Bunko, and Tokyo and Kyoto University libraries are the best for Shogunate sources. All of the libraries mentioned above have been extremely helpful. Hiramatsu Yoshiro, *Kinsei keiji soshōhō no kenkyu* 7–16 (1960) gives an extensive list of Tokugawa legal manuscripts and their locations in Japan.

The foreign lawyer in Japan will have trouble in finding the legal works which he needs on his own law. The Supreme Court Library and the Ministry of Justice Library have rather large collections and are probably the best place to start looking for foreign-language books. *Ōbun tosho mokuroku* of the Ministry of Justice is helpful for such purposes.

LIST OF JAPANESE PERIODICALS

The Japanese periodicals listed below include journals of both historical and contemporary emphasis. They are listed here to supplement the citations in the list of articles which follows immediately and also those articles listed in the section on modern legal materials. The title translations enclosed in quotation marks are those found on the periodicals themselves. For translated titles not listed below in quotations marks, we have used the translations found in the National Diet Library (compiler), *Directory of Japanese Learned Periodicals*, not because these translations are entirely satisfactory but because this directory seems to be used considerably by foreigners.

>   *Chūō kōron* 中央公論 (The Central Review). Tokyo: Chūō Kōronsha 中央公論社, from Aug. 1887. Monthly.

>   *Hanrei taimuzu* 判例タイムズ ("The Law Times Report"). Tokyo: Hanrei Taimuzusha 判例タイムズ社, first series from 1948 to 1950, five issues. Second series from 1950. Monthly.

>   *Hōgaku* 法學 ("Journal of Law and Political Science"). Sendai: Tōhoku Daigaku Hōgakkai 東北大學法學會, from 1932. Monthly.

>   *Hōgaku kyōkai zasshi* 法學協會雜誌 ("The Journal of the Jurisprudence Association"). Tokyo: Hōgaku Kyōkai 法學協會, from 1884. Monthly.

>   *Hōgaku ronsō* 法學論叢 (Fukuoka University review of law). Fukuoka: Fukuoka Daigaku Kenkyūsho 福岡大學研究所, from 1956. Quarterly. Not for sale. Supersedes *Fukuoka Shōdai Ronsō*, 1949–56 and *Heiwadai Ronshū*, 1954–56.

>   *Hōgaku ronsō* 法學論叢 ("Kyoto Law Review"; from 1906 through 1919 it was called *Kyoto Hōgakkai zasshi*.) Kyoto: Kyōto Daigaku Hōgakkai 京都大學法學會, from 1906. Bimonthly.

Hōgaku shimpō 法學新報 ("Chūō Law Review"). Tokyo: Chūō Daigaku Hōgakkai, from 1891. Monthly.

Hōritsu jihō 法律時報 (Law Journal). Tokyo: Nihon Hyōron Shinsha 日本評論新社, from 1929. Monthly. This journal contains a monthly and annual bibliography of articles and books published on legal subjects. There is an index.

Hōritsu shimbun 法律新聞 ("The Legal News"). Tokyo: Hōritsu Shimbunsha 法律新聞社, from Sept. 1900 to 1943. 12 times per month. 4,878 numbers. Second series 1956–58. 117 numbers.

Hōritsu shimpō 法律新報 ("Journal of Law and Politics"). Tokyo: Hōritsu Shimpōsha 法律新報社 from May, 1924 to 1951. Monthly. 1759 numbers.

Hōritsu taimuzu 法律タイムズ (Law Times). Tokyo: Hōritsu Taimuzusha 法律タイムズ社, 1947–50. Monthly.

Hōsei kenkyū 法政研究 ("Journal of Law and Politics"). Fukuoka: Kyūshū Daigaku Hōseigakkai 九州大學法政學會, from 1931. Quarterly.

Hōseishi kenkyū 法制史研究 ("Legal History Review"). Tokyo: Hōseishi Gakkai 法制史學會, from 1952. Annual.

Hōsō 法曹 (Legal professionals). Tokyo: Hōsōkai 法曹會 (Lawyers Association). From 1946. Monthly.

Hōsō jiho 法曹時報 ("Lawyers Association Journal"). Tokyo: Hōsōkai 法曹會 (Lawyers Association), from 1949. Monthly.

Hō to seiji 法と政治 ("The Journals of Law and Politics"). Osaka: Kansai Gakuin Daigaku Hōseigakkai 關西學院大學法政學會, from Dec. 1949. Quarterly.

Jurisuto ジュリスト (Jurist). Tokyo: Yūhikaku 有斐閣, from Jan. 1952. Twice monthly.

Keizai ronsō 經濟論叢 ("The Economic Review"). Kyoto: Kyōto Daigaku Keizai Gakkai 京都大學經濟學會, from 1915. Monthly.

Kēsu kenkyū ケース研究 (Case study). Tokyo: Tōkyō Katei Saibansho Katei Jiken Kenkyūkai 東京家庭裁判所家庭事件研究會, from 1949. Bimonthly.

Kinseishi kenkyū 近世史研究 (Studies in Modern History). Ōsaka: Ōsaka Rekishi Gakkai Kinseishi Bukai, from 1954. Monthly.

Kokka gakkai zasshi 國家學會雜誌 ("The Journal of the Association of Political and Social Science"). Tokyo: Kokka Gakkai 國家學會, from 1887. Monthly.

Kokugakuin zasshi 國學院雜誌 ("Journal of Kokugakuin University"). Tokyo: Kokugakuin Daigaku 國學院大學, from 1894. Monthly.

Minji soshō zasshi 民事訴訟雜誌 ("Journal of Civil Procedure"). Tokyo: Minji Soshōhō Gakkai 民事訴訟法學会, from 1954. Yearly.

Minshōhō zasshi 民商法雑誌 (Journal of Civil and Commercial Law). Tokyo: Yūhikaku 有斐閣, from 1935. Monthly.

Minzoku to rekishi 民族と歴史 (Race and history). Tokyo: Nihon Gakujutsu Fukyūkai 日本學術普及會, from 1919 to 1922. Monthly. Title varies: *Shakaishi kenkyū*, 1923; superseded by *Rekishi chiri*, 1924.

Mita gakkai zasshi 三田學會雑誌 ("Mita Journal of Economics"). Tokyo: Keio Gijuku Daigaku Keizaigakkai 慶応義塾大學經濟學會, from 1909. Monthly.

Nihon hōgaku 日本法學 (Journal of Law and Politics). Tokyo: Nihon Daigaku Hōgakkai 日本大學法學會, from May 1935. Bimonthly.

Nihon rekishi 日本歴史 ("The Journal of the Japanese History"). Nihon Rekishi Gakkai 日本歴史學會, from 1946. Monthly.

Nihonshi kenkyū 日本史研究 (Studies in Japanese history). Kyoto: Nihonshi Kenkyūkai 日本史研究会, from 1946. Quarterly.

Rekishi chiri 歴史地理 (History and historical geography of Japan). Tokyo: Nihon Rekishi Chiri Gakkai 日本歴史地理學會, from 1899. Quarterly.

Rekishigaku kenkyū 歴史學研究 ("The Journal of Historical Studies"). Tokyo: Rekishigaku Kenkyūkai 歴史學研究會, from 1933. Monthly. This publication has been Marxist oriented since the war at least.

Rekishi kagaku 歴史科學 (Historical Science). Tokyo: Meiji Daigaku 明治大學, 1932–36. Monthly.

Rekishi to chiri 歴史と地理 (History and geography). Kyoto: Kyōto Shigaku Chirigaku Dōkōkai 京都史學地理學同好會, from 1917 to 1935. Monthly.

Shakaigaku zasshi 社會學雑誌 (Journal of Sociology). Tokyo: Nihon Shakai Gakkai 日本社會學會, from 1924 to 1930. Monthly.

Shakai keizai shigaku 社會經濟史學 ("The socio-economic history"). Tokyo: Shakai Keizaishi Gakkai 社會經濟史學會, from 1930. Bimonthly.

Shichō 史潮 ("The Journal of History"). Tokyo: Tōkyō Bunrika Daigaku Otsuka Shigakkai 東京文理科大學大塚史學會, from 1931. Quarterly.

Shien 史苑 (The Journal of historical studies). Tokyo: Rikkyō Daigaku Shigaku Kenkyūkai 立教大學史學研究會, from 1928. Semi-annually.

Shien 史淵 ("The Journal of History"). Fukuoka: Kyūshū Shigakkai 九州史學會, from 1929. Five times a year.

Shigaku kenkyū 史學研究 ("Review of Historical Studies"). Hiroshima:

Hiroshima Shigaku Kenkyūkai in Hiroshima Daigaku Bunga-
kubu 廣島史學研究會 廣島大學文學部, from 1929. Quarterly.

Shigaku zasshi 史學雜誌 ("The Historical Journal of Japan"). Tokyo:
Tōkyō Daigaku Shigakkai 東京大學史學會, from 1889. Monthly.

Shihō kenshūjohō 司法研修所報 ("Law Journal of the Legal Training
and Research Institute"). Tokyo: Shihō Kenshūjo 司法研修所,
from 1948. Irregular.

Shikan 史觀 ("The Historical Review"). Tokyo: Waseda Daigaku
Shigakkai 早稲田大學史學會, from 1908. Quarterly.

Shirin 史林 ("Journal of History"). Kyoto: Kyōto Daigaku Shigaku
Kenkyūkai 京都大學史學研究會, from 1916. Bimonthly.

Shisō 思想 (Ideas). Tokyo: Iwanami Shoten 岩波書店, from 1921.
Monthly.

Waseda shōgaku 早稲田商學 (Waseda Commercial Review). Tokyo:
Waseda Shōgaku Dōkōkai 早稲田商學同好會, from June 1925.
Bimonthly.

PART I: JAPANESE LANGUAGE SOURCES
SECTION A: TOKUGAWA SOURCES
a. References and Primary Materials

In the subsection below on Tokugawa "General References and Primary Materials," the items are listed by title instead of author. The bibliographies and catalogues are confined to those dealing specifically with
law. The legal historian finds most of his material in the collections of law
and decrees, but inevitably his inquiry will lead to chronologies, diaries,
official records, general histories, and other literature. For an understanding of the voluminous collections of such materials, a few general
historical catalogues, indices, guides and dictionaries are essential. For a
convenient guide to such materials, see John W. Hall's, *Japanese History:
A Guide to Japanese Reference and Research Materials* (University of Michigan
Press, 1954), 165 pp.

1. *Bibliographies of Legal History.*
    Daijūsankai bunken mokuroku 第十三回文獻目録 (Thirteenth list of
    literature [for 1961]). Ed. by Hōseishi Gakkai 法制史學會 (Legal
    History Association). Tokyo: mimeographed, 1962. 87 pp.
        There are twelve prior annual lists starting with 1949. These
    annual bibliographies are the most convenient to keep abreast of
    the current scholarly output by contemporary Japanese legal
    historians.

Hōseishi bunken mokuroku 法制史文献目録 (List of literature on legal history). Ed. by Hōseishi Gakkai 法制史学会 (Legal History Association). Tokyo: Sōbunsha 創文社, 1962. 290 pp.

A complete list of studies on Japanese legal history published in books and periodicals between Aug. 15, 1945, and Dec. 31, 1959.

Kinsei keiji soshōhō no kenkyū 近世刑事訴訟法の研究 (A study of the law of criminal procedure in the recent era). Hiramatsu Yoshirō 平松義郎. Tokyo: Sōbunsha 創文社, 1960. 1084 pp.

This work contains at pp. 7–16 the best up-to-date list of Tokugawa primary (manuscript) materials on Shogunate offices, their jurisdiction and procedure. It shows the library location and number of volumes for about 350 manuscripts.

Kokusho sōmokuroku 国書総目録 (Complete list of writings). Ed. by Iwanami Yūjirō 岩波雄二郎. Tokyo: Iwanami Shoten 岩波書店, 1964. Vols. 1, 2———.

This is to be a multivolume set which claims to cover all premodern Japanese literature.

Nihon hōseishi 日本法制史 (Japanese legal history). Takayanagi Shinzō 高柳眞三. Tokyo: Yūhikaku 有斐閣, 1948. 383 pp.

A list of literature on Japanese legal history is included at pp. 367–83. Since Takayanagi lists all of the Tokugawa sources together, instead of mixing them with those on the same subject from other periods, in some ways it is more convenient to use but not quite as comprehensive as Ishii's.

Nihon hōseishi gaisetsu 日本法制史概説 (General survey of Japanese legal history). Ishii Ryōsuke 石井良助. Rev. ed. Tokyo: Kōbundō 弘文堂, 1960. 607 pp.

The chapter on sources of law, pp. 369–78, lists many of the primary sources of Tokugawa law, both printed and unprinted.

Nihon hōseishi gaiyō 日本法制史概要 (General essentials of Japanese legal history). Ishii Ryōsuke 石井良助. Tokyo: Sōbunsha 創文社, 1952. 247 pp.

In arabic paging the author includes twenty pages of bibliography. This list is the most comprehensive coverage of earlier literature on the whole of Japanese legal history to be found in one place. The materials are classified in subject-matter divisions with chronological listing in each division.

Nihon hōseishi shomoku kaidai 日本法制史書目解題 (Annotated bibliography on Japanese legal history). Ed. by Ikebe Yoshikata 池邊義象. Tokyo: Daitōkaku 大鐙閣, 1918. 2 vols. Paper bound.

Three parts: (1) primary sources; (2) general historical sources; (3) special subjects.

Zōtei kokusho kaidai 増訂國書解題 (Revised and supplemented, annotated bibliography of national literature). Ed. by Samura Hachirō 佐村八郎. Rev. by Samura Toshirō 佐村敏郎. Tokyo: Rikugōkan 六合館, 1926. 2 vols.

The second volume has a subject-matter index of 154 pages (separate pagination). See pp. 27–33 for descriptions of pre-Meiji works on legal subjects. Nowhere near all of the important sources of legal history are listed, but occasionally a helpful description of a manuscript may be found.

2. *Encyclopediae and Miscellaneous Reference Works*

Chihōshi kenkyū hikkei 地方史研究必携 (Essential manual for the study of local history). Ed. by Chihōshi Kenkyū Kyōgikai 地方史研究協議會. Tokyo: Iwanami Shoten 岩波書店, 1952. 316 pp.

Dai bukan 大武鑑 (Large registry of warriors). Ed. by Hashimoto Hiroshi 橋本博. Tokyo: Daikōsha 大治社, 1935–36. 12 vols.

The *Bukan* were compiled regularly in the Edo period, and sold by enterprising townsmen in Edo as early as the Genroku period. A number of them are printed in this work by Hashimoto Hiroshi.

Dai Nihon dokushi chizu 大日本讀史地圖 (Maps of great Japan for history readers). Compiled by Yoshida Tōgo 吉田東伍 and Ashida Koreto 蘆田伊人. 10th reprint rev. ed. Tokyo: Fuzambō 富山房, 1940. 141 pp.

Dokushi biyō 讀史備要 (Stock of essentials for reading history). Compiled by Tōkyō Teikoku Daigaku Shiryō Hensanjo 東京帝國大學史料編纂所. 5th ed. Tokyo: Naigai Shoseki K.K. 内外書籍株式會社, 1935. 2154 pp.

Enkaku kōshō Nihon dokushi chizu 沿革考證日本讀史地圖 (Developmental treatment of maps for reading Japanese history). Compiled by Kawada 河田, Yoshida 吉田, and Takahashi 高橋. Tokyo: Fuzanbō 富山房, 1897. 51 maps, no pagination.

Hansei ichiran 藩制一覧 (Synopsis of the domain systems). Tokyo: Nihon Shiseki Kyōkai 日本史籍協會, 1928. 2 vols.

Koji ruien 古事類苑 (Encyclopedia of ancient matters). Compiled by Jingūshichō 神宮司廳. Nishimura Shigeki 西村茂樹, editor-in-chief. Tokyo: Koji Ruien Kankōkai 古事類苑刊行會, 1896–1914. 51 vols. Rev. ed. 1936. 60 vols.

The following are particularly relevant: *Hōritsu bu* 法律部 (section on law), 3 vols; *Kan-i bu* 官位部 (section on official positions), 3 vols; and *Seiji bu* 政治部 (section on governance), 4 vols.

Kōza Nihon kindaihō hattatsushi 講座日本近代法發達史 (Series on history

of the development of modern Japanese law). Tokyo: Keisō
Shobō 勁草書房, 1958–61. 10 vols.

Nihon keizaishi jiten 日本經濟史辭典 (Dictionary of Japanese economic
history). Ed. by Nihon Keizaishi Kenkyūjo 日本經濟史研究所.
Honjō Eijirō 本庄榮次郎, editor-in-chief. Tokyo: Nihon Hyōronsha 日本評論社, 3 vols. Vol. 1, 1936; Vol. 2, 1940; Vol. 3, 1940.

Nihon rekishi chizu 日本歷史地圖 (Japanese historical maps). Ed. by
Nishioka Toranosuke 西岡虎之助 and Hattori Shisō 服部之總.
Tokyo: Zenkoku Kyōiku Tosho Kabushiki Kaisha 全國教育圖
書株式會社, 1956. 482 pp.

Osaka shūhen no sonraku shiryō 大阪周辺の村落史料 (Historical materials
of the Osaka area). Ed. by Kansai Daigaku, Hōseishi Gakkai
関西大学法制史学会. Osaka: Kansai Daigaku, 1956. 203 pp.

Seigyō bukka jiten 生業物價事典 (Dictionary of commodity cost of
living). Ed. by Miyoshi Ikkō 三好一光. Tokyo: Seiabō 青蛙房,
1960. 561 pp.

Tokugawa Ieyasu monjo no kenkyū 德川家康文書の研究 (A study of the
documents of Tokugawa Ieyasu). Ed. by Nakamura Kōya
中村孝也. Tokyo: Gakujutsu Shinkōkai 學術振興會, 1958–61.
4 vols.

Tokugawa Yoshimune kōden 德川吉宗公伝 (Record of Shōgun Tokugawa
Yoshimune). Nikko: Nikkō Tōshōgū Shamusho 日光東照宮
社務所, 1962. 347 pp.

3. *Printed Collections of Tokugawa Laws and Precedents*

Explanations of some of these sources may be found in Dan F.
Henderson, "Japanese Legal History of the Tokugawa Period:
Scholars and Sources," University of Michigan Center of Japanese
Studies. *Occasional Papers* (no. 7) 100–21 (1957).

Bokumin kinkan 牧民金鑑 (Golden guide of rustic folk). Originally
compiled by Arai Akimichi 荒井顯道 (1853). Ed. by Yokogawa
Shirō 橫川四郎 and supervised by Takigawa Masajirō 瀧川政次郎.
Tokyo: Seibundō Shinkōsha 誠文堂新光社, 1935. 2 vols.

This is a valuable work on rural administration by Arai
Akimichi, a deputy. The manuscript copy is available at the
Naikaku Bunko.

Edo no hankachō 江戶の犯科帳 (Edo records of crimes). Ed. by Higuchi
Hideo 樋口秀雄. Tokyo: Jimbutsu Oraisha 人物往來社, 1963.
2 vols.

Goningumichō no kenkyū 五人組帳の研究 (Study of the five-man-groups
registry). Nomura Kentarō 野村兼太郎, author and editor.
Tokyo: Yūhikaku 有斐閣, 1944. 682 pp.

Goningumi hōkishū 五人組法規集 (Collection of regulations for the five-man groups). Compiled by Hozumi Nobushige 穗積陳重. Tokyo: Yūhikaku, 有斐閣, 1921. 705 pp.

Goningumi hōkishū zokuhen 五人組法規集續編 (Later collection of laws of the five-man groups). Compiled by Hozumi Shigetō 穗積重遠. Tokyo: Yūhikaku 有斐閣, 1944. 2 vols.

Hampōshū Okayama-han (jō, ge) 藩法集 岡山藩 (Collection of Okayama domain law). Compiled by Hampō Kenkyūkai 藩法研究會. Tokyo: Sōbunsha 創文社, 1959. 2 vols.

Hampōshū 藩法集 (Collection of domain law). Compiled by Hampō Kenkyūkai 藩法研究會. Tokyo: Sōbunsha 創文社, 1961–64. 5 vols. (Tottori, Tokushima, Kanazawa, and Shohan [small *fudai* daimyō].)

Ijō narabini buke gofuchinin reisho 以上並武家御扶持人例書 (Book of precedents for warriors over [the rank of audience, *omemie* 御目見]). This is summarized by Miura Kaneyuki 三浦周行 in *Ushinawa retaru kinsei hōsei shiryō* 失はれたる近世法制史料 (Lost materials of legal history of the recent era), in *Hōseishi no kenkyū* 1389–1458 at 1418.

Kempō shiryō 憲法志料 (Materials of [ancient] law). Originally compiled by Kimura Seiji 木村政辭. Translated from *kambun* to Japanese by Hashimoto Hiroshi 橋本博. Tokyo: Shihōshō 司法省, 1935. 2 vols.

This is a collection of legal materials from Empress Suiko 推古 (seventh century) to the Keichō period (1596–1614), not to be confused with *Kempō shiryō* 憲法資料 (Source of material on the [Meiji] constitution).

Kentei hikki 謙亭筆記 (Notes of Kentei). Komiyama Kentei 小宮山謙亭. In 13 *Nihon keizai taiten* 144.

Komiyama Kentei became a deputy for the Shogunate in the Kyōho period (1716–36). This and the book of *Zōho den-en ruisetsu* are on local administration.

Kikizutae sōsho 聞傳叢書 (Collected writings of traditions heard). In 25 *Nihon keizai taiten*.

Bunyō Inshi (pen-name) edited the *Kikizutae sōsho*, together with *Jikata ochiboshū* and *Zoku jikata ochiboshū*. Together the three writings constitute about 1600 pp. in 24–25 *Nihon keizai taiten*. A manuscript copy may be found at Naikaku Bunko.

Kinsei hampō shiryō shūsei 近世藩法資料集成 (Compilation of materials on the law of the feudal domains of the recent era). Ed. by Kyōto Daigaku, Hōgakubu 京都大學法學部. Kyoto: Kōbundō 弘文堂, 1942–44. 3 vols.

Volume 1 includes the code of the Kameyama 亀山 domain

and Morioka 盛岡 domain; volume 2, the Kumamoto 熊本 domain; and volume 3, the Matsue 松江 domain.

Kinsei hōseishiryo sōsho 近世法制史料叢書 (Compilation of writings on legal history of the recent era). Compiled by Ishii Ryōsuke 石井良助. Tokyo: Kōbundō Shobō 弘文堂書房, 1938–41. 3 vols.

These volumes include important early collections of laws and precedents. They are mostly private compilation by officials before the *Osadamegaki* (1742).

Kōdōkanki 弘道館記 (Records of the Kōdōkan School [of the Mito domain]). In 3 *Kinnō bunko* 119.

This is an introduction by Tokugawa Nariaki 徳川齊昭 to *Kōdōkanki jutsugi* by Fujita Hyō 藤田彪. *Id.* at 121–90.

Kyōhō nenkan zakki 享保年間雑記 (Miscellaneous notes on the Kyōhō period, 1716–36). In 17 *Mikan zuihitsu hyakushu* no. 118.

Kyōhō sen-yō ruishū 享保撰要類集 (Classified collection of essential regulations of the Kyōhō era, 1716–1735). Ed. by Ishii Ryōsuke 石井良助. Tokyo: Kōbundō 弘文堂, 1944. 236 pp.

This is a printed copy of part of a collection of important regulations issued by the North Edo Town Commissioner from 1716–53. Only three books *(kan)* of thirty-two are printed in this volume.

Minji kanrei ruishū 民事慣例類集 (Classified collection of civil customary practices). Ed. by Takimoto Seiichi 瀧本誠一. Tokyo: Hakutōsha 白東社, 1932. 390 pp.

Originally compiled by a commission from the Ministry of Justice in 1877.

Nihon kindai keiji hōreishū 日本近代刑事法令集 (Collection of criminal law of modern Japan). Compiled by Shihōshō Hishoka 司法省秘書課. Tokyo: Shihōshō, 1945. 641 pp.

This volume contains one of the best versions of the *Osadamegaki, gekan* 御定書下巻 (Written decisions, second book). It also contains the body of precedents (*Osadamegaki reisho* 御定書例書) which grew up in applying the *Osadamegaki* after 1742 (See *id.* at 145–205) and *Sharitsu* 赦律 (Law of amnesty) promulgated near the end of the Tokugawa period and important to studies of criminal law.

Nihon kinsei sompō no kenkyū 日本近世村法の研究 (A study of village law of the Japanese recent era). Maeda Masaharu 前田正治, author and compiler. Tokyo: Yūhikaku 有斐閣, 1952. 319 pp.

This is an important assemblage of laws established by the villages and hence complements the collections of Shogunate regulations for the five-man groups.

Nihon kodai hōten 日本古代法典 (Compilation of ancient Japanese laws). Compiled by Konakamura Kiyonori 小中村清矩 and others. Tokyo: Hakubunkan 博文館, 1892. 986 pp.

This volume contains some of the more important "legislation" of the various periods in Japanese history. It contains the *Buke Shohatto, "Osadamegaki* Hyakkajō," etc.

Ofuregaki Kampō shūsei 御觸書寛保集成 (Compilation of proclamations of the Kampō era, 1741–43). Ed. by Ishii Ryōsuke 石井良助 and Takayanagi Shinzō 高柳眞三. Tokyo: Iwanami Shoten 岩波書店, 1934. 1356 pp.

This volume, covering decrees from 1615 to 1743, is one of five volumes. The other four were compiled by the Tokugawa Conference Chamber *(hyōjōsho)* in the periods of Hōreki (1751–63) 1 volume, Temmei (1781–88) 1 volume, and Tempō (1830–43) 2 volumes. There was a reprint of this five-volume set in 1958.

Oshioki reiruishū 御仕置例類集 (Classified collection of precedents on executions). In *Shihō shiryō bessatsu*, vols. 8, 10, 11, 12, 18, and 20. Tokyo: Shihōshō Chōsabu 司法省調査部, 1941–46. 6 vols.

These precedents are the instructions of the conference chamber in response to requests put to the senior council by the various commissioners and in turn referred to the chamber for opinions.

Saikyodome 裁許留 (Records of judgments). In *Shihō shiryō bessatsu*, vol. 19. Tokyo: Shihōshō Hishoka 司法省秘書課, 1943. 607 pp.

This is a printed copy of all that remains of the forty-five volumes of records kept between 1702 and 1867 of civil cases in the conference chamber. The greater part were lost in the Tokyo earthquake (1923).

Shōji kanrei ruishū 商事慣例類集 (Classified collection of commercial customary practices). Ed. by Takimoto Seiichi 瀧本誠一. Tokyo: Hakutōsha 白東社, 1932. 1130 pp.

This collection also may be found in 49 *Nihon keizai taiten* 3–732 and 50 *id.* 735–1130. The original collection was made by teams of investigators from the Ministry of Justice 1883–84.

Tokugawa jidai minji kanreishū 德川時代民事慣例集 (Collection of civil customary precedents of the Tokugawa period). In *Shihō shiryō*, vols. 187, 192, 205, 213, and 216. Tokyo: Shihōshō Chōsaka 司法省調査課, 1936. 5 vols.

This collection is mostly court decisions and volume 216 on procedure is of great value to the study of Tokugawa procedure.

Tokugawa jidai saiban jirei 德川時代裁判事例 (Precedents of trials in the Tokugawa period). In *Shihō shiryō*, vols. 221 and 273. Tokyo:

Shihōshō Chōsaka 司法省調査課, 1936 and 1942. 2 vols.
These are criminal precedents.

Tokugawa kinreikō 徳川禁令考 (Consideration of Tokugawa regulations). Compiled by Ishii Ryōsuke 石井良助. Tokyo: Sōbunsha 創文社, 1959–61. 11 vols. (*zenshū*, 6 vols; *kōshū*, 4 vols; *bekkan*, 1 vol.).

This new edition of Tokugawa materials is conveniently numbered and more clearly identifies the original sources than the prior editions of Kikuchi Shunsuke 菊地駿助 (see next two items).

Tokugawa kinreikō 徳川禁令考 (Consideration of Tokugawa regulations). Kikuchi Shunsuke 菊地駿助, editor-in-chief. Compiled between 1878–1895. Tokyo: Shihōshō 司法省, 1933–34. 6 vols.

Tokugawa kinreikō kōshū 徳川禁令考後聚 (Consideration of Tokugawa regulations, latter part). Kikuchi Shunsuke 菊地駿助, editor-in-chief. Tokyo: Shihōshō 司法省, 1929–31. 6 vols.

Toyotomi-shi hattokō 豐臣氏法度考 (Consideration of the decrees of the House of Toyotomi). Ed. by Miyake Chōsaku 三宅長策. Tokyo: Tetsugaku Shoin 哲學書院, 1893. 122 pp.

Zenkoku minji kanrei ruishū 全國民事慣例類集 (Country-wide classified collection of civil customary practices). Compiled by Shihōshō 司法省 in 1880. Found in 50 *Nihon keizai taiten* 3–390.

Zenkoku minji kanrei ruishū 全國民事慣例類集 (Country-wide classified collection of civil customary practices). Compiled by Kazahaya Yasoji 風早八十二. Tokyo: Nihon Hyōronsha 日本評論社, 1944. 353 pp.

This compilation is based primarily on the Shihōshō version by the same name, but it assimilates the best features of the *Minji kanrei ruishū* (1877) also. Hence it is perhaps the most convenient source for the Tokugawa customary law.

4. *Printed Specific Tokugawa Literature Included in Various Collections*

Many of the writings by authors of the Tokugawa period listed below are printed in the *Nihon keizai taiten*. Also several of the important legal guidebooks of the middle of the Tokugawa period are printed in Ishii, *Kinsei hōsei shiryō sōsho*. Both of these collections include, in the introductions to each of the items printed therein, what facts are known of the authors and circumstances which produced the writing. Consequently, only a few comments are included with our listing here, and further data may be found, as indicated, in the prefaces of the printed copies.

The Tokugawa guides to judicial practice for officials were usually books of decrees and precedents selected and systematically arranged by the more talented and studious clerks in the various judicial offices. Handwritten copies were then circulated informally to other officials. Such books became one of the most important sources of insight into the Tokugawa court practices.

Buke meimokushō 武家名目抄 (Titles of warrior houses). In *Zōtei kojitsu Sōsho,* 8 vols.

Chōseidan 廳政談 (Discussion on administration). In 3 Ishii, *Kinsei hōsei shiryō sōsho* 257–76 (1941).

From a note in the back of the manuscript, this was approved by Yoshimune as a legal guide in 1737, but it may have been a private collection adopted by the conference chamber at that time. It has 370 articles. A manuscript copy is available in the Naikaku Bunko.

Genroku gohōshiki 元祿御法式 (Rules of the Genroku period, 1688–1703). In 1 Ishii, *Kinsei hōsei shiryō sōsho* 451–64 (1938).

Abstracts from the prison records of convictions by the town commissioners in Edo.

Gotōke reijō 御當家令條 (Articles of the Incumbent House [Shogunate]). In 2 Ishii, *Kinsei hōsei shiryō sōsho* 1–295 (1939).

This collection of decrees and precedents was written by Fujiwara Chikanaga 藤原親長. If we can assume that it was written when the introduction was signed, its date is about 1711. It consists of six hundred articles with dates ranging from 1597 to 1696.

Heirisaku 平理策 (Policy for peace through reason). Niwa Tsutomu 丹羽勗. In 33 *Nihon keizai taiten* 48.

Niwa Tsutomu wrote this short passage in 1819 as instruction for deputies and headmen. He was a clerk [*yūhitsu* 右筆] of the Owari domain and was quite accomplished in literature, but very conservative in politics.

Honchō tōin hiji 本朝藤陰比事. In *Kinsei bungei sōsho* 近世文藝叢書 (Compilation of literature of the recent era). 1911.

An anonymous writing on trials. The title is styled after a Chinese title.

Imagawa kanamokuroku, tsuika 今川かな目録追加 (Supplement to the code of the Imagawa domain). In *Zoku gunsho ruijū* (1925).

Jikata hanreiroku 地方凡例録 (Records of common precedents of rural administration). In 13 *Nihon keizai taiten.*

A valuable source book of regulations and practices in the local areas by Ōishi Hisataka, a vassal of the Tokugawa clan. Ōishi died in 1794, before it was finished.

Jikata ochiboshū 地方落穂集 (Miscellaneous gleanings on rural administration). In 24–25 *Nihon keizai taiten.*

    Edited under pen name of Bunyo Inshi (1751–64). There is a supplement, *Zoku jikata ochiboshū*, also in 24–25 *Nihon keizai taiten.*

Junshi kundōhen 荀子君道篇, in 8 *Kokuyaku kambun taisei* Vol. 8.

Kadōkun 家道訓 (Lessons in the ways of the house). Kaibara Ekken 貝原益軒. In Book 1 *Ekken zenshū* (Complete collection of Ekken), Vol. 3, p. 423 (upper).

Kannō wakumon 勸農或問 (Problems in the advancement of farming). Fujita Yūkoku 藤田幽谷. In 32 *Nihon keizai taiten* 199–287.

    Fujita was born in 1773, died in 1826, and served as a local administrator in the Mito domain and later as director of the Mito school.

Minkan shōyō 民間省要 (Essence of administering among the populace). Tanaka Kyūemon 田中丘隅右衛門. In 5 *Nihon keizai taiten* 110.

    Tanaka Kyūemon worked as an engineer for the Shogunate. He recorded his experience in the *Minkan shōyō*, which pleased the Shogunate, and Tanaka received a rice stipend. He was later given charge of certain lands for the Shogunate near Edo.

Ritsuryō yōryaku 律令要略 (Essentials of the prohibitions and regulations). In 2 Ishii, *Kinsei hōsei shiryō sōsho* 301–57 (1939).

    Dated 1741, this collection has several passages of interest on court practice and the basic ideas of law of the time.

Seken tedai katagi 世間手代氣質 (Disposition of the world's clerks). Written in 1730 by Ejima Kiseki 江島其磧 (1679–1736). In *Teikoku bunko kōtei Kiseki jishō kessakushū*, Vol. 1.

Suijinroku 吹塵録 (Records of blowing dust). In 3 and 4 *Kaishū zenshū* (1928).

    A miscellaneous collection of source material assembled by Katsu Kaishū for the finance minister during the Meiji period. There are statistics on population and rice production divided by province in the Tokugawa period. Despite inaccuracies, it is an important source of material on various subjects.

Tamakushige 玉くしげ (Jewel box [means inner-most thought]). Motoori Norinaga 本居宣長. 23 *Nihon keizai taiten* 89.

    Motoori Norinaga (1730–1801) wrote this book in 1787 in response to questions on administration put to him by the daimyō of Kii, who gave him a three-hundred *koku* stipend. His criticism is quite frank and concrete.

Teijō zakki 貞丈雑記 (Miscellaneous notes of Teijō). In 616 *Zōtei kojitsu sōsho* 157.

Tokugawa jikki 徳川實紀 (Actual records of the Tokugawa). 38–44 *Shintei zōho kokushi taikei.*

> A daily chronicle of affairs of the Shogunate in first part of the Edo period.

Tsurumi Kyūko isaku 鶴見九臯遺策 (Remaining works of Tsurumi Kyūko). Tsurumi Heizaemon 鶴見平左衞門. 5 *Nihon keizai taiten* 582.

> Tsurumi was a Mito retainer. Although the date of this book is not given, we know that it was presented after Tsurumi's death to the Mito elders in 1799 by a Tachibana Suiken.

Yabureya no tsuzukuri banashi 破れ家のつゞくり話 (A tale of patching a tumble-down house). Shingū Ryōtei 新宮涼庭. 33 *Nihon keizai taiten* 164.

> Shingū Ryōtei wrote this book in 1845. He was a famous Kyoto physician and quite critical of the Shogunate.

Zōho den-en ruisetsu 増補田園類説 (Supplemented classified explanations of rice lands). Komiyama Kentei 小宮山謙亭. In 13 *Nihon keizai taiten* 5–134.

> This book has been mistakenly attributed to the author who revised it, Tanimoto Oshie 谷本教.

5. *Unprinted Tokugawa Manuscripts (brush written)*

The most complete list of manuscript material on Tokugawa courts and procedures is Hiramatsu Yoshirō, *Kinsei keiji soshōhō no kenkyū* 7–16 (1960), and the most important depositories for Tokugawa Shogunate manuscripts and documents are the Naikaku Bunko, the National Diet Library, the Ministry of Justice Library, Tokyo University Library and Kyoto University Library. Most of the manuscripts which were used in this study are at Kyoto University, but other important ones are at other libraries as indicated.

Many of these valuable manuscripts, brush-written and worm-eaten, only exist in one copy. *Mokuhi, Soshō hikan tsuika,* and *Bunshō hikan* were of sufficient value to civil trial practices to warrant having a personal copy made by hand. Several of the other manuscripts used in this study are owned by the present writer, such as *Aoyama hiroku.* Among others, the Kiuchi 木内 old book shop in front of Tokyo University (Akamon) usually has quite a stock of Tokugawa manuscripts, and the Shibunkaku 思文閣 in Kyoto also deals in such materials.

Aoyama hiroku 青山秘録 (Private records of Aoyama). 5 vols.

> The present writer has a manuscript copy of this private guide of a member of the senior council.

Bunshō hikan 聞詔秘鑑 (Private guide of petitions heard). 2 vols.

This appears to be a sort of summary of the *Jichōkan hibunshū* 寺町勘秘聞集. The general coverage of the *Jichōkan hibunshū* and *Sampishū* 三秘集 are practically the same. Like many of the other manuscripts in this list, the *Bunshō hikan* was a private manual made by an official as a guide in his judicial work, but it is one of the most abstract, brief, and general manuscripts of its type, and consequently it is quite convenient on questions of jurisdiction and procedure. The present writer has a hand-written copy (1954) of the Tokyo University original.

Bunshō hikanroku 聞詔秘鑑録 (Record of private guidance of petitions heard).

This Kyoto manuscript is in two small volumes of 104 sections (*ten* 天) and 86 sections (*chi* 地). It appears to be a copy of or at least of the same origin as the *Bunshō hikan*.

Chōso hiroku 聰訴秘録 (Private records of petitions heard).

A Kyoto manuscript in five volumes (ten books). Since the material follows the order of the *Osadamegaki*, it was probably written after 1742.

Edo jidai soshō sumikuchi shōmon 江戸時代訴訟濟口證文 (Documents of settlements for lawsuits in the Edo period).

A manuscript dated 1842 at Kyoto University.

Gokenin oshioki ukagai 御家人御仕置伺 (Request for execution of housemen [of the Shogunate]).

This manuscript is in several large volumes and includes cases from 1784–88. The Kyoto version was copied under the supervision of Miura Kaneyuki 三浦周行. It served as precedents for judges to follow in their application of the *Osadamegaki* to the Shōgun's housemen.

Goyōdome 御用留 (Notes for official use). One vol.

At Kyoto this manuscript is entitled both *Goyōdome* and *Hōsō kōkan* 法曹後鑑. This is probably an extract for the use of a certain official, hence *Goyōdome*.

Harigamidome 張紙留 (Notes on pasted papers). 6 vols. at Naikaku Bunko.

The conference chamber customarily pasted its decision to letters of inquiry. These pasted decisions were called *harigami*.

Hikan 秘鑑 (Private guide).

This is a private legal guidebook in five manuscript volumes (ten books). It is a collection of ordinances from about the time of Yoshimune 吉宗 (1716–45). There are copies at Kyoto Univeristy and the Naikaku Bunko.

Hōsō kōkan 法曹後鑑 (Later guide for legal officials).

A manuscript at Kyoto University including conference chamber decisions and opinions in answer to inquiries from daimyō and Shogunate officials. It covers the period from roughly 1765 to 1800. There is a much larger manuscript by the same name at Tokyo University containing criminal cases.

Hyōgiritsu 評議律 (Conferences on criminal law).

This appears to be a private collection of criminal precedents extracted from the *Oshioki reiruishū*. There are copies at Tokyo University and Kyoto University.

Hyōjōsho kakurei 評定所格例 (Rules and precedents of the conference chamber).

This is a description of the conference chamber as it was after 1772. There is also detailed description of the practice in the chamber (dated 1788). The only copy, made by Miura Kane-yuki, seems to be at Kyoto University.

Hyōjōsho okite 評定所掟 (Conference chamber regulations).

Kyoto University manuscript.

Itakura seiyō 板倉政要 (Essentials of the administration of Itakura).

This is a manuscript in three volumes (eight books) at Kyoto. Presumably this is a guidebook based on the practices established and regulations issued by the Itakura's while they were the first two Deputy Governors *(Shoshidai)* of Kyoto.

Jichōkan hibunshū 寺町勘秘聞集 (Collection of private questions of the temple, town, and finance commissions). 2 vols.

This is a private manuscript, presently at Kyoto University, copied by an unidentified person in 1791. The contents are legal questions from the various daimyō and officials to the temple and shrine, Edo town, and finance commissioners. The commissioners then attached their answers [*tsukefuda* 附札]. Since it shows the legal relationship in concrete situations between private domains of daimyō and the Shogunate, it is valuable for a study of the conformity of the daimyō to Edo practice.

Jishakata oshioki reisho 寺社方御仕置例書 (Written precedents for execution of temple and shrine persons).

This is a very small manuscript, but well known as a supplemental law to implement the *Osadamegaki* vis-a-vis bonzes. There are copies at Kyoto and Tokyo universities.

Keizai daihiroku 刑罪大秘録 (Great private records of crimes and penalties).

A copy of this manuscript may be found at the Naikaku Bunko.

Kenkyō ruiten 憲教類典 (Classified compilation of wise instructions).

A private collection of Shogunate laws compiled by Kondō Shujū 近藤守重.

This is a detailed work of 122 manuscript volumes classified by subject matter and offices. It covers materials from Keichō (1596–1614) to Kansei (1789–1800). Manuscript at Naikaku Bunko.

Kōsai hiroku 公裁秘録 (Private records of public trials).

A manuscript in six volumes at Kyoto, including cases through the Bunka 文化 period (1804–18) and valuable for details of adjudication. There is a three-volume manuscript by the same name at Naikaku Bunko.

Kōsai kikanroku 公裁亀鑑録 (Records of model cases of public trials).

This is a manuscript in three volumes (*ten, chi, jin* 天地人) and appears to be another collection of precedents and rules as a guidebook for an official (copied 1854).

Kōsai zuihitsu 公裁随筆 (Miscellaneous notes on public records). 2 vols. at Kyoto.

Kujiyō zuihitsu 公事用随筆 (Miscellaneous notes on practice in suits).

This is a record of the Hashimoto family and the brush manuscript is at Kyoto Daigaku Fuzoku Toshokan.

Kyōchōfuin kiji 京兆府尹記事 (Notes on officials of Kyoto). 3 vols. (6 books 巻).

This manuscript by Okafuji Toshitada 岡藤利忠 has an interesting description of the duties of the commissioners of distant provinces in 1799 and also a detailed chart of the ranks of bannermen (vol. 2).

Kyōto kiroku 京都記録 (Written records of Kyoto).

This is a small Kyoto manuscript valuable for details on Kyoto jurisdiction and the domains of the Imperial court—a handbook of Kyoto administration. Since the eight Kansai provinces had been split for jurisdictional purposes, we can assume it was written after 1722.

Machi bugyōsho toiawase aisatsudome 町奉行所問合挨拶留 (Notes of questions and answers of the town commission).

The manuscript is at Tokyo University.

Mokuhi 目秘 (Private articles).

This is an unprinted manuscript, a copy of which may be found in the Kyoto University Library. It is quite valuable for Tokugawa civil procedures. The present writer has a copy made by hand from the original in the fall of 1954.

Nagasaki bugyōsho shohōrei hikae 長崎奉行所諸法令控 (Copy of various decrees of the Nagasaki Commissioner Office).

A manuscript in two volumes at Kyoto University.

Ōsaka sode kagami 大阪袖鑑 (Pocket guide to Osaka).

The manuscript at Kyoto has a detailed list of the Osaka officials and their duties. There is also a copy at the Naikaku Bunko.

Otomegaki 御留書 (Written notes). 4 vols.

This manuscript at Kyoto is in very poor condition and unclearly marked. However someone has numbered the volumes 1, 2, 3, 4 in the lower left corner in red and these numbers may be used for identification.

Ryūei hikan 柳営秘鑑 (Private guides of the Willow Camp [Shogunate]).

There is a copy at Kyoto University. The contents concern the rank, ceremony, and manners of the Shōgun's castle.

Sambugyō mondō 三奉行問答 (Inquiries and replies of the three commissions). 16 vols.

This is a comprehensive compilation of daimyō interrogations and the commissioners' answers (Tokyo University).

Shintōrei 新東令 (New eastern [Shogunate] decrees). One vol.

This manuscript, dated 1789, in seventy-four pages, can be found at Kyoto University.

Shōei bukan (ken) 昇栄武鑑 (乾) (Registry of higher warriors [first book]). 1864.

This is a two-volume, brush-written document of 1864, listing all bannermen with rice ratings in excess of three thousand *koku*. It is in Hiramatsu Yoshirō's library.

Shōmon hinagatachō 證文雛形帳 (Form book for documents).

Tokyo University manuscript.

Shoyō ukagai tomegaki 諸用伺留書 (Written notes on requests for various purposes).

A one-volume manuscript including legal questions referred to the Shogunate up to 1852. There are 127 entries in all.

Sogan tegata ambun 訴願手形案文 (Forms of instruments for filing suit). Ishii Ryōsuke's copy.

Sojō hentōsho uragakian 訴状返答書裏書案 (Form book for petitions, answers, and endorsements).

Signed by Kotani Jirozaemon 小谷次郎左衛門. Kyoto University.

Sosho hikan tsuika 訴所秘鑑追加 (Supplement to the private guide to the petition place).

This Tokyo University document is very valuable for its detailed explanations of the trial practices in the temple and shrine commission. The title indicates that it is a supplement to a prior volume, but the whereabouts of this first work is unknown. The present writer has a copy made by hand in the fall of 1954.

Tekirei mondō 的例問答 (Model inquiries and replies). 7 vols. at the Naikaku Bunko.

Tōto kanron hikan 東都官論秘鑑 (Private guide of explanation on offices of the eastern capital, Edo). 5 vols. Vol. 1 is missing at Kyoto.

This manuscript is a description of various offices in the Edo Shogunate and also includes a report by Etagashira Danzaemon on his genealogy and feudal duty to the Shogunate in 1719.

Tōyō ichiran 當用一覽 (Table of present practices).

The Kyoto manuscript dates back to 1672 (in the back) and is concerned largely with protocol and ceremonial detail. However, the part on the composition of the conference chamber is valuable.

b. Secondary Studies on Tokugawa Institutions by Modern Authors

6. *Books, Pamphlets, and Monographs*

Many of the books used in this study are difficult to find in libraries or to buy, even though the old-book business is well organized in Japan. Such shops as Isseidō 一誠堂, Gannandō 巖南堂, Meijidō, 明治堂, Shinshōdō 伸松堂, Takayama Shoten 高山書店 and Tōyōdō 東陽堂 in Tokyo; Rinsen 臨川 and Shibunkaku 思文閣 in Kyoto; and Manjiya 萬字屋 in Osaka are very helpful in searching for old books on the Tokugawa period. See a useful list by Naomi Fukuda (compiler), *List of Major Second-hand Book Stores in Tokyo.* International House of Japan, 1962. 16 pp.

Of the list of general treatises below, Ishii Ryōsuke, *Nihon hōseishi gaisetsu,* Hiramatsu, *Kinsei keiji soshōhō no kenkyū,* Fujino, *Bakuhan taiseishi no kenkyū,* and Matsudaira Tarō, *Edo jidai seido no kenkyū* contain a wealth of factual material on Tokugawa institutions. On civil litigation, Kobayakawa Kingo, *Kinsei minji soshō seido no kenkyū,* which is a collection of Kobayakawa's articles published earlier in *Hōgaku ronsō,* and Kobayakawa, *Nihon kinsei minji saiban tetsuzuki no kenkyū* are the only one-volume works.

Andō Seiichi 安藤精一. *Kinsei zaikata shōgyō no kenkyū* 近世在方商業の 研究 (A study of rural commerce in the recent era). Tokyo: Yoshikawa Kōbunkan 吉川弘文館, 1958. 423 pp.

Chiyoda-ku shi 千代田區史 (A history of Chiyoda ward). Tokyo: Chiyoda kuyakusho 千代田區役所, 1960. 3 vols.

Fujino Tamotsu 藤野保. *Bakuhan taiseishi no kenkyū* 幕藩体制史の研究

(A study of the history of the Shogunate-domain system). Tokyo: Kōbunkan 弘文館, 1961. 730 pp.

————. *Daimyō; sono sakoku keiei* 大名；その鎖国経営 (Daimyō; their exclusive provincial enterprises). Tokyo: Jimbutsu Ōraisha 人物往來社, 1964. 299 pp.

Fukuo Takeichirō 福尾猛市郎. *Nihon kazoku seidoshi* 日本家族制度史 (History of the Japanese family system). Tokyo: Ōyashima Shuppansha 大八州出版社, 1948. 230 pp.

Hanseishi Kenkyūkai 藩制史研究会. *Hansei seiritsushi no sōgō kenkyū; Yonezawahan* 藩制成立史の綜合研究；米沢藩 (Comprehensive study of the history of establishing domain government; the Yonezawa domain). Tokyo: Yoshikawa Kōbunkan, 1963. 839 pp. Period covered: 1555–1711.

Haruhara Gentarō 春原源太郎. *Osaka no machi bugyōsho to saiban* 大阪の町奉行所と裁判 (The Osaka town commission and litigation). Tokyo: Fuzambo 富山房, 1962. 241 pp.

Hayashi Tōichi 林董一. *Owari-han kōhōshi no kenkyū* 尾張藩公法史の研究 (A study of the history of the public law of the Owari domain). Tokyo: Nihon Gakujutsu Shinkōkai 日本學術振興会, 1961. 882 pp.

Hiramatsu Yoshirō 平松義郎. *Kinsei keiji soshōhō no kenkyū* 近世刑事訴訟法の研究 (A study of the law of criminal procedure in the recent era). Tokyo: Sōbunsha 創文社, 1960. 1084 pp.

Honjō Eijirō 本庄榮治郎. *Nihon jinkōshi* 日本人口史 (History of Japanese population). Tokyo: Nihon Hyōronsha 日本評論社, 1941. 429 pp.

Hosokawa Kameichi 細川亀市. *Nihon hōseishi taikō* 日本法制史大綱 (General outline of Japanese legal history). Tokyo: Jichōsha 時潮社, 1935. 232 pp.

Hozumi Nobushige 穂積陳重. *Goningumi seidoron* 五人組制度論 (Treatise on five-man-group system). Tokyo: Yūhikaku 有斐閣, 1921. 634 pp.

————. *Inkyoron* 隠居論 (Treatise on retirement as head of the house). Tokyo: Yūhikaku 有斐閣, 1915. 746 pp.

————. *Yui Shōsetsu jiken to Tokugawa bakufu no yōshihō* 由井正雪事件と徳川幕府の養子法 (The Yui Shōsetsu incident and the Tokugawa Shogunate adoption law). Tokyo: No publisher, 1912. 42 pp.

There is a copy at the Tokyo Bengoshikai Library.

Hozumi Shigetō 穂積重遠. *Rienjō to enkiridera* 離縁狀と縁切寺 (Divorce documents and divorce temples). 2nd ed. Tokyo: Nihon Hyōronsha 日本評論社, 1943. 270 pp.

Ikebe Yoshikata 池邊義象. *Nihon hōseishi* 日本法制史 (Japanese legal history). Tokyo: Hakubunkan 博文館, 1912. 1022 pp.

Inokuma Kaneshige 猪熊兼繁. *Nihon seikatsushi* 日本生活史 (History of Japanese living). Tokyo: Sekai Shisōsha 世界思想社, 1952. 210 pp.

Inoue Kazuo 井上和夫. *Kirishitan no hankachō* 切支丹の犯科帳 (Record of Christian crimes). Tokyo: Jimbutsu Ōraisha 人物往來社, 1963. 312 pp.

———. *Nihon tochihō-shi* 日本土地法史 (History of Japanese land law). Tokyo: Nihon Hōri Kenkyūkai 日本法理研究會, 1943. 372 pp.

Inoue Tetsujirō 井上哲治郎. *Nihon shushigaku no tetsugaku* 日本朱子學の哲學 (The philosophy of the Japanese school of Chu Hsi). Tokyo: Kōbundō 弘文堂, 1906. 607 pp.

Ishii Ryōsuke 石井良助. *Chūsei buke fudōsan soshō no kenkyū* 中世武家不動産訴訟の研究 (Study of litigation concerning immovables of military families in the medieval period). Tokyo: Kōbundō 弘文堂, 1938. 633 pp. Ishii's doctoral dissertation.

———. *Edo jidai mampitsu* 江戸時代漫筆 (A miscellany on the Edo period). Tokyo: Shinkai Shoseki 信海書籍, 1961. 328 pp.

———. *Edo no keibatsu* 江戸の刑罰 (Edo crimes and punishments). Tokyo: Chūō Kōronsha 中央公論社, 1964. 202 pp. (Chūō shinsho, no. 31).

———. *Han* はん (Seals). Tokyo: Gakuseisha 学生社, 1964. 225 pp.

———. *Nihon hōseishi gaisetsu* 日本法制史概説 (General survey of Japanese legal history). Tokyo: Sōbunsha 創文社, 1960. 607 pp.

———. *Nihon hōseishi gaiyō* 日本法制史概要 (General essentials of Japanese legal history). Tokyo: Sōbunsha 創文社, 1952. 247 pp.

———. *Tennō* 天皇 (Emperor). Tokyo: Kōbundō 弘文堂, 1952. 250 pp.

———. *Zoku Edo jidai mampitsu* 續江戸時代漫筆, (Supplement to a miscellany on the Edo period). Tokyo: Shinkai Shoseki 信海書籍, 1961. 328 pp.

Ishikawa Junkichi 石川準吉. *Edo jidai daikan seido no kenkyū* 江戸時代代官制度の研究 (Study of the deputy system of the Edo period). Tokyo: Nihon Gakujutsu Shinkōkai 日本学術振興会, 1963. 937 pp.

Ishikawa Ken 石川謙. *Nihon kinsei kyōikushi* 日本近世教育史 (History of education in the recent era of Japan). Tokyo: Kōshisha Shobō 甲子社書房, 1938. 474 pp.

Itō Tasaburō 伊東多三郎. *Nihon hōken seidoshi* 日本封建制度史 (History of the Japanese feudal system). 5th printing. Tokyo: Yoshikawa Kōbunkan 吉川弘文館, 1953. 354 pp.

————. *Nihon kinseishi* 日本近世史 (History of Japan of the recent era). Vol. 2. Tokyo: Yūhikaku 有斐閣, 1953. 358 pp.

This book covers from 1716 to 1829 and has a thirty-page index.

Kanai Madoka 金井圓. *Hansei* 藩政 (Domain government). Tokyo: Shibundō 至文堂, 1962. 240 pp. (Nihon rekishi shinsho).

Kaneda Heiichirō 金田平一郎. *Kinsei saikenhō* 近世債權法 (The law of obligations in the recent era). *Shihō shiryō*, no. 298, 1948. 262 pp.

Kanno Watarō 菅野和太郎. *Ōmi shōnin no kenkyū* 近江商人の研究 (A study of the Ōmi merchants). Tokyo: Yūhikaku 有斐閣, 1941. 329 pp.

Katsumoto Masaakira 勝本正晃. *Hōritsu yori mitaru Nihon bungaku* 法律より見たる日本文學 (Japanese literature from the standpoint of law). Tokyo: Ganshōdō Shoten 嚴松堂書店, 1934. 278 pp.

Kawashima Takeyoshi 川島武宜. *Iriaiken no kaitai* 入會權の解体 (The breakup of the right to commons). Tokyo: Iwanami Shoten, Vol. I: 1959 (361 pp.); Vol. II: 1961 (526 pp.); Vol. III: in preparation.

————. *Nihon shakai no kazokuteki kōsei* 日本社會の家族的構成 (The familial structure of Japanese society). Tokyo: Nihon Hyōron Shinsha 日本評論新社, 1961 reprint. 207 pp.

Kida Teikichi 喜田貞吉. *Bakumatsu daimyō fōyū kyosho enkaku ichiran* 幕末大名封邑居所沿革一覽 (A glance at the development of daimyō fiefs and residences at the end of the Shogunate). Tokyo: Chirigaku Kōza 地理學講座, no date. 280 pp.

Kikuchi Sansai 菊地山哉. *Etazoku ni kansuru kenkyū* 穢多族に關する研究 (A study concerning the outcast group). Tokyo: Sanseisha Shoten 三星社書店, 1923. 400 pp.

Kitagawa Morisada 喜田川守貞. *Ruishū kinsei fūzokushi* 類聚近世風俗志 (Collections and records on modern customs). Tokyo: Bunchō-sha 文潮社, 1927. 621 pp.

Kitajima Masamoto 北島正元. *Edo jidai* 江戸時代 (The Edo period). Tokyo: Iwanami Shoten 岩波書店, 1959. 248 pp.

Kobayakawa Kingo 小早川欣吾. *Kinsei minji soshō seido no kenkyū* 近世民事訴訟制度の研究 (A study of the civil litigation system in the recent era). Ed. by Maki Kenji. Tokyo: Yūhikaku 有斐閣, 1957. 696 pp.

————. *Nihon kinsei minji saiban tetsuzuki no kenkyū* 日本近世民事裁判手續の研究 (A study of civil trial procedure in the Japanese recent era). *Nihon hōri sōsho* 日本法理叢書 (Series on Japanese legal theory), Vol. 18. Tokyo: Nihon Hōri Kenkyūkai 日本法理研究會, 1942. 141 pp.

Kodama Kōta 兒玉幸多. *Kinsei nōmin seikatsushi* 近世農民生活史 (History of the life of farming people in the recent era). 3rd ed. Tokyo: Yoshikawa Kōbunkan 吉川弘文館, 1952. 347 pp.

————. *Sakura Sōgorō* 佐倉惣五郎 (Sakura Sōgorō [personal name]). Tokyo: Yoshikawa Kōbunkan 吉川弘文館, 1958. 194 pp.

————. *Shukueki* 宿駅 (Post-towns). Tokyo: Shibundō 至文堂, 1960. 230 pp.

Kōda Shigetomo 幸田成友. *Edo to Ōsaka* 江戸と大阪 (Edo and Osaka). 2nd rev. ed. Tokyo: Fuzambō 冨山房, 1942. 445 pp.

————. *Ōsakashishi* 大阪市史 (History of Osaka City). Osaka: Ōsakashi Sanjikai 大阪市參事會, 1911–15. 8 vols.

Konakamura Kiyonori 小中村清矩 [posthumously]. *Kansei enkaku ryakushi* 官制沿革略史 (Brief history of the development of the bureaucracy). Tokyo: Yoshikawa Hanshichi 吉川半七, 1900. 169 pp.

Kumasaki Wataru 隈崎渡. *Nihon hōseishi gairon* 日本法制史概論 (General discussion of Japanese legal history). Tokyo: Shunjūsha 春秋社, 1951. 163 pp.

Kure bunsō 吳文聰. *Tōkei shūshi* 統計集誌 (Compilation of statistics). Tokyo, 1882.

Kure Fumiaki 吳文炳. *Hōsei o chūshin to seru Edo jidai shiron* 法制を中心とせる江戸時代史論 (Historical discussion of the Edo period centered around the legal institutions). Tokyo: Ganshōdō Shoten 巖松堂書店, 1923. 346 pp.

Kurita Mototsugu 栗田元次. *Edo jidaishi* 江戸時代史 (History of the Edo period). *Sōgō Nihonshi taikei* 綜合日本史大系 (Consolidated compendium of Japanese history), Vols. 17, 18, and 19. Tokyo: Naigai Shoseki Kabushiki Kaisha 内外書籍株式會社, 1939–40. 3 vols.

Kurita Mototsugu, Nakamura Koya, and Inobe Shigeo 栗田元次, 中村孝也, 井野邊茂雄. *Edo bakufu seiji* 江戸幕府政治 (The government of the Edo Shogunate). *Iwanami kōza, Nihon rekishi* (Iwanami lecture series on Japanese history), no. 6. Tokyo: Iwanami Shoten 岩波書店, 1934. 68 pp.

Kyōdo no rekishi (Shikoku hen) 郷土の歴史 (四國編) (History of the localities [Part on Shikoku]). Tokyo: Hōbunkan 寳文館, 1959. 479 pp. There are eight volumes, together covering most of Japan.

Kyūji shimonroku 舊事咨問録 (Records of inquiries and answers on ancient matters). Tokyo: Gosanrō Bunko 五三樓文庫, 1891. One volume without continuous paging.

    This is a record of early Meiji interviews with Shogunate

officials speaking from their memories about the Shogunate bureaucracy. Reprinted in 1964 by Seiabō 青蛙房.

Maeda Masaharu 前田正治. *Nihon kinsei sompō no kenkyū* 日本近世村法 の研究 (A study of village law of the Japanese recent era). Tokyo: Yūhikaku 有斐閣, 1952. 319 pp.

Maki Kenji 牧健二. *Nihon hōken seido seiritsushi* 日本封建制度成立史 (History of the formation of the Japanese feudal system). Tokyo: Kōbundō 弘文堂, 1935. 526 pp.

―――. *Nihon hōseishi gairon* 日本法制史概論 (General treatise of Japanese legal history). 2nd ed. Tokyo: Kōbundō 弘文堂, 1949. 542 pp.

―――. *Seiyōjin no Nihon rekishikan* 西洋人の日本歴史觀 (Westerners' views of Japanese history). 2nd ed. Tokyo: Kōbundō 弘文堂, 1951. 286 pp.

Maruyama Masao 丸山眞男. *Nihon seiji shisōshi kenkyū* 日本政治思想史 研究 (A study of the history of Japanese political thought). Tokyo: Tōkyō Daigaku Shuppankai 東京大學出版會, 1952. 363 pp.

Matsudaira Tarō 松平太郎. *Edo jidai seido no kenkyū* 江戸時代制度の研究 (A study of the system of the Edo period). Tokyo: Buke Seido Kenkyūkai 武家制度研究會, 1919. 1100 pp. Reprinted 1964.

Matsuyoshi Sadao 松好貞夫. *Kanekashi to daimyō* 金貸と大名 (Money lenders and daimyō). Tokyo: Kōbundō (Athenes shinsho) 弘文堂(アテネ新書), 1957. 190 pp.

Mitamura Engyo 三田村鳶魚. *Edo jidai no samazama* 江戸時代のさまざ ま (Various aspects of the Edo period). Tokyo: Hakubunkan 博文館, 1929. 814 pp.

Miura Kikutarō 三浦菊太郎. *Nihon hōseishi* 日本法制史 (Japanese legal history). Tokyo: Hakubunkan 博文館, 1900. 324 pp.

Miyagiken 宮城縣, compiler. *Miyagi kenshi (keisatsu)* 宮城縣史 (警察) (History of Miyagi prefecture [Part on police]). Ed. by Taka-yanagi Shinzō. Tokyo: Miyagikenshi Kankōkai 宮城縣史刊行會, 1960. Vol. 7. 717 pp.
    This volume contains material on the Sendai domain's judicial system.

Miyake Chōsaku 三宅長策 *Toyotomishi hatto kō* 豊臣氏法度考 (Con-sideration of decrees of the houses of Toyotomi). Tokyo, 1893. 122 pp.

Miyamoto Mataji 宮本又次. *Kabunakama no kenkyū* 株仲間の研究 (A study of joint-stock associations). Tokyo: Yūhikaku 有斐閣, 1958. 436 pp.

―――. *Kinsei shōnin ishiki no kenkyū* 近世商人意識の研究 (A study of

the mentality of merchants in the recent era). Tokyo: Yūhikaku
有斐閣, 1941. 320 pp.

————. *Nihon shōgyōshi* 日本商業史 (Japanese commercial history).
Tokyo: Ryūginsha 龍吟社, 1949. 310 pp.

————. *Nihon shōgyōshi gairon* 日本商業史概論 (An outline treatise of
Japanese commercial history). Kyoto: Sekai Shisōsha 世界思想社,
1954. 367 pp.

————. *Ōsaka bunkashi* 大阪文化史 (Osaka cultural history). Tokyo:
Yūhikaku 有斐閣, 1955. 145 pp.

————. *Ōsaka shōnin—zoku Ōsaka chōnin* 大阪商人―續大阪町人 (Merchants of Osaka—a supplement to Osaka townsmen). Tokyo:
Kōbundō 弘文堂, 1958. 279 pp.

Nagasaki goyōdomeshoshū tōsen fūsetsusho 長崎御用留所収唐船風説書 (Reports presented by Chinese ships found in Nagasaki official
records). Ed. by Tōyō bunko 東洋文庫. Tokyo: Tōyō Bunko
東洋文庫, 1960. 27 pp.

Nakada Kaoru 中田薫. *Tokugawa jidai no bungaku ni mietaru shihō* 徳川
時代の文學に見えたる私法 (Private law as seen in the literature
of the Tokugawa period). 2nd ed. Tokyo: Meijidō Shoten
明治堂書店, 1935. 262 pp.

Nakagawa Zennosuke 中川善之助. *Saishōron* 妻妾論 (Discussion of
wives and concubines). Tokyo: Chūō Kōronsha 中央公論社,
1936. 202 pp.

Nakai Nobuhiko 中井信彦. *Bakuhan shakai to shōhin ryūtsū* 幕藩社會と
商品流通 (Shogunate-domain society and commodity circulation). Tokyo: Hanawa Shobō 塙書房, 1961. 251 pp.

Nakamura Kichiji 中村吉治. *Hōken shakai* 封建社會 (Feudal society).
Tokyo: Kawade Shobō 河出書房, 1943. 398 pp.

————. *Nihon hōkensei saihenseishi* 日本封建制再編成史 (A history of the
reformation of Japanese feudalism). Tokyo: Mikasa Shobō
三笠書房, 1939. 248 pp.

Nakamura Kōya 中村孝也. *Tokugawa Ieyasu monjo no kenkyū* 徳川家康
文書の研究 (A study of the documents of Tokugawa Ieyasu).
Tokyo: Maruzen, 1958. 4 vols.

Nakamura Naokatsu 中村直勝 ed. *Hikone shishi (jō)* 彦根市史 (上)
(History of Hikone City). Hikone: Hikone shiyakusho 彦根市役所,
1960–64. 3 vols.

Nakayama Tarō 中山太郎. *Baishō sanzen-nen shi* 賣笑三千年史 (History
of three thousand years of prostitution). Tokyo: Shunyōdō
春陽堂, 1927. 692 pp.

Noma Kōshin 野間光辰 *et al.*, compilers. *Teihon Saikaku zenshū* 定本
西鶴全集 (Complete collections of standard books of Ihara

Saikaku). Tokyo: Chūō Kōronsha 中央公論社, 1950–59. 11 vols. There are three other volumes yet to be published.

Nomura Kentarō 野村兼太郎. *Mura meisaichō no kenkyū* 村明細帳の研究 (Study of village registries). Tokyo: Yūhikaku 有斐閣, 1949. Separate paging, 1122 and 136 pp.

Numata Raisuke 沼田頼輔. *Ōoka Echizen no kami* 大岡越前守 (A biography of Judge Ōoka). Tokyo: Meiji Shoin 明治書院, 1929. 207 pp.

Ōita Shiyakusho 大分市役所, ed. *Ōita shishi* 大分市史 (History of Ōita city). Tokyo: Zenkoku Shichōsonshi Kankōkai 全国市町村誌刊行会, 1937. 758 pp.

Ōito Toshio 大絲年夫. *Bakumatsu heisei kaikakushi* 幕末兵制改革史 (History of the reforms in the military organization at the end of the Shogunate). In *Nihon rekishi bunko,* Vol. 2. Tokyo: Hakuyō-sha 白揚社, 1939. 274 pp.

Okazaki Kōatsu 岡崎高厚. *Kyūshi seiki* 旧市制記 (Annals of the system of old cities). (1888).

Okuno Hikoroku 奥野彦六. *Kinsei Nihon koyūhō ronkō* 近世日本固有法論考 (Inquiry into the Japanese traditional law of the recent era). Tokyo: Kasahara Shoten 笠原書店, 1943. 284 pp.

———. *Nihon hōseishi ni okeru fuhō kōihō* 日本法制史における不法行為法 (Torts in Japanese legal history). Tokyo: Sōbunsha 創文社, 1960. 480 pp.

Ono Hitoshi 小野均. *Kinsei jōkamachi no kenkyū* 近世城下町の研究 (A study of castle towns in the recent era). Tokyo: Shibundō 至文堂, 1928. 298 pp.

Ono Takeo 小野武夫. *Gōshi seido no kenkyū* 郷士制度の研究 (A study of the local gentry). Tokyo: Ōokayama Shoten 大岡山書店, 1925. 201 pp.

———. *Nihon sonrakushi gaisetsu* 日本村落市概説 (General survey of the history of Japanese village). 5th ed. Tokyo: Iwanami Shoten 岩波書店, 1942. 483 pp.

Ōoka seidan 大岡政談 (Chats about Ōoka governance). *Kinsei mono-gatari bungaku, dai-ikkan* 近世物語文学第一巻 (Literary stories of the recent era), Vol. 1. Tokyo: Yūzankaku 雄山閣, 1960. 300 pp.

Osakashi, Sanjikai. *Osaka shishi* 大阪市史 (History of Osaka city). Osaka: Osakashi 大阪市, 1911–15. 7 vols.

Ōtsu Shiyakusho 大津市役所, ed. *Ōtsu shishi* 大津市史 (History of Ōtsu City). Ōtsu: Ōtsu Shiyakusho 大津市役所, 1942. 3 vols.

Saitō Ryūzō 齊藤隆三. *Edo no sugata* 江戸のすがた (Figures of Edo). Tokyo: Yūzankaku 雄山閣, 1936. 249 pp.

Sakamoto Tarō 坂本太郎. *Nihonshi gaisetsu* 日本史概説 (General

survey of Japanese history). 10th ed. Tokyo: Shibundō 至文堂, 1945. 2 vols.

Sakata Yoshio 坂田吉雄. *Chōnin* 町人 (Townsmen). Tokyo: Kōbundō 弘文堂, 1939. 158 pp.

―――. *Meiji ishinshi* 明治維新史 (History of the Meiji restoration). Tokyo: Miraisha 未來社, 1960. 266 pp.

Sakuma Osahiro 佐久間長敬. *Tokugawa shōgun ojiki saiban jikki* 徳川将軍御直裁判實記 (Actual records of trials before the Tokugawa Shōgun). Tokyo: Namboku Shuppan Kyōkai 南北出版協會, 1893. 94 pp.

Satō Shin-ichi 佐藤進一. *Kamakura bakufu soshō seido no kenkyū* 鎌倉幕府訴訟制度の研究 (Study on the system for litigation under the Kamakura Shogunate). Tokyo: Unebi Shobō 畝傍書房, 1943. 353 pp.

Sekiyama Naotarō 關山直太郎. *Kinsei Nihon jinkō no kenkyū* 近世日本人口の研究 (A study of population of the recent era of Japan). Tokyo: Ryūginsha 龍吟社, 1948. 282 pp.

―――. *Kinsei Nihon no jinkō kōzō* 近世日本の人口構造 (Population structure of Japan in the recent era). Tokyo: Kōbunkan 弘文館, 1958. 326 pp.

Shigaken 滋賀縣, ed. *Shiga kenshi* 滋賀縣史 (History of Shiga Prefecture). Tokyo: Sanshūsha 三秀社, 1928. 6 vols.

Shinji Yoshimoto 進士慶幹. *Edo jidai no buke no seikatsu* 江戸時代の武家の生活 (Life of the warriors in the Edo period). Tokyo: Shibundō 至文堂, 1961. 202 pp.

Takahashi Sadaki 高橋貞樹. *Tokushu burakushi* 特殊部落史 (History of special [outcast] villages). 5th ed. Kyoto: Kōseikaku 更生閣, 1925. 300 pp.

Takamure Itsue 高群逸技, *Nihon josei shakaishi* 日本女性社會史 (A social history of Japanese women). Osaka: Shin Nihonsha 新日本社, 1948. 318 pp.

Takayanagi Shinzō 高柳眞三. *Tokugawa jidai keihō no gaikan* 徳川時代刑法の概觀 (A survey of criminal law in the Tokugawa period). *Shihō shiryō bessatsu* 司法資料別冊, no. 9. Tokyo: Shihōshō Chōsabu 司法省調査部, 1942. 94 pp.

Takigawa Masajirō 瀧川政次郎. *Hōritsu shiwa* 法律史話 (Stories on [Japanese] legal history). Tokyo: Ganshōdō Shoten 嚴松堂書店, 1932. 280 pp.

―――. *Hōshi kanwa* 法史閑話 (Talks on legal history). Tokyo: Sōgensha 創元社, 1951. 236 pp.

―――. *Hōshi sadan* 法史瑣談 (Tales of legal history). Tokyo: Jichōsha 時潮社, 1934. 202 pp.

———. *Kujiyado no kenkyū—Nihon bengoshi zenshi—kujiyado henjutsu "Hikae" no shōkai* 公事宿の研究——日本辯護士前史——公事宿編述秘下會の紹介 (A study of the suit inns—a prehistory of the Japanese lawyer—an introduction to the "Hikae" compiled by a *kujiyado*). Tokyo: Waseda Daigaku Hikakuhō Kenkyūjo 早稲田大學比較法研究所, 1959. 166 pp.

———. *Nihon dorei keizaishi* 日本奴隷經濟史 (History of Japanese slave economy). Tokyo: Tōkō Shoin 刀江書院, 1930. 553 pp.

———. *Nihon hōseishi* 日本法制史 (Japanese legal history). Rev. ed. Tokyo: Kadokawa Shoten 角川書店, 1959. 542 pp.

———. *Nihon hōseishi no tokushoku* 日本法制史の特色 (Special characteristics of Japanese legal history). Tokyo: Nomura Shoten 野村書店, 1948. 205 pp.

———. *Nihon rekishi kaikin* 日本歴史解禁 (Japanese history revealed). Tokyo: Sōgensha 創元社, 1951. 260 pp.

Tamura Eitarō 田村榮太郎. *Kinsei Nihon kōtsūshi* 近世日本交通史 (History of Japanese transport in the recent era). Tokyo: Seiwa Shoten 清和書店, 1935. 366 pp.

———. *Yakuzakō* やくざ考 (Consideration of *yakuza*). Tokyo: Yūzankaku 雄山閣, 1958. 366 pp.

Toyoda Takeshi 豐田武. *Nihon no hōken toshi* 日本の封建都市 (Japan's feudal cities). Tokyo: Iwanami Shoten 岩波書店, 1952. 301 pp.

———. *Nihon shūkyō seidoshi no kenkyū* 日本宗教制度史の研究 (A study of history of the Japanese religious system). Tokyo: Kōseikaku 更生閣, 1938. 297 pp.

Tsuda Hideo 津田秀夫. *Edo jidai no sandai kaikaku* 江戸時代の三大改革 (The three great reforms in the Edo period). Tokyo: Kōbundō (Athenes Bunko) 弘文堂 (アテネ文庫), 1956. 72 pp.
This book is not as useful as the title might indicate.

Tsuda Sōkichi 津田左右吉. *Bungaku ni arawaretaru waga kokumin shisō no kenkyū* 文學に現はれたる我國民思想の研究 (A study of the thought of our people as it appears in literature). Tokyo: Rakuyōdō 洛陽堂, 1918 and 1921. 2 vols.

Watanabe Ichirō 渡邊一郎, compiler. *Bakushin Iwaseshi kankei shiryō* 幕臣岩瀬氏関係資料 (Historical materials relative to Mr. Iwase, a retainer of the Shogunate). Tokyo: Yamashita Insatsu 山下印刷, 1958. 198 pp.
This book contains the article, "Tokugawa ichi jikisan no kasei kaikaku," published in *Tōkyō kyōiku daigaku shigaku kenkyū* (no. 16).

Watsuji Tetsurō 和辻哲郎. *Sakoku* 鎖國 (Isolated country). 5th printing. Tokyo: Chikuma Shobō 筑摩書房, 1953. 415 pp.

Yamane Shinjirō 山根眞次郎. *Nihon karyūshi* 日本花柳史 (History of

the gay quarters of Japan). Tokyo: San-yōdō 山陽堂, 1913.
414 pp.

Yamazaki Tasuku 山崎佐. *Nihon chōtei seido no rekishi* 日本調停制度の
歴史 (History of the Japanese conciliation system). Tokyo:
Nihon chōtei kyōkai rengōkai 日本調停協會連合會, 1957. 126 pp.

Yazaki Takeo 矢崎武夫. *Nihon toshi no hatten katei* 日本都市の發展過程
(The developmental process of Japanese cities). Tokyo:
Kōbundō 弘文堂, 1962. 464 pp.

7. *Collections of Articles and Essays*

Much of the most valuable secondary material on the Japanese
legal system is found in collections of essays. There are several types:
collections of articles of a single author previously printed; collections
of essays by different authors as contributions to a volume in commemoration of a retiring professor; essays by several authors in a
cooperative research project; or essays by a single author not previously published. All of these various collections used in this study
have been included below by title so that this list can be used for
reference in the section on articles and essays.

Edo jidai shiron 江戶時代史論 (Historical essays on the Edo period).
Compiled by Nihon Rekishi Chiri Gakkai 日本歷史地理學會
(Japanese History and Geography Association). Tokyo: Jin-
yūsha 仁友社, 1915. 644 pp.

Hōsei ronsan 法制論纂 (Compilation of essays on legal institutions).
Compiled by Kokugakuin 國學院. Tokyo: Dai Nihon Tosho
Kabushiki Kaisha 大日本圖書株式會社, 1904. 1446 pp.

Hōsei ronsan zokuhen 法制論纂續編 (Supplement to the Compilation of
essays on legal institutions). Compiled by Kokugakuin 國學院.
Tokyo: Dai Nihon Tosho Kabushiki Kaisha 大日本圖書株式會社,
1904. 914 pp.

Hōseishi no kenkyū 法制史の研究 (A study of legal history). A compilation of the articles of Miura Kaneyuki. 三浦周行 Tokyo:
Iwanami Shoten 岩波書店, 1918. 1174 pp.

Hōseishi ronshū 法制史論集 (Collection of essays on legal history). A
compilation of the essays of Nakada Kaoru 中田薫. Tokyo:
Iwanami Shoten 岩波書店, 1926–43. 3 vols.
    Vol. 1 — Family and succession law, 1926
    Vol. 2 — Property law, 1938
    Vol. 3 — Law obligations and miscellaneous, 1943.
    Vol. 4 — 1964.

Jusshūnen kinen hōgaku ronshū 十周年記念法學論集 (Collection of essays
on jurisprudence as a tenth-anniversary memorial). Compiled

by Tōhoku Teikoku Daigaku Hōgakubu 東北帝國大學法學部.
Tokyo: Iwanami Shoten 岩波書店, 1934. 690 pp.

Keibatsu to kokka kenryoku 刑罰と國家権力 (National power and criminal penalties). Compiled by Hōseishi gakkai 法制史學會. Tokyo: Sōbunsha 創文社, 1960. 596 pp.

Kinsei minji soshō seido no kenkyū 近世民事訴訟制度の研究 (A study of the civil litigation system in the recent era). Kobayakawa Kingo 小早川欣吾. Ed. by Maki Kenji. Tokyo: Yūhikaku 有斐閣, 1957. 696 pp.

This is a collection of seven of the twelve articles by Kobayakawa published in *Hōgaku ronsō* between 1934 and 1942, but the editor, Maki Kenji, has changed the titles somewhat. See Maki's introduction, *id.* at 1–25.

Kinsei Nihon no jugaku 近世日本の儒學 (Confucianism of Japan of the recent era). Compiled by Tokugawa-kō Keisō Shichijūnen Shukuga Kinenkai 徳川公繼宗七十年祝賀記念會 (Commemorative Service for celebrating the seventieth anniversary of Prince Tokugawa's succession). Tokyo: Iwanami Shoten 岩波書店, 1939. 1149 pp.

Kokka Gakkai gojusshūnen kinen kokkagaku ronshū 國家學會五十周年記念國家學論集 (Collections of the essays on the national polity as a memorial on the fiftieth anniversary of the Political Science Association). Compiled by Kokka Gakkai 國家學會. Ed. by Rōyama Masamichi 蠟山政道. Yūhikaku 有斐閣, 1937. 815 pp.

Miyake hakushi koki shukuga kinen rombunshū 三宅博士古稀祝賀記念論文集 (A collection of essays in commemoration of Doctor Miyake's seventieth anniversary). Compiled by Ōtsuka Shigakkai 大塚史學會. Tokyo: Oka Shoin 岡書院, 1929. 830 pp.

Miyazaki sensei hōseishi ronshū 宮崎先生法制史論集 (Collection of essays of Professor Miyazaki on legal history). Compiled by Nakada Kaoru 中田薫. Tokyo: Iwanami Shoten 岩波書店, 1929. 766 pp.

Nakada sensei kanreki shukuga hōseishi ronshū 中田先生還曆祝賀法制史論集 (Collection of essays on legal history in honor of Professor Nakada's sixty-first anniversary). Ed. by Ishii Ryōsuke 石井良助. Tokyo: Iwanami Shoten 岩波書店, 1937. 717 pp.

Nihon hōseishi kenkyū 日本法制史研究 (A study of Japanese legal history). Takigawa Masajirō 瀧川政次郎. Tokyo: Yūhikaku 有斐閣, 1941. 790 pp.

Nihon keizaishi kenkyū 日本經濟史研究 (A study of Japanese economic history). Kōda Shigetomo 幸田成友, author and compiler. Tokyo: Ōokayama Shoten 大岡山書店, 1928. 854–61 pp.

Saitō hakushi kanreki kinen, hō to saiban 齊藤博士還曆記念法と裁判 (Mem-

morial to Doctor Saitō on his sixty-first anniversary, law and
litigation). Compiled by Kitamura Gorō 北村五郎. Tokyo:
Yūhikaku 有斐閣, 1942. 720 pp.

Tokugawa seido shiryō 德川制度資料 (Historical materials on the Tokugawa system). Compiled by Ono Kiyoshi 小野清. Tokyo:
Rikugōkan 六合館, 1927. 2 parts. Part 1, 209 pp.; part 2, 273 pp.

Tōkyō teikoku daigaku gakujitsu taikan 東京帝國大學學術大觀 (Survey of
studies at Tokyo Imperial University). Compiled by Tōkyō
Teikoku Daigaku, Hōgakubu, Keizaigakubu 東京帝国大學法學部
經濟學部. Tokyo: Kokusai Shuppan Insatsusha 國際出版印刷社,
1942. 786 pp.

Zoku hōseishi no kenkyū 續法制史の研究 (Supplement to a study of
legal history). A compilation of later articles of Miura Kaneyuki.
Tokyo: Iwanami Shoten 岩波書店, 1925. 1563 pp.

8. *Articles and Essays from Periodicals and Collections*

The articles in scholarly journals and the essays to be found in
various collections are often the best introductions to the voluminous
source material which is available on almost any phase of Tokugawa
law.

In this study, several articles deserve special mention. Kobayakawa
Kingo's series of articles in *Hōgaku ronsō* listed below have been relied
on heavily in the treatment of jurisdiction and procedure. As mentioned, these articles (seven of twelve) are collected in *Kinsei minji
soshō seido no kenkyū* (1957). In digging deeper into the sources, one
will find that Kobayakawa's profuse documentation is also generally
accurate. The same can be said for the articles of Nakada Kaoru,
Hōseishi ronshū. On conciliation, Maki Kenji, "Kinsei bukehō no
wakai oyobi chōtei," Kaneda Heiichirō, "Tokugawa jidai ni okeru
soshōjō no wakai," and Ōtake Hideo, "Kinsei suiri soshōhō ni okeru
naisai no gensoku," have been helpful in leading to other sources.
The analysis of Takayanagi Shinzō, "Wakaishugi ni tatsu saiban,"
is provocative, but it was written for semipopular reading and hence
is not documented. The articles of the outstanding Kyoto scholar,
Miura Kaneyuki, are often still the best on their subjects, but his
method of documentation is general and not very useful in searching
out other materials.

The essays on Confucianism in *Kinsei Nihon no jugaku* are of uneven
quality, but some, such as Morohashi Tetsuji, "Kansei igaku no
kin," have been quite valuable.

Aikawa Haruki 相川春喜. "Kenchi—bakuhan hōkensei seiritsu no
    kiso katei" 檢地－幕藩封建制成立の基礎過程 (Inspection of land

—the fundamental process of forming the feudal system of the Shogunate and domains), 3 *Rekishi kagaku* (no. 9) 19–32; (no. 10) 58–77; and (no. 12) 56–84 (1934).

Andō Seiichi 安藤精一. "Kinsei zaikata ni okeru ichi ni tsuite" 近世在方における市について (Concerning rural markets in the recent era), 37 *Nihonshi kenkyū* 52–64 (1958).

———. "Kinsei zaikata shōgyō to kyokuchiteki shijōken" 近世在方商業と局地的市場圏 (Rural trade in the recent era and the effective marketing area), 6 *Rekishi kyōiku* (no. 1) 13–19 (1958).

Arai Kōjirō 荒井貢次郎. "Seisai" 制裁 (Village adjudication), in *Shakai to minzoku* of the series, *Nihon minzokugaku taikei* 173–88 (1962).

Arami Yoshiharu 新見吉治. "Dōshin (ashigaru) kabu yuzurikin kanjōgaki" 同心（足軽）株譲り金勘定書 (Money receipt for the transfer of police [foot-soldier] status), 19 *Shakai keizai shigaku* (no. 2) 81–92 (1953).

Dohi Noritaka 土肥鑑高. "Kyōhō kaikaku ni tsuite—tokuni saikin no kenkyū to kanren shite" 享保改革について—特に最近の研究と關連して (Concerning the Kyōhō reform especially in relation to the recent studies), *Tōhō gakuhō* (no. 10) 30–38 (1960).

Etō Tsuneji 江頭恒治. "Shōka no i-shoku-jū—Hino no gōshō Nakai Genza" 商家の衣食住—日野の豪商中井源左 (A merchant's clothing, food, and shelter—Nakai Genza, a wealthy merchant of Hino), in *Kinsei Nihon no keizai to shakai (Honjō sensei koki kinen)* 23–54 (1958).

Fujiki Hisashi 藤木久志. "Uesugi-shi chigyōsei no kōzōteki tokushitsu 上杉氏知行制の構造的特質 (Special structural characteristics of the fief system of the Uesugi family), 69 *Shigaku zasshi* 1414–39 (1960).

Fuji Naomoto 藤直幹. "Daimyō ryōchihō no seikaku" 大名領地法の性格 (Character of law in daimyō's fief), 28 *Shirin* 244–62 (1943).

Fuse Yaheiji 布施彌平治 "Edo jidai ni okeru saiban kankatsu, ichi" 江戸時代に於ける裁判管轄一 (Trial jurisdiction in the Edo period, part one), 22 *Nihon hōgaku* 207–28 (1956).

———. "Murahachibu no soshō" 村八分の訴訟 (A suit involving "*murahachibu*"), 23 *Nihon hōgaku* 376–89 (1957).

Haga Noboru 芳賀登. "Gōnō Hirayama-ke no gakumon" 豪農平山家の學問 (Study of the wealthy rural Hirayama family), 8 *Chihōshi kenkyū* 36–58 (1958).

Hagino Yoshiyuki 萩野由之. "Kinsei no dōrohō" 近世の道路法 (Law

concerning roads in the Tokugawa period), *Hōsei ronsan zokuhen* 369–85 (1904).

———. "Kinsei no kosekihō" 近世の戸籍法 (Registration law of the recent era), *Hōsei ronsan* 1347–1411 (1903).

———. "Tokugawa-shi kansei tsūkō" 徳川氏官制通考 (Directory of Tokugawa administrative system), *Hōsei ronsan zokuhen* 408–51 (1904).

Harafuji Hiroshi 服藤弘司. "'Aitai sumashi' reikō" "相對濟" 令考 (Considering the "Mutual-settlement" decrees), *Kanazawa daigaku hōbungakubu ronshū hōkei hen* (no. 2) 1–32 (1955).

———. "Kinsei saikenhō jō ni okeru shōsho no kinō" 近世債權法上における証書の機能 (Function of documents in the law of obligations in the recent era), 4 *Kanazawa hōgaku* (no. 2) 77–116 (1958); 5 *id.* (no. 2) 47–79 (1959); 6 *id.* (no. 1) 35–68 (1960).

Haruhara Gentarō 春原源太郎. "Deiri atsukai nikki" 出入曖日記 (Diary of conciliation in Tokugawa disputes), 12 *Hōseishi kenkyū* 194–206 (1961).

———. "Edo jidai no kōtō benron" 江戸時代の口頭弁論 (Oral argument in the Edo period), 2 *Kinsei minji saiban shiryō* 1–12 (1963).

———. "Kinsei Osaka no senso kōso dōjitsunegai" 近世大坂の先訴後訴.同日願 (*Senso, kōso, dōjitsunegai* practices in Osaka in the recent era), 6 *Hōseishi kenkyū* 164–76 (1955).

———. "Kujiyado no senden bira" 公事宿の宣伝ビラ (Advertising handbills of a suit inn), 15 *Jiyū to seigi* (no. 1) 39–40 (1964).

———. "Minzoku kankō no hōteki shōnin" 民族慣行の法的承認 (Legal recognition of folk customs), *Kansai daigaku gakuhō* (no. 283) 2–3 (Sept. 1955).

———. "Toiya hisashitsuki deiri—Mino-no-kuni Hino Shinden" 問屋庇附出入—美濃國日野新田 (Suit involving wholesalers' eaves accessories—a case in Hino Shinden of Mino province), 9 *Hōseishi kenkyū* 172–82 (1958).

———. "Wakamonogumi gōyado mittsū murahachibu" 若者組郷宿密通村八分 (Youth groups, local [suit] inns, adultery, and village-eight-parts [ostracism]), *Kansai daigaku gakuhō* (no. 317) 2–4 (July 1958).

———. "Yūjo to hōtei" 遊女と法廷 (Prostitutes and courts), *Kansai daigaku shimpō* (June 1956).

Hayashi Tōichi 林董一. "Gosanke no kakushiki to sono seiritsu" 御三家の格式とその成立 (The ranking of the three houses and their establishment), 69 *Shigaku zasshi* 1440–63 (1960).

Hiramatsu Yoshirō 平松義郎. "Daimyō no keibatsuken" 大名の刑罰權 (The authority of daimyō to impose criminal penalties), *Keibatsu to kokka kenryoku* 刑罰と國家權力 (Sovereign power and criminal penalties), 125–62 (1960).

———. "Hatamoto no keibatsuken" 旗本の刑罰權 (The authority of bannermen to impose criminal penalties), 9 *Hōseishi kenkyū* 1–54 (1958).

———. "Tokugawa bakufu keihō ni okeru settōzai" 徳川幕府刑法に於ける窃盗罪 (The crime of larceny in the criminal law of the Tokugawa Shogunate), 65 *Kokka gakkai zasshi* 342–82 and 618–52 (1952).

Hirano Hikojirō 平野彦次郎. "Hayashi Razan to Honchō Tsugan" 林羅山と本朝通鑑 (Hayashi Razan and his Japanese history), *Kinsei Nihon no jugaku* 279–96 (1939).

———. "Yoshimune to jugaku" 吉宗と儒學 (Yoshimune and confucianism), *Kinsei Nihon no jugaku* 53–72 (1939).

Hiranuma Yoshirō 平沼淑郎. "Jiin monzen machi to shite no Nagano no hattatsu" 寺院門前町としての長野の發達 (The growth of Nagano as a town in front of the gate to a temple), 7 *Waseda shōgaku* (no. 1) 1–17; (no. 2) 1–42 (1931).

———. "Jiin to rinsetsu ryōshu to no keisō jiken no ichirei" 寺院と隣接領主との係爭事件の一例 (An example of a dispute between a temple and the neighboring feudal lord), 1 *Shakai keizai shigaku* 154 (1931).

Hirayama Kōzō 平山行三. "Shomuzata ni okeru wayo no kōsatsu" 所務沙汰に於ける和與の考察 (Consideration of conciliation in proceedings concerning fiefs), 4 *Shakai keizai shigaku* 1341–65 (1935).

Honjō Eijirō 本庄榮治郎. "Daimyō no ryōchi ni tsuite" 大名の領地について (Concerning the daimyō's fiefs), 25 *Keizai ronsō* 1225–29 (1927).

———. "Hyakushō to chōnin" 百姓と町人 (Farmers and townsmen), 17 *Keizai ronsō* 434–39 (1923).

———. "Sankin kōtai seido no keizaikan" 參勤交代制度の經濟觀 (An economic view of the system requiring daimyō to alternately spend time at Edo and their fiefs), 3 *Keizai ronsō* 828–41 (1916) and 4 *id.* 521–40 (1917).

Horie Eiichi 堀江英一. "Watakushi wa 'Kyōdōtai riron' ni hantai suru" 私は共同体理論に反對する (I oppose the "Cooperative body" theory), *Nihon kenkyū* (no. 37) 65–72 (1957).

Horiguchi Sadayuki 堀口貞幸. "Shinshū chūma Hōreki ikken" 信州中馬寶暦一件 (The case of the [pack-horse drivers of] Chūma

[village] in Shinshū during the Hōreki period [1751–64]),
2 *Inaji* (no. 4) 31–40 (1958).

Hozumi Shigetō 穗積重遠. "Tokugawa shomin seikatsu hōten" 徳川
庶民生活法典 (Code of laws regulating life of the commoners of
the Tokugawa period), 61 *Hōgaku kyōkai zasshi* 1–52, 193–231
(1943).

Iida Yoneaki 飯田米秋. "Sanron" 山論 (A dispute over mountain),
Geibi chihōshi kenkyū (no. 35) 14–19 (1960).

Inobe Shigeo 井野邊茂雄. "Tashidaka no sei o ronzu" 足高の制を論ず
(Discussion of the system of supplementary rice allowances)
20 *Kokugakuin zasshi* (no. 10) 36–41; (no. 11) 32–35 (1914).

Inoue Kazuo 井上和夫. "Kinsei shoki no soshō gijutsu" 近世初期の
訴訟技術 (The trial techniques in the early part of the recent
era), *Saikō saibansho shihō kenshūjohō* (no. 8) 34–54 (1953).

Ishii Ryōsuke 石井良助. "Futatabi Seii-taishōgun to Minamoto no
Yoritomo ni tsuite" 再び征夷大將軍と源頼朝に就いて (Again
concerning the position of *Seii-taishōgun* and Minamoto no
Yoritomo), 46 *Kokka gakkai zasshi* 1028–35 (1932).

———. "Gofunai" 御府内 (Inside of the capital), 53 *Kokka gakkai
zasshi* 314–21 (1939).

———. "Gōriki" 合力 (Mutual aid), 52 *Kokka gakkai zasshi* 407–21
and 561–72 (1935).

———. "Kamakura bakufu no seiritsu jiki" 鎌倉幕府の成立時期 (The
period of the formation of the Kamakura Shogunate), 62 *Kokka
gakkai zasshi* 229–32 (1948).

———. "Kinsei no ukenin to shōnin" 近世の請人と證人 (Guarantor
and witness in the later feudal period), 62 *Kokka gakkai zasshi*
166–68 (1948).

———. "Kinsei rikonhō nidai" 近世離婚法二題 (Two problems of
divorce law of the recent era), *Kokka gakkai gojusshūnen kinen kokkagaku ronshū* 3–52 (1937).

———. "Kohōsei zakkō" 古法制雑考 (Notes on ancient legal history),
51 *Kokka gakkai zasshi* 959–66 (1937).

———. "Machi shikimoku" 町式目 (The town regulations), 61
Hōgaku kyōkai zasshi 1274–87 and 1417–42 (1943).

———. "Nihon hōseishi kenkyū no hattatsu" 日本法制史研究の發達
(Development of the study of Japanese legal history), *Tōkyō
teikoku daigaku gakujitsu taikan* 277–93 (1942).

———. "Ofuregaki hensan no enkaku" 御觸書編纂の沿革 (A history
of the compilations of proclamations), 2 *Ofuregaki Tempō shūsei*
913–30 (1958).

———. "Ofuregaki senjutsu kakurei oyobi oshioki reiruishū" 御觸書

選述格例及び御仕置例類集 (Proclamations, selected regulations and the classified collections of precedents on execution), 53 *Kokka gakkai zasshi* 1660–68 (1939); and 54 *id.* 921–26 (1940).

———. "Ofuregaki shūsei ni tsuite" 御觸書集成に就て (Concerning the compilation of proclamations), 49 *Kokka gakkai zasshi* 734–66 (1935).

———. "Saiban no rekishi" 裁判の歴史 (History of adjudication), 23 *Hōritsu jihō* 110–16 (1951).

———. "Seii-taishōgun to Minamoto no Yoritomo (Kamakura bakufu shokusei nidai no ichi)" 征夷大將軍と源賴朝 (鎌倉幕府職制二題の一) (The position of *Seii-taishōgun* and Minamoto no Yoritomo [one of two problems of the Kamakura Shogunate]), 45 *Kokka gakkai zasshi* 793–98 (1931).

———. "Shomuzata no kenkyū" 所務沙汰の研究 (Study of civil proceedings involving fiefs in the Kamakura period), 49 *Hōgaku kyōkai zasshi* 2093–2141 (1931); 50 *id.* 77–127, 274–316, and 437–97 (1932).

Itō Kōichi 伊藤好一. "Ōme-ichi Shinmachi-ichi ni okeru ichibi funsō" 青梅市新町市における市日紛爭 (Disputes over market-days in Ōme and Shinmachi markets), 8 *Chihōshi kenkyū* (no. 3) 31–35 (1958).

Kaneda Heiichirō 金田平一郎. "Hanrei kinsei Osaka shihō ippan" 判例近世大坂私法一斑 (An aspect of Osaka private law of the recent era as seen by the precedents), *Nakada sensei kanreki shukuga hōseishi ronshū* 119–248 (1937).

———. "Kinsei no shiteki sashiosae keiyaku" 近世の私的差押契約 (Private servitude contracts in the recent era), 14 *Hōsei kenkyū* 110–36 (1946).

———. "Kinsei saiken hō" 近世債權法 (The law of obligations in the recent era), 298 *Shihō shiryō* 124 (1948).

———. "Kohanrei kenkyū" 古判例研究 (Study of ancient precedents), 3 *Hōsei kenkyū* 59–116 (1932).

———. "Kujigata osadamegaki no songai baishō hōki ni tsuite" 公事方御定書の損害賠償法規について (Concerning indemnity for damages as provided in the *Osadamegaki*), 5 *Hōsei kenkyū* 107–47 (1934).

———. "Tokugawa bakufu no karyō shōkō" 徳川幕府の過料小考 (Brief study of fines under the Tokugawa Shogunate), *Kokka gakkai gojusshūnen kinen kokkagaku ronshū* 53–84 (1937).

———. "Tokugawa jidai ni okeru koyōhō no kenkyū" 徳川時代に於ける雇傭法の研究 (A study of the law of personal services in the Tokugawa period), 41 *Kokka gakkai zasshi* 1103–39, 1299–1341, 1441–73, and 1650–74 (1927).

———. "Tokugawa jidai ni okeru saiken oyobi saimu no iten" 徳川時代に於ける債權及債務の移轉 (Assignment of rights and liabilities in the Tokugawa period), 1 *Hōsei kenkyū* 1–77 (1931).

———. "Tokugawa jidai ni okeru soshōjō no wakai" 徳川時代に於ける訴訟上の和解 (Compromise from the standpoint of litigation in the Tokugawa period), 1 *Shien* 174–98 and 266–75 (1928).

———. "Tokugawa jidai no tanin no kōi ni taisuru sekininsei ippan" 徳川時代の他人の行為に對する責任制一斑 (An aspect of the system of responsibility for the conduct of other persons during the Tokugawa period), 47 *Kokka gakkai zasshi* 1499–1534 (1933).

———. "Tokugawa jidai no tokubetsu minji soshōhō—kanekuji no kenkyū" 徳川時代の特別民事訴訟法—金公事の研究 (Special civil procedural law of the Tokugawa period—a study of money suits), 42 *Kokka gakkai zasshi* 1934–84 (1928); and 43 *id.* 1136–64 and 1423–45 (1929).

———. "Waga kinseihō jō no 'nakamagoto'" 我近世法上の"仲間事" (Mutual affairs in the law of our recent era), 46 *Kokka gakkai zasshi* 545–63 and 683–708 (1932).

Kanesashi Shōzō 金指正三. "Edo jidai no nansen naisai ni tsuite" 江戸時代の難船内濟について (Concerning the settlement out of court of shipwreck in the Edo period), 25 *Shakai keizai shigaku* (no. 5) 30–57 (1959).

Katō Toranosuke 加藤虎之亮. "Tsunayoshi to jugaku" 綱吉と儒學 (Tsunayoshi and Confucianism), *Kinsei Nihon no jugaku* 35–52 (1939).

Kawashima Takeyoshi 川島武宜. "Hōkenteki keiyaku to sono kaitai" 封建的契約とその解體 (The feudal contract and its dissolution), *Shisō* (no. 302) 43–55; and *id.* (no. 303) 39–48 (1949).

Kawaura Kōji 川浦康次. "Kabunakama saikōrei to chihō shōhin no ryūtsū kikō" 株仲間再興令と地方商品の流通機構 (The decrees to re-establish the stock guilds and the local mechanisms for commodity circulation), 9 *Meijō shōgaku* (no. 1) 123–50 (1959).

Kida Teikichi 喜田貞吉. "Daimyō" 大名 (Great names [feudal lord with ten thousand *koku*]), *Edo jidai shiron* 549–90 (1915).

———. "Ishin zengo ni okeru daimyō ryōchi" 維新前後に於ける大名領地 (The daimyō domains at the time of the Meiji restoration), 8 *Rekishi chiri* 32–36 and 124–27 (1906).

———. "Seii-taishōgun no meigi ni tsuite" 征夷大將軍の名義に就いて

(Concerning the title of *Seii-taishōgun*), 7 *Minzoku to rekishi* 431–46 (1922).

Kikuta Tarō 菊田太郎. "Shūmon nimbetsu aratame seido no enkaku" 宗門人別改制度の沿革 (History of the system of census according to Buddhist sects), 25 *Keizai ronsō* 86–108 (1927).

Kobayakawa Kingo 小早川欣吾. "Futatabi kinsei soshō ni okeru kankatsu oyobi shinkyū ni tsuite" 再び近世訴訟に於ける管轄及審級について (Again about appeals and jurisdiction in litigation of the recent era), 33 *Hōgaku ronsō* 287–322 and 604–36 (1935).

———. "Iwayuru shihai chigai e kakaru deiri ni tsuite" 所謂支配違へ懸る出入に就て (Concerning the so-called disputes involving diversity of jurisdiction), 34 *Hōgaku ronsō* 408–39 and 756–99 (1936).

———. "Kinsei minji saiban ni okeru mibunteki seikaku to tōkyū-sei ni tsuite" 近世民事裁判に於ける身分的性格と等級性について (Concerning the graded nature and status character of the civil trials of the recent era), 46 *Hōgaku ronsō* 20–56 and 388–423 (1942).

———. "Kinsei minji saiban ni okeru ni san no mondai" 近世民事裁判に於ける二, 三の問題 (Two or three problems in civil litigation of the recent era), 39 *Hōgaku ronsō* 527–72 and 777–816 (1938).

———. "Kinsei minji saiban no gainen to tokushitsu" 近世民事裁判の概念と特質 (General concepts and special characteristics of civil litigation of the recent era), 45 *Hōgaku ronsō* 1–36, 372–404, and 614–43 (1941).

———. "Kinsei minji saiban tetsuzuki ni okeru 'kuji'—toku ni honkuji ni tsuite 近世民事裁判手續に於ける公事—特に本公事について ("Suits" in the civil trial procedure of the recent era—especially concerning main suits), 47 *Hōgaku ronsō* 176–205 and 343–81 (1942).

———. "Kinsei ni okeru shindai kagiri oyobi bunsan ni tsuite" 近世に於ける身代限及分散について (Concerning *shindai kagiri* and *bunsan* in the recent era), 43 *Hōgaku ronsō kigen 2600 nen kinen ronbunshū no bu* 262–92 (1940).

———. "Kinsei ni okeru shindai kagiri oyobi bunsan zokkō" 近世に於ける身代限り及分散續考 (Further consideration of *shindai kagiri* and *bunsan* in the recent era), 44 *Hōgaku ronsō* 133–68, 299–331, and 619–49 (1941).

———. "Kinsei no saiban soshiki to shinkyū oyobi kankatsu ni kansuru jakkan no kōsatsu" 近世の裁判組織と審級及び管轄に關

する若干の考察 (Some considerations of the organization, appeals, and jurisdiction of the courts of the recent era), 31 *Hōgaku ronsō* 994–1020 (1934); and 32 *id.* 100–21 and 801–44 (1935).

———. "Kinsei saiban ni okeru 'hikiai' oyobi soshō tōjisha" 近世裁判に於ける引合及訴訟當事者 ("Interrelated matters" and parties to the suit in litigation of the recent era), 31 *Hōgaku ronsō* 565–631 and 807–51 (1939).

———. " 'Ronsho' ni kansuru soshō tetsuzuki ni tsuite" 論所に關する訴訟手續について (Concerning the litigation procedure involving land suits), 37 *Hōgaku ronsō* 65–116 and 603–60 (1937).

———. "Wagakuni kinsei no minji soshō tetsuzuki ni tsuite" 我國近世の民事訴訟手續について (Concerning the procedure in civil litigation in our country in the recent era), 38 *Hōgaku ronsō* 315–41, 551–85, and 700–44; and 39 *id.* 89–144 (1938).

Kobayashi Bunzui 小林文瑞. "Genroku-Kyōhōki ni okeru zaikata shōnin no seichō" 元禄享保期における在方商人の成長 (Growth of provincial merchants in the Genroku [1688–1703]–Kyōhō [1717–35] era), 6 *Rekishi kyōiku* (no. 1) 20–24 and 45; and 6 *id.* (no. 2) 61–65 and 72 (1958).

Kobayashi Seiji 小林清治. "Kinsei jōkamachi no seiritsu to shoki chōnin no keifu" 近世城下町の成立と初期町人の系譜 (Establishment of castle-towns in the recent era and the genealogy of townsmen in the early stages), *Rekishi hyōron* (no. 109) 10–20 (1959).

Kobayashi Shigeru 小林茂. "Keiō gannen kokuso no oboegaki, chū, ge" 慶應元年國訴の覺書, 中, 下 (A memorandum on the rebellion of 1865, Part 2 and Part 3), *Rekishi hyōron* (no. 93) 41–52; and (no. 94) 60–69 (1958).

Kōda Shigetomo 幸田成友. "Edo no chōnin no jinkō" 江戸の町人の人口 (Population of Edo townsmen), 8 *Shakai keizai shigaku* 1–23 (1938).

———. "Edo no nanushi" 江戸の名主 (Headmen of Edo), in *Nihon keizaishi kenkyū* 615–67 (1928).

———. "Hinin yoriba" 非人寄場 (Gathering place for nonhumans), *Nihon keizaishi kenkyū* 575–97 (1928).

———. "Kabu nakama no kaihō" 株仲間の解放 (The dissolution of the stock guilds), *Nihon keizaishi kenkyū* 358–84 (1928).

Kodama Kōta 兒玉幸多. "Edo Temmachō to Kai Kuisshikigō no keisō" 江戸傳馬町と甲斐九一色郷の係爭 (The dispute between Temmachō in Edo and the village of Kuisshikigō in Kai), *Kai shigaku* (no. 4) 1–16 (1958).

———. "Kinsei nōson no daikazoku seido" 近世農村の大家族制度

(The large family system of the rural village in the recent era), *Shisō* (no. 302) 504–14 (1949).

Koide Yoshio 小出義雄. "Osadamegaki hyakkajō hensan no jijō ni tsuite" 御定書百ヶ條編纂の事情に就いて (Concerning the conditions of compilation of the *Osadamegaki hyakkajō* [*gekan*]), *Shichō* (no. 3) 112–37 (1934).

Komiyama Yasusuke 小宮山綏介. "Edo machi bugyō no koto" 江戸町奉行の事 (Concerning the town commissioners of Edo), *Hōsei ronsan* 1115–50 (1903).

―――. "Edo machi no kaeki" 江戸町の課役 (Duty officers [at traffic posts] of Edo towns), *Hōsei ronsan* 1169–88 (1903).

Kondō Masaharu 近藤正治. "Seidō to Shōheizaka Gakumonjo" 聖堂と昌平坂學問所 [Confucian institutions of the Hayashi family], *Kinsei Nihon no jugaku* 199–217 (1939).

Kumagai Kaisaku 熊谷開作. "Iwayuru Nihon hōseishi no seiritsu to sono genkai" いわゆる日本法制史の成立とその限界 (The establishment of the so-called Japanese legal history and its proper sphere), 4 *Hōritsu bunka* (no. 1) 62–66 (1949).

Kuwada Tadachika 桑田忠親. "Toyotomi Hideyoshi no shirowari" 豊臣秀吉の城割 (Castle destruction by Toyotomi Hideyoshi), 59 *Kokugakuin zasshi* (no. 5) 1–5 (1958).

Kyōguchi Motokichi 京口元吉. "Tokugawa kyūbakuhan taisei no ichi kōsatsu" 徳川舊幕藩体制の一考察 (A consideration of the structure of the Tokugawa Shogunate and the local domains), 36 *Shikan* 35–63 (1951).

Maeda Masaharu 前田正治. "Mura seisai o tsūjite mitaru wagakuni kinsei sonraku no jishusei" 村制裁を通じて見たる我國近世村落の自主性 (The autonomous character of the village in the recent era of our country as seen through village adjudication), 52 *Hōgaku ronsō* 318–52 (1946).

―――. "Ryōshuhō jō no keibatsu to mura seisai to no kankei" 領主法上の刑罰と村制裁との關係 (The relationship between punishment under the laws of the feudal loads and village adjudication), *Keibatsu to kokka kenryoku* 101–23 (1960).

Maki Kenji 牧健二. "Buke seiji no taisei ni kansuru Edo jidai gakusha no kenkai" 武家政治の體制に關する江戸時代學者の見解 (Opinions of scholars in the Edo period concerning the political structure of the *buke*), 35 *Hōgaku ronsō* 1229–65 (1936).

―――. "Daimyō no shakaiteki oyobi hōteki gainen" 大名の社會的及び法的概念 (Social and legal concepts of the daimyō), 10 *Hōgaku ronsō* 457–82 (1923).

———. "Daimyō ron" 大名論 (A treatise on daimyō), 12 *Rekishi to chiri* 345–52 and 557–63 (1923).

———. "Hōken seido seiritsuki no goon to hōkō" 封建制度成立期の御恩と奉公 (Service and beneficence of the formative period of the feudal system), 27 *Hōgaku ronsō* 171–201 (1932).

———. "Kinsei bukehō no wakai oyobi chōtei" 近世武家法の和解及調停 (Conciliation and private settlement in law of the military houses of the recent era), *Saitō hakushi kanreki kinen, Hō to saiban* 201–34 (1942).

———. "Muromachi makki ni okeru daimyō ryōchi no seiritsu" 室町末期に於ける大名領地の成立 (The establishment of daimyō domains in the latter part of the Muromachi period), 38 *Hōgaku ronsō* 813–47 and 1054–94 (1938).

———. "Wagakuni kinsei no sonraku dantai no kigen" 我國近世の村落團體の起源 (The origins of our village associations in the recent era of our country), 34 *Hōgaku ronsō* 833–913 (1936).

Matsumoto Sannosuke 松本三之介. "Kinsei Nihon ni okeru kokugaku no seijiteki kadai to sono tenkai" 近世日本に於ける國學の政治的課題とその展開 (The political role of classical nationalism and its growth in Japan of the recent era), 66 *Kokka gakkai zasshi* 59–92 (1952).

Mikami Sanji 三上参次. "Edo bakufu no jūyō naru seisaku" 江戸幕府の重要なる政策 (Important policies of the Edo Shogunate), *Edo jidai shiron* 31–65 (1915).

Mitsuda Shinzō 満田新造. "Tokugawa jidai ni okeru chōson jichi no han-i" 徳川時代に於ける町村自治の範圍 (The scope of village and town autonomy in the Tokugawa period), 10 *Shigaku zasshi* 717–28, 837–49, 913–39, 1017–34, and 1246–54 (1899).

Miura Kaneyuki 三浦周行. "Edo bakufu no chōtei ni taisuru hōsei" 江戸幕府の朝廷に對する法制 (The legal system of the Edo Shogunate for the Imperial court), *Zoku hōseishi no kenkyū* 1347–78 (1925).

———. "Edo jidai no saiban seido" 江戸時代の裁判制度 (The judicial system of the Edo period), *Hōseishi no kenkyū* 1041–82 (1925).

———. "Enzahō ron" 縁座法論 (Essay on the law of liability of relatives), *Hōsei no kenkyū* 1026–40 (1925).

———. "Eta hinin no hōseishi jō no chii" 穢多非人の法制史上の地位 (The position of the outcasts and nonhumans from the standpoint of legal history), *Hōseishi no kenkyū* 1132–42 (1925).

———. "Goningumi seido no kigen" 五人組制度の起源 (Origins of the five-man-group system), *Hōseishi no kenkyū* 697–751 (1925).

————. "Hōseishi yori mitaru Osaka" 法制史より見たる大阪 (Osaka from the viewpoint of legal history), *Zoku hōseishi no kenkyū* 1500–14 (1925).

————. "Kinsei bushi kaikyū ni kansuru ichi kōsatsu" 近世武士階級に關する一考察 (A view of the military classes of the recent era), 1 *Shigaku kenkyū* 29–37 (1929).

————. "Oda, Toyotomi nishi no hōsei to zaisei" 織田豐臣二氏の法制と財政 (Legal institutions and finance of the Oda and Toyotomi), *Hōseishi no kenkyū* 226–43 (1925).

————. "Rekidai hōsei no kōfu to sono kōfushiki" 歷代法制の公布とその公布式 (Promulgation and promulgation formality in the legal systems of successive periods), *Hōseishi no kenkyū* 63–157 (1925).

————. "Shakai o chūshin to seru Edo bakufu no hōsei" 社會を中心とせる江戸幕府の法制 (Legal institutions of the Edo Shogunate with emphasis on social conditions), *Hōseishi no kenkyū* 244–82 (1925).

————. "Sōni ni kansuru hōsei no kigen" 僧尼に關する法制の起源 (The origin of legal regulations concerning monks and nuns), *Hōsei no kenkyū* 1113–32 (1925).

————. "Ushinawaretaru kinsei hōsei shiryō" 失はれたる近世法制史料 (Lost materials of legal history of the recent era), *Zoku hōseishi no kenkyū* 1389–1458 (1925).

————. "Yōshi kō" 養子考 (A consideration of adoption), 6 *Shigaku zasshi* 193–206, 338–49, 419–27, and 571–78 (1895).

Miyazaki Dōsei 宮崎道生. "Arai Hakuseki to Hōei Buke Shohatto" 新井白石と寶永武家諸法度 (Arai Hakuseki and the *Buke Shohatto* of the Hōei period [1704–1711]), *Nihon rekishi* (no. 107) 6–19 (1957).

Miyazaki Michisaburō 宮崎道三郎. "Nihon hōseishi no kenkyū jō ni okeru Chōsen-go no kachi" 日本法制史の研究上に於ける朝鮮語の價值 (The value of the Korean language in the study of Japanese legal history), *Miyazaki sensei hōseishi ronshū* 204–40 (1929).

Mori Ōgai 森鷗外. "Kuriyama Taizen" 栗山大膳 (Kuriyama Taizen [name of a person]), 4 *Mori Ōgai zenshū* 3–18 (1961).

Mori Yasuhiro 森泰博. "Hatamoto no ryōchi shihai to zaisei" 旗本の領地支配と財政 (Bannerman fief management and finance), 9 *Handai keizaigaku* (no. 1) 92–132 (1959).

Morohashi Tetsuji 諸橋轍次. "Kansei igaku no kin" 寬政異學の禁 (Decree against unorthodox learning in the Kansei period [1789–1800]), *Kinsei Nihon no jugaku* 157–78 (1939).

Naitō Chisō 内藤恥叟. "Bakufu tairō no haichi" 幕府大老の廢置 (The abolition and creation of the great elder of the Shogunate), *Hōsei ronsan zokuhen* 514–20 (1904).

———. "Daimyō ryōchi no yurai" 大名領地の由來 (The origins of the daimyō fiefs), *Hōsei ronsan zokuhen* 509–13 (1904).

———. "Kirishitan aratame no koto" 切支丹改の事 (Concerning the Christian renunciations), *Hōsei ronsan* 1188–1206 (1903).

———. "Kunōzan hyakkajō wa itsuwari naru koto" 久能山百箇條は偽なること (Concerning the fraud of the Kunōzan One Hundred Articles ["Legacy of Ieyasu"]), *Hōsei ronsan zokuhen* 529–34 (1904).

———. "Tokugawa-shi kansei" 徳川氏官制 (The Tokugawa bureaucracy), *Hōsei ronsan* 1241–1347 (1903).

———. "Tokugawa-shi shisei no taii" 徳川氏施政の大意 (A synopsis of the Tokugawa administration), *Hōsei ronsan* 1206–34 (1903).

———. "Tokugawa-shi kansei taikōzu" 徳川氏官制大綱圖 (A chart of the core of the Tokugawa bureaucracy), *Hōsei ronsan* 1235–41 (1903).

Nakada Kaoru 中田薫. "Eiyo no shichi-ire" 榮譽の質入 (Pledges of honor), 3 *Hōseishi ronshū* 295–308 (1943).

———. "Itakura-shi shinshikimoku ni tsuite" 板倉氏新式目に就て (Concerning the new code of the Itakura house), 3 *Hōseishi ronshū* 653–725 (1943).

The *Itakura Shinshikimoku* was a code drawn up by Itakura Shigemune, first Kyoto Shoshidai (1622). This article is valuable for the study of the law of the early part of the Tokugawa period.

———. "Kenri" 權利 (Right), 3 *Hōseishi ronshū* 1160–64 (1943).

———. "Kohō zakkan" 古法雑感 (Miscellaneous views on ancient law), 1 *Hōseishi kenkyū* 1–44 (1951).

———. "Taihō" 大法 (Great law), 3 *Hōseishi ronshū* 1096–1100 (1943).

———. "Tokugawa jidai ni okeru bō shōka no kafū-sho" 徳川時代に於ける某商家の家風書 (Documents showing the household customs of a certain merchant family in the Tokugawa period), 1 *Hōseishi ronshū* 357–74 (1926).

———. "Tokugawa jidai ni okeru jimbai oyobi hitojichi keiyaku" 徳川時代に於ける人賣及び人質契約 (Contracts for the sale and pledging of humans in the Tokugawa period), 3 *Hōseishi ronshū* 365–432 (1943).

———. "Tokugawa jidai ni okeru mura no jinkaku" 徳川時代に於ける村の人格 (Personalities in the village of the Tokugawa period), 2 *Hōseishi ronshū* 963–1106 (1938).

———. "Tokugawa jidai no minji saiban jitsuroku" 徳川時代の民事

裁判實録 (Actual records of civil trials in the Tokugawa period), 3 *Hōseishi ronshū* 753–832 (1943).

———. "Tokugawa jidai no minji saiban jitsuroku zokuhen" 徳川時代の民事裁判實録続編 (Supplement to actual records of civil trials in the Tokugawa period), 3 *Hōseishi ronshū* 833–904 (1943).

———. "Tokugawa jidai no sonraku jichisei" 徳川時代の村落自治制 (The system of village autonomy in the Tokugawa period), *Hōritsu shimpō* (no. 743) 1–4 (1948).

Nakada Yasunao 中田易直. "Kan-ei jūninen Kambun sannen Buke Shohatto kō" 寛永十二年寛文三年武家諸法度考 (A consideration of the regulations for the military houses of 1635 and 1663), *Shichō* (no. 46) 40–44 (1952).

Nakamura Kichiji 中村吉治. "Kinsei hōkensei no seikaku" 近世封建制の性格 (Nature of feudalism of the recent era), *Shisō* (no. 302) 481–90 (1949).

———. "Kokudakasei to hōkensei" 石高制と封建制 (The *koku* system and feudalism), 69 *Shigaku zasshi* 817–63 and 965–79 (1960).

Nakamura Kōya 中村孝也. "Daimyō no kenkyū" 大名の研究 (A study of the daimyōs), *Miyake hakushi koki shukuga kinen ronshū* 329–85 (1929).

Nakayama Kyūshirō 中山久四郎. "Rin-ke to bunkyō" 林家と文教 (The house of Hayashi and education), *Kinsei Nihon no jugaku* 73–94 (1939).

Nishizawa Takehiko 西澤武彦. "Kinsei jōkamachi ni okeru chōnin-machi no keizai" 近世城下町における町人町の經濟 (Economy of a townsmen's block in the castle town in the recent era), 10 *Shinano* (no. 8) 22–34 (1958).

Nomura Kentarō 野村兼太郎. "Tokugawa jidai sonraku kenkyū josetsu" 徳川時代村落研究序説 (An introduction to the study of villages of the Tokugawa period), 34 *Mita gakkai zasshi* (no. 10) 1019–65 and 1405–38 (1940).

Ōde Yukiko 大出由紀子. "Kinsei sompō to ryōshuken" 近世村法と領主權 (Village law and the authority of the feudal lords in the recent era), *Hōsei ronshū* (no. 18) 1–32; and (no. 19) 73–128 (1962).

Ohara Naka 小原仲. "Ōoka Echizen-no-kami no saibansho" 大岡越前守の裁判書 (Judicial records of Ōoka Echizen-no-kami), *Hōsō* (no. 65) 1–4 (1956).

Ōishi Shinzaburō 大石愼三郎. "Kyōhō kaikaku ni okeru chihō shihai kikō no seibi to nōmin taisaku (ichi)" 享保改革における地方支配機構の整備と農民對策(一) (Installation of rural control mechanisms during the Kyōhō [1716–35] reforms and peasant countermeasure [part 1]), *Rekishi hyōron* (no. 117) 54–70 (1960).

Ono Masao 小野正雄. "Kambun-ki ni okeru chūkei shōgyō toshi no kōzō" 寛文期における中繼商業都市の構造 (The structure of a transit commercial town in the Kambun [1661–1673] era), 12 *Rekishigaku kenkyū* 17–27 (1960).

Osatake Takeshi 尾佐竹猛. "Eta hinin no shōgō haishi ni tsuite" 穢多非人の稱號廢止に就て (Concerning the abolition of the terms *eta* and *hinin*), 34 *Rekishi chiri* 397–406 (1919).

———. "Yūjo kaihōrei no zengo" 遊女解放令の前後 (Before and after the decree releasing women of pleasure), 3 *Hōritsu jihō* 838–42 (1931).

Ōta Heisaburō 大田兵三郎. "Fujiwara Seika no gakuteki taido" 藤原惺窩の學的態度 (Scholarly attitudes of Fujiwara Seika), *Kinsei Nihon no jugaku* 261–78 (1939).

Ōtake Hideo 大竹秀男. "Kinsei suiri soshōhō ni okeru 'naisai' no gensoku" 近世水利訴訟法に於ける内濟の原則 (The general principle of "private settlement" in the procedural law of water use in the recent era), 1 *Hōseishi kenkyū* 183–212 (1951).

Sakudō Yōtarō 作道洋太郎. "Andō Seiichi cho 'Kinsei zaikata shōgyō no kenkyū'" 安藤精一著近世在方商業の研究 (Review of Ando Seiichi, *A study of rural commerce in the recent era*), 5 *Shakai keizai shigaku* 98–102 (1959).

Saku Takashi *et al.* 左久高士他. "Kinsei chihōshi no kenkyū" 近世地方史の研究 (A study of local history of the recent era), 6 *Rekishi kyōiku* 7–63 (1958).

Sasaki Kiichirō 佐々木喜一郎. "Ōoka Echizen-no-kami otazune jūsan yashi no koto" 大岡越前守お尋ね十三香具師の事 (Thirteen kinds of showmen questioned by Ōoka Echizen-no-kami), 20 *Sendai kyōdo kenkyū* (no. 4) 49–51 (1960).

Satō Shōsuke 佐藤昌介. "Ahen sensō to Tempō-ki no seikyoku" 阿片戰爭と天保期の政局 (The opium war and the political situation in the Tempō period [1830–43]), 69 *Shigaku zasshi* 1–30 (1960).

Sekiyama Naotarō 關山直太郎. "Tokugawa jidai no jinkō kōzō to sono hendō—toku ni mibun oyobi shokugyō betsu kōsei ni tsuite" 徳川時代の人口構造とその變動 ― 特に身分及び職業別構成に就て (The structure and trend of population in the Tokugawa period —concerning the structure classified by status and occupation in particular), *Keizai riron* (no. 32) 1–23 (1956).

Shinji Yoshimoto 進士慶幹. "Buke shohatto" 武家諸法度 (Regulations for the military houses), 7 *Rekishi kyōiku* (no. 10) 58–65 (1959).

Suenaka Tetsuo 末中哲夫. "Jōkamachi no keisei to hisabetsu buraku" 城下町の形成と被差別部落 (The formation of the castle town and the partitioned [*eta*] sections), 6 *Shōkei gakusō* 117–32 (1958).

Sukeno Kentarō 助野健太郎. "Kinsei shoki no jōkamachi seisaku" 近世初期の城下町政策 (Provisions for castle towns in the early part of the recent era), *Nihon rekishi* (no. 123) 64–75 (1958).

Sumi Tōyō 鷲見等曜. "Bakuhan kōki Sennan kigyō chitai nōmin no tōsō—kokuso o chūshin to shite" 幕藩後期泉南機業地帯農民の闘争—國訴を中心として (Peasant struggles in the Sennan textile industrial zone in the latter part of Shogunate-domain period—centering around rebellions), *Historia* (no. 14) 1–19 (1956).

Suzuki Naoharu 鈴木直治. "Muro Kyūsō to Shushigaku" 室鳩巣と朱子學 (Muro Kyūsō and the philosophy of Chu Hsi), *Kinsei Nihon no jugaku* 427–52 (1939).

Takayanagi Shinzō 高柳真三. "Kyōhō no kaikaku to Osadamegaki" 享保の改革と御定書 (The Kyōhō [1716–1735] reforms and the *Osadamegaki*), *Nihon rekishi* (no. 53) 19–26 (1952).

———. "Mittsūzai to sono tokuisei" 密通罪とその特異性 (The crime of adultery and its special peculiarities), 9 *Hōgaku* 680–704 (1940).

———. "Noyamazakai-ron—sono ichirei" 野山境論—その一例 (Lawsuit concerning boundaries of fields and mountain land—one example), 9 *Hōgaku* 1155–76 (1940).

———. "Tokugawa jidai no jūkon" 徳川時代の重婚 (Bigamous marriages in the Tokugawa period), 3 *Hōgaku* 656–66 (1934).

———. "Tokugawa jidai buke kazokuhō no kōsei ni tsuite" 徳川時代武家家族法の構成に就いて (Concerning the structure of the family law of the warrior house in the Tokugawa period), *Tōhoku daigaku hō-bun-gakubu jusshūnen kinen hōgaku ronshū* 593–656 (1934).

———. "Tokugawa jidai no mekake" 徳川時代の妾 (Concubines in the Tokugawa period), 5 *Hōgaku* 823–46 (1936).

———. "Tokugawa jidai no mimoto hoshō" 徳川時代の身元保證 (Personal suretyship in the Tokugawa period), 3 *Hōritsu jihō* 612–15 (1931).

———. "Wakaishugi ni tatsu saiban" 和解主義に立つ裁判 (Trials based on the principle of compromise), 56 *Chūō kōron* (no. 4) 139–47 (1941).

Takeuchi Makoto 竹内誠. "Kansei kaikaku to 'kanjōsho goyōtatsu' no seiritsu" 寛政改革と勘定所御用達の成立 (The Kansei [1789–1801] reform and the establishment of "purveyors of the finance commission"), *Nihon rekishi* (no. 128) 23–32; and (no. 129) 49–56 (1959).

Takeuchi Toshimi 竹内利美. "Mura no seisai—shu to shite hōritsu-teki no mono ni tsuite" 村の制裁―主として法律的のものについて (Village adjudication—chiefly concerning legal matters), 8 *Shakai keizai shigaku* 603–33 and 743–72 (1938).

Takeyasu Shigeji 竹安繁治. "Kinsei kosakuryō no kinō" 近世小作料の機能 (The function of farm rent in the recent era), *Nihon rekishi* (no. 123) 32–47 (1958).

Takigawa Masajirō 瀧川政次郎. "Bengokan" 辯護官 (The advocating official), 2 *Jiyū to seigi* (no. 8) 38–40 (1951).

———. "Hōseishi jō ni okeru josei no chii" 法制史上に於ける女性の地位 (The position of woman in legal history), *Nihon hōseishi kenkyū* 541–54 (1941).

———. "Kujishi to gannimbō" 公事師と願人坊 (Suit solicitor and mendicant), 2 *Jiyū to seigi* (no. 5) 43–44 (1951).

———. "Kujishi to kujiyado" 公事師と公事宿 (Suit solicitor and suit inn), 2 *Jiyū to seigi* (no. 2) 12–17 (1951).

———. "Kujishi Magoshi Kyōheiō no kotodomo" 公事師馬越恭平翁のことども (About old Mr. Kyōhei Magoshi, suit solicitor [who was born in 1844 and later became king of the brewing business]), 2 *Jiyū to seigi* (no. 4) 49–52 (1951).

———. "Sambyaku daigen" 三百代言 (The three-hundred-advocate [mouthpiece or shyster]), 2 *Jiyū to seigi* (no. 6) 39–41 (1951).

Tanaka Hisao 田中久夫. "Sengoku jidai ni okeru sōryo no mibun" 戰國時代に於ける僧侶の身分 (The status of priests in the warring period), 78 *Rekishi chiri* 187–98 and 286–91 (1941).

Tanigawa Iwao 谷川盤雄. "Nihon josei no chii no hensen" 日本女性の地位の變遷 (Changes in the position of Japanese women), 31 *Kokugakuin zasshi* (no. 4) 23–45 (1925).

Tsuboi Kumazō 坪井九馬三. "Edo bakufu no kenchi tetsuzuki" 江戸幕府の檢地手續 (The procedure for land inspection under the Edo government), 5 *Shigaku zasshi* 315–41 and 413–19 (1894).

Tsuchiya Takao 土屋喬雄. "Tokugawa jidai ni okeru mibun to kaikyū" 德川時代に於ける身分と階級 (Class and status in the Tokugawa period), *Shisō* (no. 114) 677–91 (1931).

Tsuji Tatsuya 辻達也. " 'Tenna no chi' ni tsuite" 「天和の治」について (Concerning good governance in the Tenna period [1681–83]), 69 *Shigaku zasshi* 34–60 (1960).

Tsuruoka Takashi 鶴岡隆. "Hatamotoryō no seiritsu to bungō" 旗本領の成立と分郷 (The establishment and division of bannermen's fiefs), *Nihon daigaku shigakkai kenkyū ihō* (no. 3) 46–55 (1959).

Yamaguchi Satsujō 山口察常. "Ieyasu to jugaku" 家康と儒學 (Ieyasu

and Confucianism), *Kinsei Nihon no jugaku* 21–34 (1939).

Yamaguchi Tōru 山口徹. "Obama Tsuruga ni okeru kinsei shoki gōshō no sonzai keitai" 小濱敦賀における近世初期豪商の存在形態 (The form in which the wealthy merchants in Obama and Tsuruga existed in the early recent era), 12 *Rekishigaku kenkyū* 1–16 (1960).

Yamaguchi Yukio 山口之夫. "Temmei hachi-nen Kansei roku-nen no hiryō kokuso" 天明八年寛政六年の肥料國訴 (Rebellions relating to fertilizer in 1788 and in 1794), 27 *Kinseishi kenkyū* 15–22 (1959).

Yamanaka Einosuke 山中永之佑. "Mittsū no shioki to naisai" 密通の仕置と内濟 (Punishment for adultery and private settlement), *Handai hōgaku* (no. 38) 23–79 (1956).

Yamori Kazuhiko 矢守一彦. "Kinsei jōkamachi puran no hatten ruikei—josetsu" 近世城下町プランの發展類型—序説 (An introduction to developmental types of plans for castle towns in the recent era), 41 *Shirin* (no. 6) 561–80 (1958).

Yokoyama Tatsuzō 横山達三. "Edo jidai no kyōiku" 江戸時代の教育 (Education of the Edo period), *Edo jidai shiron* 499–526 (1915).

SECTION B: SOURCES AND WRITINGS ON
MODERN (1868–1964) JAPANESE LAW

As an introduction to the legal materials used by the Japanese lawyer, Shihō Kenshūjo, *Hōrei hanrei gakusetsu no chōsa ni tsuite* (1962), published by the Legal Training and Research Institute as a manual for its students, who are training to become judges, lawyers and procurators is a convenient guide. For historical studies in the modern period, *Hōgaku kenkyū no shiori*, 2 volumes (1948) provides a good listing and evaluation of studies and treatises up to the end of World War II.

Since modern Japanese law is a derivative of the European code law, the starting place for research on any Japanese legal problem are the statutes found most conveniently in the ubiquitous *Roppō zensho*, which gives the codes, the most important special statutory and cabinet or ministry regulations with cross references and legislative history. Perhaps the next step in research would be to go to a treatise by the leading jurists in the field to see whether they have covered the application of the code to the specific problem. A convenient collection of treatises is the *Hōritsugaku zenshū* (1957–64, 44 vols.—60 vols. projected), which has been in the process of publication in the last few years. It furnishes an analysis of major Japanese legal topics written by outstanding living scholars in their respective fields.

Of course, precedent does not have the same importance that it does in Anglo-American law, although the difference is only a matter of degree. As will be noted from the listings below, in the post-1945 period, new sets of laws and regulations, as well as completely revised and supplemented sets of case reports, have been published. However, it should be noted that even the *Saikō Saibansho hanreishū* (a collection of Supreme Court decisions) is not a complete set of decisions. Japanese lawyers rely more heavily on jurists to edit and interpret the case materials than we do in the Anglo-American system.

9. *Modern Legal Bibliographies*

Hōbun hōritsu zasshi kiji sakuin nempō 邦文法律雜誌記事索引年報 (Annual index to articles in legal periodicals). Compiled by Saikō Saibansho Toshokan 最高裁判所圖書館. Tokyo: Author, annual volumes since 1957.

Hōgaku kenkyū no shiori 法學研究の栞 (A guide to the study of jurisprudence). Compiled by Kikui Tsunahiro 菊井維大, Yokota Kisaburō 横田喜三郎, and Wagatsuma Sakae 我妻榮. Tokyo: Tōkyō Daigaku Gakusei Bunka Shidōkai 東京大學學生文化指導會, 1950. 2 vols.

This is a useful annotated guide to legal literature for law students. It is arranged by subject matter and is quite selective; of course, it does not cover most of the important postwar literature.

Hōrei hanrei gakusetsu no chōsa ni tsuite 法令判例學説の調査について (Concerning investigation on laws, judicial decisions and theories). Shihō Kenshūjo 司法研修所. Tokyo: Author, 1962. 131 pp.

Hōritsu jihō 法律時報 (Law journal).

This monthly contains listings and comments on new literature regularly, especially in the December issue each year. See listing on p. 317.

Hōritsu jihō sōsakuin 法律時報總索引 (Law journal index). Tokyo: Nihon Hyōron Shinsha, 1954 and 1963.

The 1954 index covers volumes 1 through 25. The 1963 index covers volumes 26 through 35.

Hōritsu kankei zasshi kiji sakuin 法律關係雜誌記事索引 (Index to articles in legal periodicals). Compiled by Hōmu Toshokan 法務圖書館 (Library of the Ministry of Justice). Tokyo: Author, biennial volumes since 1957.

These volumes cover all articles published since 1945 in legal periodicals received by the Ministry of Justice Library in Tokyo.

The coverage is similar but not identical to that of the Supreme Court annual index.

Hōritsu nenkan 法律年鑑 (Law annual). Compiled by Hōritsu jihō henshūbu 法律時報編集部. Tokyo: Nihon Hyōron Shinsha 日本評論社, Annual volumes since 1924.

Minji chōteihō gaisetsu 民事調停法概説 (General survey of civil conciliation law). Koyama Noboru 小山昇. Tokyo: Yūhikaku 有斐閣, 1953. 245 pp.

See pp. 237–41 for the most complete list of writings on conciliation.

Sengo hōgaku bunken sōmokuroku 戰後法學文獻總目録 (A general list of postwar literature on jurisprudence). Compiled by Hōritsu jihō henshūbu 法律時報編集部編. Tokyo: Nihon Hyōron Shinsha 日本評論新社, 1954. 2 vols.

These two volumes list all Japanese publications (books and articles) on legal subjects published between 1946 and 1953. The listing is quite complete for postwar literature to 1953, but it lacks annotation.

10. *Modern Legal Dictionaries*

Hōgaku jiten 法學辭典 (Dictionary of jurisprudence). Ed. by Suekawa Hiroshi 末川博. Tokyo: Nihon hyōronsha 日本評論社, 1951. 1140 pp.

Hōritsugaku jiten 法律學辭典 (Dictionary of jurisprudence). Ed. by Suehiro Izutarō 末弘嚴太郎 and Tanaka Kōtarō 田中耕太郎. Tokyo: Iwanami Shoten 岩波書店, 1934–37. 5 vols.

Minji hōgaku jiten 民事法學辭典 (Dictionary of civil jurisprudence). Ed. by Suekawa Hiroshi 末川博. Tokyo: Yūhikaku 有斐閣, 1960. 2 vols.

11. *Modern Legal Encyclopediae, Series, and Miscellaneous References*

Gendai hōgaku zenshū 現代法學全集 (A complete compilation on modern jurisprudence). Suehiro Izutarō 末弘嚴太郎, editor-in-chief. Tokyo: Nihon Hyōronsha 日本評論社, 1928–31. 39 vols.

Hōritsugaku kōza 法律学講座 (Series on legal studies). Tokyo: Kōbundō 弘文堂.

Hōritsu gakusetsu hanrei sōran 法律學説判例總覧 (Consolidated legal theories and decisions). Ed. by Takakubo Kihachirō 高窪喜八郎. Tokyo: Chūō Daigaku Shuppambu 中央大学出版部, 1950————. 27 vols. to date (34 vols. projected).

This work was first published by Hōritsu Hyōronsha in 1935 (Takakubo Kihachirō 高窪喜八郎, ed.) 37 vols., but his original edition is now out of print.

Hōritsugaku taikei 法律學體系 (A compendium on legal studies). Suekawa Hiroshi 末川博, editor-in-chief. Tokyo: Nihon Hyōronsha 日本評論社.

This series is in three parts: (1) *Komentāru* コメンタール (Commentary); (2) *Hōgaku riron* 法學理論 (Theory of jurisprudence); (3) *Hōritsu kōwa* 法律講話 (Lectures on law).

Hōritsugaku zenshū 法律學全集 (Complete works of jurisprudence). Ed. by Wagatsuma Sakae 我妻榮 *et al.* Tokyo: Yūhikaku 有斐閣, 1957 (first vol. published). 42 vols. to date (60 vols. projected).

Hōritsu jitsumu kōza 法律實務講座 (Series on legal practices). Ed. by Iwamatsu Saburō 岩松三郎 and Kaneko Hajime 兼子一. Tokyo: Yūhikaku 有斐閣.

This series is in two parts:

1) *Minji soshō hen* (Civil procedure part): Vols. 2, 4 and 5 (7 vols. projected).

2) *Keiji hen* (Criminal part) 12 vols.

Kōza Nihon kindaihō hattatsushi 講座日本近代法發達史 (Series on history of the development of modern Japanese law). Compiled by Ukai Nobushige 鵜飼信成 *et al.* Tokyo: Keisō Shobō 勁草書房, 1958–61. 10 vols. to date (14 vols. projected).

Mimpō kōgi 民法講義 (Series on civil code). Wagatsuma Sakae 我妻榮. Tokyo: Iwanami Shoten 岩波書店, 1961. 6 vols.

Minji soshōhō kōza 民事訴訟法講座 (Series on civil procedure law). Compiled by Minji Soshōhō Gakkai 民事訴訟法學會. Tokyo: Yūhikaku 有斐閣, 1961. 5 vols.

Nihon bengoshi meibo 日本弁護士名簿 (Directory of Japanese lawyers). Tokyo: Nihon bengoshi rengō kai, 1963. 360+43+13 pp.

Shihō kenkyū 司法研究 (Judicial study). Compiled by Shihōshō chōsabu 司法省調査部. Tokyo: Shihōshō, 1926–48. 130 vols.

This series continued after 1949 as *Hōmu kenkyū* 法務研究 and the compilers changed to Hōmushō Hōmu Sōgō Kenkyūjo 法務省法務總合研究所 in 1952. 71 vols. to date.

Shihō shiryō 司法資料 (Judicial materials). Compiled by Shihōshō Chōsabu 司法省調査部. Tokyo: Shihōshō 司法省, 307–46. 1921 vols.

This series continued after Volume 307 as *Hōmu shiryō* 法務資料, and compilers changed to Hōmushō Shihō Hōsei Chōsabu 法務省司法法制調査部. Also there is a series, *Shihō shiryō bessatsu* 司法資料別冊 (Extra judicial materials), Vols. 1–23 to date.

Shin hōgaku zenshū 新法學全集 (A complete compilation on newer jurisprudence). Ed. by Suehiro Izutarō 末弘嚴太郎. Tokyo: Nihon Hyōronsha 日本評論社, 1936–40. 31 vols.

The writers of this collection were somewhat different from *Gendai hōgaku zenshū*, but it is the latest treatment of the pre-war law on many topics.

Sōgō hanrei kenkyū sōsho 總合判例研究叢書 (Collections of consolidated case studies). Tokyo: Yūhikaku 有斐閣, 1956 (first vol. published) 73 vols. to date.

A postwar series.

12. *Modern Collection of Laws and Precedents*

Chōtei kankei hōkishū 調停關係法規集 (A collection of regulations concerning conciliation). Compiled by Saikō Saibansho Jimu Sōkyoku Minjikyoku 最高裁判所事務總局民事局. Tokyo: Compiler, 1953. 100 pp.

In Miyazaki, *Chōteihō no riron to jissai* 237–95 and Koyama, *Minji chōteihō gaisetsu* 185–236 there are also collections of laws and regulations on conciliation.

Chōtei roppō 調停六法 (Conciliation six-codes). Compiled by Nihon Chōtei Kyōkai Rengokai. Tokyo: Compiler, 1964. 328 pp.

Daishin-in minji hanreishū 大審院民事判例集 (The case reports of the Court of Cassation). Compiled by Daishin-in 大審院. Tokyo: Hōsōkai, 25 vols. (from 1922 to 1946).

Genkō hōki sōran 現行法規總覽 (General coverage of currently effective laws and regulations). Compiled by Shūgiin Hōseikyoku, Sangiin Hōseikyoku 衆議院法制局, 參議院法制局. Tokyo: Daiichi Hōki Shuppan Kabushiki Kaisha 第一法規出版株式會社, 1950——————. 52 vols.

Volume 6 is on civil procedures.

Genkō Nihon hōki 現行日本法規 (Currently effective Japanese laws and regulations). Compiled by Hōmu Daijin Kambō Hōkishitsu 法務大臣官房法規室. Tokyo: Teikoku Chihō Gyōsei Gakkai 帝國地方行政學會. 1951——————. 52 vols.

This set of regulations and the one above bring together the currently effective laws and regulations of importance to the practising lawyers. There is little difference between the two sets.

Hanrei jihō 判例時報 (Reports of decisions). Compiled by Hanrei jihō kankōkai 判例時報刊行会. Tokyo: Nihon Hyōron Shinsha 日本評論新社, bimonthly since June 1, 1953; tri-monthly since no. 78, July 1, 1956.

Hanrei taikei 判例體系 (Compendium of decisions). Tokyo: Keihōsha 啓法會, 1932–43. 30 vols.

Volumes 27, 28, 29, and 30 are on civil procedure. This set of cases is useful for pre-war decisions and is organized by the sections of the various Japanese codes.

Hanrei taikei 判例体系 (Compendium of decisions). Compiled by
Inoue Noboru 井上登, Iwamatsu Saburō 岩松三郎, Wagatsuma
Sakae 我妻榮, Tanaka Haruhiko 田中治彦, Tanaka Jirō 田中二郎,
Kaneko Hajime 兼子一, Ishii Teruhisa 石井照久, Dandō
Shigemitsu 團藤重光. Tokyo: Daiichi Hōki Shuppan Kabushiki
Kaisha 第一法規出版株式會社, 1962.

    124 volumes published up to November 1964. The organiza-
tion follows the sections of the various codes.

Hōrei zensho 法令全書 (Complete compilations of laws and ordinances).
Compiled by Naikaku Kampōkyoku 内閣官報局. Tokyo:
Naikaku Insatsukyoku 内閣印刷局, 1887————.

    This is a monthly collection of the materials of the Kampō,
classified according to types of regulation, i.e., laws, cabinet
orders, ministerial orders, etc.

Kampō 官報 ("The Official Gazette"). Tokyo: Naikaku Insatsukyoku
内閣印刷局, 1886————.

    There is an English translation, *The Official Gazette*, from 1946
to 1952. A copy may be found in the *Horei-ka* on the third floor
of the Diet Library. All laws and regulations are promulgated in
this official publication.

Kankei hōkishū 關係法規集 (Collection of laws and regulations related
to lawyers). Compiled by Nihon Bengoshi Rengōkai 日本辯護士
連合會. Tokyo: Compiler, Undated. 67 pp.

Kōtō Saibansho hanreishū 高等裁判所判例集 (Compilation of high court
decisions). Compiled by Saikō Saibansho Hanrei Chōsakai 最高
裁判所判例調査會. Tokyo: Saikō Saibansho Jimu Sōkyoku 最高
裁判所事務總局. Annual volumes.

Roppō zensho 六法全書 (Complete collections of the six codes). Compiled by Wagatsuma Sakae 我妻榮, Miyazawa Toshiyoshi
宮澤俊義. Tokyo: Yūhikaku 有斐閣, 1964. 2142 pp.

    The various *Roppō zensho* are revised and republished by their
respective compilers annually, and they consist of the codes and
other selected laws and regulations. There are various types of
Roppō zensho, but they usually include more than the "six codes."

Saikō Saibansho hanreishū 最高裁判所判例集 (Compilation of Supreme
Court decisions). Compiled by Saikō Saibansho Hanrei Chōsakai
最高裁判所判例調査會. Tokyo: Saikō Saibansho Jimu Sōkyoku
最高裁判所事務總局.

    This set does not include all of the cases decided by the
Supreme Court, but this is the standard set of reports. They
came out in annual volumes.

13. *Japanese Government Records and Statistics*

Dai jū kokkai sangiin iinkai kaigiroku 第十國會參議院委員會會議録 (Records of the Committees of the House of Councillors of the tenth Diet). 1951.

Dai jū kokkai sangiin kaigiroku 第十國會參議院會議録 (Records of the meeting of the House of Councillors of the tenth Diet). 1951.

Dai jū kokkai shūgiin iinkai kaigiroku 第十國會衆議院委員會會議録 (Records of the Committees of the House of Representatives of the the tenth Diet). 1951.

Dai jū kokkai shūgiin kaigiroku 第十國會衆議院會議録 (Records of the meeting of the House of Representatives of the tenth Diet). 1951.

Kempō seitei no keika ni kansuru shōiinkai hōkokusho 憲法制定の經過に關する小委員會報告書 (Report by the subcommittee concerning the process of establishment of the Constitution). Kempō Chōsakai 憲法調査會 (Takayanagi Kenzō 高柳賢三, chairman). Tokyo: Kempō Chōsakai Jimukyoku 憲法調査會事務局, 1961. 612 pp.

Kempō un-yō no jissai ni tsuite no dai ichi iinkai hōkokusho 憲法運用の實際についての第一委員會報告書 (Report by the first committee on practical operation of the Constitution). Kempō Chōsakai 憲法調査會 (Takayanagi Kenzō 高柳賢三, chairman). Tokyo: Kempō Chōsakai Jimukyoku 憲法調査會事務局, 1961. 466 pp.

Kempō un-yō no jissai ni tsuite no dai ni iinkai hōkokusho 憲法運用の實際についての第二委員會報告書 (Report by the second committee on practical operation of the Constitution). Kempō Chōsakai 憲法調査會 (Takayanagi Kenzō 高柳賢三, chairman). Tokyo: Kempō Chōsakai Jimukyoku 憲法調査會事務局, 1961. 408 pp.

Kempō un-yō no jissai ni tsuite no dai san iinkai hōkokusho 憲法運用の實際についての第三委員會報告書 (Report by the third committee on practical operation of the Constitution). Kempō Chōsakai 憲法調査會 (Takayanagi Kenzō 高柳賢三, chairman). Tokyo: Kempō Chōsakai Jimukyoku 憲法調査會事務局, 1961. 308 pp.

Kempō un-yō no jissai ni tsuite no iinkai hōkokusho sakuin 憲法運用の實際についての委員會報告書索引 (Index of report by the committee on practical operation of the Constitution). Kempō Chōsakai 憲法調査會 (Takayanagi Kenzō 高柳賢三, chairman). Tokyo: Kempō Chōsakai Jimukyoku 憲法調査會事務局, 1961. 49 pp.

Minji chōtei hōki no kaisetsu 民事調停法規の解説 (Explanation of laws and regulations of civil conciliation). Saikō Saibansho 最高裁判所. Tokyo: Saikō Saibansho Jimu Sōkyoku Minjikyoku 最高裁判所事務總局民事局, 1951. 103 pp.

Minji jiken no gaikyō 民事事件の概況 (The general conditions of civil cases). Saikō Saibansho 最高裁判所. Tokyo: Saikō Saibansho Jimu Sōkyoku 最高裁判所事務總局, 1957. 190 pp.

Minji saibankan kaidō yōroku 民事裁判官會同要録 (Essential record of the conference of judges in civil matters). Saikō Saibansho Jimu Sōkyoku 最高裁判所事務總局. In series *Minji saiban shiryō* (no. 78) 民事裁判資料. Tokyo: Author, 1960. 415 pp.

Minji soshōhō kaisei chōsa iinkai giji sokkiroku 民事訴訟法改正調査委員會議事速記録 (Stenographic records of the research committee's discussions of the revisions of the code of civil procedure). Compiled by Hōsōkai 法曹會. Tokyo: Compiler, 1929.

Minji soshō no un-yō ni kansuru kenkyū tōron 民事訴訟の運用に關する研究討論 (Discussion of research concerning the operations in civil suits). Shihō Kenshūjo 司法研修所. Tokyo: Author, 1950. 96 pp.

Shihō tōkei nempō 司法統計年報 (The annual report of the judicial statistics). Compiled by Saikō Saibansho Jimu Sōkyoku 最高裁判所事務總局. Tokyo: Compiler, annually.

These reports are divided into three parts: civil, criminal, and family. Recently each volume contains about four hundred pages of statistics on the number of cases filed and the manner of disposition. They are unusually good judicial statistics.

14. *Modern Books, Pamphlets, and Monographs on Law*

On the general outlines of the modern Japanese legal system from the historical point of view, Ishii Ryōsuke, *Meiji bunkashi, hōseihen* (1954) and Ukai Nobushige *et al.*, *Kōza Nihon kindaihō hattatsushi* (1958–62) contain a wealth of information.

Koyama Noboru, "Chōteihō, chūsaihō," in 38 *Hōritsugaku zenshū* (1959) and Koyama's book, *Minji chōteihō gaisetsu* (1954) and Miyazaki Sumio, *Chōteihō no riron to jissai* (1942) are the best introductions to modern conciliation from different points of view and under prewar (Miyazaki) and postwar (Koyama) circumstances.

Adachi Motonosuke 安達元之助, compiler. *Tōkyō bengoshikaishi* 東京辯護士會史 (History of the Tokyo Bar Association). Tokyo: Tōkyō Bengoshikai Jimusho 東京辯護士會事務所, 1935. 987 pp.

Harada Keikichi 原田慶吉. *Nihon mimpōten no shiteki sobyō* 日本民法典の史的素描 (A historical sketch of the Japanese civil code). Tokyo: Sōbunsha 創文社, 1954. 396 pp.

Hoshino Tōru 星野通. *Meiji mimpō hensanshi kenkyū* 明治民法編纂史研究 (A study of the history of the Meiji compilation of the civil law). Tokyo: Daiyamondo-sha ダイヤモンド社, 1943. 545 pp.

———. *Mimpōten ronsōshi* 民法典論爭史 (History of the civil code dispute). Tokyo: Nihon Hyōronsha 日本評論社, 1944. 262 pp.

Hōsōkai 法曹會, ed. *Shin minji soshōhō jisshi kinengō* 新民事訴訟法實施記念號 (Memorial number to the execution of the new Code of Civil Procedure), in 8 *Hōsōkai zasshi* (no. 12) 1–610 (1930).

Hosono Nagayoshi 細野長良. *Minji soshōhō yōgi* 民事訴訟法要義 (Essential meaning of the code of civil procedure). Tokyo: Ganshōdō Shoten 嚴松堂書店, 1930–37. 5 vols.

Ichikawa Shirō 市川四郎. *Kaji shimpanhō gaisetsu* 家事審判法概説 (General survey of the law for settling family affairs). Tokyo: Yūhikaku 有斐閣, 1954. 197 pp.

Ikeda Torajirō 池田寅二郎. *Chūsai to chōtei* 仲裁と調停 (Arbitration and conciliation). Tokyo: Iwanami Shoten 岩波書店, 1932. 261 pp.

———. *Hōten hensan* 法典編纂 (Codification of laws), in *Iwanami kōza, Nihon rekishi* (no. 1). Tokyo: Iwanami Shoten 岩波書店, 1933.

Inoue Kazuo 井上和夫. *Hampō bakufuhō to ishinhō* 藩法幕府法と維新法 (Laws of the feudal domains, the law of the Shogunate, and law of the restoration). Tokyo: Ganshōdō Shoten 嚴松堂書店, 1941. 2 vols.

Ishii Ryōsuke 石井良助. *Meiji bunkashi, hōseihen* 明治文化史, 法制編 (History of Meiji culture, part on legal institutions). Tokyo: Kaikoku Hyakunen Kinen Bunka Jigyōkai 開國百年記念文化事業會, 1954. 679 pp.

This is the latest and most complete history of Japanese law from 1868 to 1912. It includes a useful chronology of events important to legal history, pp. 651–76. It has been translated into English under the title: Ishii, *Japanese Legislation in the Meiji.* Translated by Chambliss, 1958. 741 pp.

Iwamatsu Saburō 岩松三郎. *Minji saiban no kenkyū* 民事裁判の研究 (A study of civil litigation). Tokyo: Kōbundō 弘文堂, 1961. 179 pp.

Kaneko Hajime 兼子一. *Hanrei minji soshōhō* 判例民事訴訟法 (Precedents on the Code of Civil Procedure). Tokyo: Kōbundō 弘文堂, 1950. 479 pp.

———. *Minji soshōhō* 民事訴訟法 (Law of civil procedure, part 1). 3rd ed., 7th printing. Tokyo: Yūhikaku 有斐閣, 1962. 333 pp.

———. *Minji soshōhō* 民事訴訟法 (Law of civil procedure). *Hōritsugaku kōza* 法律學講座 (Lecture series on legal studies). Tokyo: Kōbundō 弘文堂, 1954. 256 pp.

———. *Minji soshōhō gairon* 民事訴訟法概論 (General discussion of the Code of Civil Procedure). Tokyo: Iwanami Shoten 岩波書店, 1937–38. 3 vols.

———. *Minji soshōhō taikei* 民事訴訟法体系 (Outline of the Code of Civil Procedure). Tokyo: Sakai Shoten 酒井書店, 1956. 537 pp.

Katayama Tetsu 片山哲. *Jinji chōteihō gaisetsu* 人事調停法概説 (General survey of the conciliation law for personal affairs). Tokyo: Ganshōdō 巖松堂, 1939. 197 pp.

Katō Masaharu 加藤正治. *Kaisei minji soshōhō gaisetsu* 改正民事訴訟法概説 (General survey of the revised Code of Civil Procedure). Tokyo: Yūhikaku 有斐閣, 1937. 198 pp.

Kawashima Takeyoshi 川島武宜 *et al.* compilers. *Iriaiken no kaitai* 入會權の解体 (The breakup of the right to commons). Tokyo: Iwanami Shoten 岩波書店, Vol. I: 1959 (361 pp.); Vol. II: 1961 (526 pp.); Vol. III: in preparation.

————. *Nihon shakai no kazokuteki kōsei* 日本社會の家族的構成 (The familial structure of Japanese society). Tokyo: Nihon Hyōronsha 日本評論社, 1959. 207 pp.

Kikui Tsunahiro 菊井維大. *Minji soshōhō* 民事訴訟法 (Law of civil procedure) (part 2). 20th printing. Tokyo: Yūhikaku 有斐閣, 1962. 414 pp.

Kiyoura Keigo 清浦奎吾. *Meiji hōseishi* 明治法制史 (Legal history of the Meiji era). Tokyo: Meihōdō 明法堂, 1899. 614 pp.

Kobayakawa Kingo 小早川欣吾. *Meiji hōseishi ron* 明治法制史論 (A treatise on the legal history of the Meiji era). Tokyo: Ganshōdō Shoten 巖松堂書店, 1940. 2 vols.

Koyama Noboru 小山昇. *Minji chōteihō gaisetsu* 民事調停法概説 (General survey of civil conciliation law). Tokyo: Yūhikaku 有斐閣, 1954. 245 pp.

Mikazuki Akira 三ヶ月章 and Nakata Junichi 中田淳一, ed. *Kēsu bukku minji soshōhō* ケースブック. 民事訴訟法 (Casebook on civil procedure law). Tokyo: Yūshindo 有信堂, 1961. 284+30 pp.

Miyazaki Sumio 宮崎澄夫. *Chōteihō no riron to jissai* 調停法の理論と實際 (The theory and practice of conciliation law). Tokyo: Tōyō Shokan 東洋書館, 1942. 295 pp.

Nakagawa Zennosuke 中川善之助 and Miyazawa Toshiyoshi 宮澤俊義, *Hōritsushi* 法律史 (History of law). 5 *Gendai Nihon bunmeishi* 現代日本文明史 (History of contemporary Japanese civilization). Tokyo: Tōyō Keizai Shimpōsha Shuppambu 東洋經濟新報社出版部, 1944. 258+256 pp.

Nakajima Hiromichi 中島弘道. *Nihon minji soshōhō* 日本民事訴訟法 (The Japanese Code of Civil Procedure). Tokyo: Shōkadō Shoten 松華堂書店, 1934. 2 vols.

Nakamura Muneo 中村宗雄. *Hanrei minji soshō kenkyū* 判例民事訴訟研究 (A study of the precedents on the Code of Civil Procedure). Tokyo: Ganshōdō Shoten 巖松堂書店, 1939. 1 vol.

Nihon Bengoshi Rengōkai 日本辯護士連合會. *Bengoshi rinri* 辯護士

倫理 (Morals for lawyers). Tokyo: Shihō Kenshūjo 司法研修所, Undated. 3 pp.

———. *Nihon bengoshi enkakushi* 日本辯護士沿革史 (Chronicle of lawyers in Japan). Tokyo: Nihon Bengoshi Rengōkai 日本辯護士連合會, 1959. 434 pp.

Nihon Chōtei Kyōkai Rengōkai 日本調停協會連合會. *Chōtei tokuhon* 調停讀本 (Conciliation reader). Tokyo: Author, 1954. 412 pp.

Ogawa Yasuo 小川保男. *Chōtei no kenkyū* 調停の研究 (A study of conciliation). Tokyo: Nikkō Shoin 日光書院, 1944.

Ōhashi Seiichi 大橋誠一. *Ōbei no chōtei seido* 欧米の調停制度 (Conciliation systems in Europe and America). Tokyo: Nihon Chōtei Kyōkai Rengōkai 日本調停協會連合會, 1958. 43 pp.

Okudaira Masayoshi 奥平昌洪. *Nihon bengoshi-shi* 日本辯護士史 (History of Japanese lawyers). Tokyo: Yūhikaku Shobō 有斐閣書房, 1914. 1439 pp.

Onogi Tsune 小野木常. *Chōteihō gaisetsu* 調停法概説 (General survey of conciliation law). Tokyo: Yūhikaku 有斐閣, 1942. 294 pp.

———. *Minji soshōhō* 民事訴訟法 (Code of Civil Procedure). Kyoto: Yūshindō Kōbunsha 有信堂高文社, 1949. 361 pp.

———. *Minji soshōhō oyobi chōteihō kōgi* 民事訴訟法及調停法講義 (Lectures on the law of civil procedure and the law of conciliation). Kyoto: Usui Shoten 臼井書店, 1949. 335 pp.

Osaka Bengoshikai 大阪辯護士會. *Osaka Bengoshi shikō* 大阪辯護士史稿 (Draft history of the Osaka lawyers). Osaka: Author, 1937. 2 vols.

Osatake Takeshi 尾佐竹猛. *Konan jiken* 湖南事件 (The southern lake incident). Tokyo: Iwanami Shoten 岩波書店, 1951. 231 pp.

———. *Meiji bunkashi to shite no Nihon baishinshi* 明治文化史としての日本陪審史 (Development of the Japanese jury system in the culture of the Meiji period). Tokyo: Hōkōdō Shoten 邦光堂書店, 1926. 176 pp.

———. *Nihon kenseishi taikō* 日本憲政史大綱 (Outline of the history of Japanese constitutional government). Tokyo: Nihon Hyōronsha 日本評論社, 1938–39. 2 vols.

Saikō Saibansho Jimu Sōkyoku 最高裁判所事務總局, compiler. *Chōtei no tebiki* 調停の手引 (A guide to conciliation). Tokyo: Supreme Court Publication, 1951. 21 pp.

———, ed. *Chōtei tokuhon* 調停讀本 (Conciliation reader). Tokyo: Supreme Court Publication, 1954. 412 pp.

———, compiler. *Saikin ni okeru chōtei jiken no gaikyō ni tsuite* 最近に於ける調停事件の概況について (Concerning the condition of contemporary conciliation cases). Tokyo: Supreme Court Publication, 1953. 31 pp.

————, compiler. *Wagakuni ni okeru chōtei seido no enkaku* わが國における調停制度の沿革 (The development of the conciliation system in our country). Tokyo: Supreme Court Publication, 1951. 101 pp.

Shihō-shō 司法省. *Shihō enkakushi* 司法沿革誌 (History of the development of the judiciary). Tokyo: Hōsōkai 法曹會, 1939. 837 pp.

Shimizu Chō 清水澄. *Meiji igo ni okeru gyōsei hōki no enkaku* 明治以後に於ける行政法規の沿革 (History of administrative regulations after the Meiji era), in *Iwanami Kōza, Nihon rekishi* (no. 11). Tokyo: Iwanami Shoten 岩波書店, 1935.

Suzuki Yasuzō 鈴木安蔵. *Hōritsushi* 法律史 (History of law), in *Nihon gendaishi taikei*. Tokyo: Tōyō Keizai Shimpōsha 東洋經濟新報社, 1961. 432 pp.

Tanimura Tadaichirō 谷村唯一郎, compiler. *Bengoshi-shi* 辯護士史 (History of [Japanese] lawyers). Tokyo: Tōkyō Bengoshikai 東京辯護士會, 1939. No continuous paging, 42＋45＋49 pp.

Terajima Yoshimatsu 寺島由松 *et al. Kaji chōtei kaisetsu* 家事調停解説 (Explanation of conciliation of family affairs). Tokyo: Nihon Bengoshi Kyōkai 日本辯護士協會, 1952. 55 pp.

Togashi Mitsusaburō 富樫光三郎. *Chōtei no tebiki* 調停の手引 (A guide to conciliation). Tokyo: Tōkyō Chihō Saibansho 東京地方裁判所, 1952. 24 pp.

Tōyama Shigeki 遠山茂樹. *Meiji ishin* 明治維新 (The Meiji restoration). Tokyo: Iwanami Shoten 岩波書店, 1951. 368 pp.

Tsuda Susumu 津田進, ed. *Chōtei no arikata* 調停の在り方 (The nature of conciliation). Kanazawa: Kanazawa Chōtei Kyōkai 金澤調停協會, 1953. 97 pp.

Ukai Nobushige 鵜飼信成 *et al.*, compilers. *Kōza Nihon kindaihō hattatsu-shi* 講座日本近代法發達史 (Series on history of the development of modern Japanese law). Tokyo: Keisō Shobō 勁草書房, 1958–61. 10 vols.

Yamazaki Tasuku 山崎佐. *Nihon chōtei seido no rekishi* 日本調停制度の歴史 (History of Japanese conciliation system). Tokyo: Nihon Chōtei Kyōkai Rengōkai 日本調停協會連合會, 1957. 126 pp.

15. *Modern Collections of Essays*

Hōken isei 封建遺制 (Remnants of feudalism). Compiled by Nihon Jimbun Kagakkai 日本人文科學會. 2nd ed. Tokyo: Yūhikaku 有斐閣, 1952. 334 pp.

Hōkensei to wa nani ka 封建制とは何か (What is the so-called feudalism?). *Shisō* no. 302, special issue. 1949.

Meiji hōsei sōkō 明治法制叢考 (Collection of essays on Meiji legal history). Kobayakawa Kingo 小早川欣吾. Kyoto: Kyōto Insho kan 京都印書館, 1945. 304 pp.

Zoku Meiji hōsei sōkō 續明治法制叢考 (Supplement to collection of essays on Meiji legal history). Kobayakawa Kingo 小早川欣吾. Kyoto: Yamaguchi Shoten 山口書店, 1944. 444 pp.

16. *Modern Articles and Essays on Law*

Although much work is now in progress in Japan, the legal history of the Meiji period is still relatively undeveloped, and consequently the most provocative work is found in specific studies scattered throughout the scholarly journals. The increase of scholarly interest in the social efficacy of law, especially during the last ten years, is also quite evident in the periodical literature, both on historical and current topics. The following list includes only articles cited or consulted in this study.

Akiyama Kazuo 明山和夫. "Kaji chōtei seido kanken" 家事調停制度管見 (Views on the system of family conciliation), *Kēsu kenkyū* (no. 80) 31–41 (1963).

Amano Takeichi 天野武一. "Hōsō jinkō" 法曹人口 (Lawyer population), *Jurisuto* (no. 249) 40–63 (1962).

Azegami Eiji 畔上英治. "Minji soshō ni okeru soshō shiki" 民事訴訟における訴訟指揮 (Supervision of lawsuits in the civil cases), *Jurisuto* (no. 156) 10–17 (1958).

———. "Minji soshō o miru kakudo" 民事訴訟をみる角度 (An angle from which to view civil suits), 30 *Hōritsu jihō* 1263–66 (1958).

Chiba Masashi 千葉正士. "Hōritsu to hōritsuka no shakaiteki seikaku" 法律と法律家の社會的性格 (Law and social character of lawyers), 10 *Jiyū to seigi* (no. 6) 12–15 (1959).

Chigusa Tatsuo 千種達夫. "Chōtei tokushū" 調停特集 (Special collection on conciliation), *Jurisuto* (no. 20) 2–31 (1952).

———. "Chūsai to chōtei no hōri" 仲裁と調停の法理 (Legal theory of arbitration and conciliation), 6 *Sōgō hōgaku* (no. 3) 2–31 (1963).

———. "Minji saibankan kara bengoshi e no kibō" 民事裁判官から弁護士への希望 (A request by a civil judge to lawyers), 10 *Jiyū to seigi* (no. 3) 11–14 (1959).

———. "Rikon to wakai, ichi, ni" 離婚と和解 (一), (二) (Divorce and compromise [nos. 1 and 2]), *Jurisuto* (no. 30) 8–11 and (no. 31) 5–7 and 18 (1953).

―――. "Saiban to wakai" 裁判と和解 (Litigation and compromise), 13 *Hanrei taimuzu* 26–30 (1951).

―――. "Saikin no chōtei jiken no dōkō" 最近の調停事件の動向 (The tendency of recent conciliation cases), *Hanrei taimuzu* (no. 3) 49–55 (1948).

Dandō Shigemitsu 団藤重光. "Shihō seido no kakuritsu" 司法制度の確立 (The establishment of the judicial system), 58 *Kokka gakkai zasshi* 148–83 (1944).

Endō Makoto 遠藤誠. "Ureubeki wakai chōtei no seikyō" 憂うべき和解調停の盛況 (The lamentable success of conciliation and compromise), 33 *Hōritsu jihō* 496–501 (1961).

Harada Keikichi 原田慶吉. "Nihon mimpō sōsokuhen no shiteki sobyō" 日本民法總則編の史的素描 (A historical sketch of the book on the general provisions of the Japanese Civil Code), 57 *Hōgaku kyōkai zasshi* 593–633, 1020–52, and 1265–87 (1939).

Hattori Sadao 服部定雄. "Kōnin kaikeishi to bengoshi to no kengyō nado ni tsuite" 公認會計士と辯護士の兼業等について (Concerning the overlap of C. P. A. and lawyer business, etc.), 10 *Jiyū to seigi* (no. 3) 16–17 (1959).

Hirano Ryūichi 平野龍一. "Shokugyō saibankan to shirōto saibankan" 職業裁判官と素人裁判官 (Professional judges and amateur judges), 29 *Hōritsu jihō* (no. 4) 11–17 (1957).

Hironaka Toshio 廣中俊雄. "Gōi ni sōtō suru shimpan no unyō o megutte" 合意に相當する審判の運用をめぐって (Involving the operation of "judgment substituted for agreement"), *Jurisuto* (no. 250) 36–38 (1962).

―――. "Hō to saiban, ichi, ni" 法と裁判 (一), (二) (Law and litigation [nos. 1 and 2]), *Jurisuto* (no. 119) 39, 72; and (no. 120) 52–58 (1956).

―――. "Keisatsukan no hatasu hōteki kinō ni tsuite" 警察官のはたす法的機能について (Concerning the legal functions performed by police officers), *Jurisuto* (no. 78) 31–35 (1955).

―――. "Shimin no kenri no kakuho to minji saiban—minji funsō no shori ni okeru saiban no kinō" 市民の權利の確保と民事裁判—民事紛爭の處理における裁判の機能 (Securing of citizens' rights and civil litigation—function of litigation in settling civil disputes), 32 *Hōritsu jihō* 1002–8 (1960).

Hizume Akimichi 樋瓜彰道. "Kanazawa katei saibansho ni okeru yakan shitsumu no jissai" 金澤家庭裁判所における夜間執務の實際 (The practice of night-time work in the Kanazawa Family Court), *Jurisuto* (no. 89) 6–11 (1955).

Hōritsu jihō henshūbu 法律時報編集部 "Wakai chōtei to wa donna

seido ka" 和解調停とはどんな制度か (What sort of systems are compromise and conciliation?), 28 *Hōritsu jihō* (no. 2) 58–60 (1956).

Horiuchi Setsu 堀内節, Ōhashi Seiichi 大橋誠一, Mori Seiichirō 森盛一郎, Akine Kyūta 秋根久太, Katō Akira 加藤晃, Ōhama Eiko 大濱英子, Shiobara Shizuka 塩原しづか. "Chōtei seido no hatten no tame ni" 調停制度の發展のために (In order to develop the conciliation system), *Jurisuto* (no. 20) 17–25 (1952).

Hozumi Shigetō 穂積重遠. *Chōteihō* 調停法 (Conciliation law), 38 *Gendai hōgaku zenshū* 現代法學全集 (Complete collection on modern jurisprudence), 229–78 (1931).

Ienaga Saburō 家永三郎. "Nihon ni okeru saiban no shisōshiteki kōsatsu" 日本における裁判の思想史的考察 (A review of the Japanese litigation from the standpoint of the history of thought), *Shisō* (no. 432) 730–52 (1960).

Ikura Hitoshi 井倉均. "Chōtei ni yoru shihō kankei no shūsei" 調停による私法關係の修正 (Adjustment of private law relations through conciliation), 29 *Shihō kenkyū* (no. 17) (1941).

Imai Michinori 今井道鑑. "Chōtei (saiban jō no wakai o fukumu) no kashi to sono kyūsai" 調停(裁判上の和解を含む)の瑕疵とその救濟 (Defects in conciliation—including compromise during trial—and their cure), 37 *Minshōhō zasshi* 35–56 (1958).

Ishii Ryōsuke 石井良助. "Mimpōten no hensan" 民法典の編纂 (Compilation of the civil code), 58 *Kokka gakkai zasshi* 184–221 (1944).

Ishii Ryōzō 石井良三. "Shakuchi shakka jiken no shihōteki shori" 借地借家事件の司法的處理 (Judicial disposition of land lease and house lease cases), *Jurisuto* (no. 117) 16–22 (1956).

Kainō Michitaka 戒能通孝. "Jijitsu nintei to saibankan" 事實認定と裁判官 (Fact-finding and judges), 9 *Jiyū to seigi* (no. 9) 4–9 (1958).

——— *et al.* "Minji chōtei—genjō to hihan" 民事調停—現狀と批判 (Civil conciliation—present condition and criticism), 28 *Hōritsu jihō* (no. 2) 148–76 and 196–211 (1956).

———. "Mimpō to kaji chōtei" 民法と家事調停 (Civil code and family conciliation), 28 *Hōritsu jihō* (no. 2) 148–53 (1956).

———. "Minsohō riron to saiban no jissai" 民訴法理論と裁判の實際 (Theories of civil procedural law and litigation practice), 28 *Hōritsu jihō* (no. 8) 22–34 (1956).

——— *et al.* "Nihon no bengoshi" 日本の辯護士 (Japanese lawyers), 32 *Hōritsu jihō* (no. 5) 432–566 (1960).

Kaneko Hajime 兼子一. "Minji soshōhō no seitei—Tehhyō no sōan o chūshin to shite" 民事訴訟法の制定—テッヒョウの草案を中心と

して (Establishment of the Code of Civil Procedure—centered around the Techow's draft), *Tōkyō daigaku gakujutsu taikan* 223–34 (1942).

———. "Soshō chien to shihō seisaku" 訴訟遅延と司法政策 (Delay of litigation and judicial policy), 30 *Hōritsu jihō* 1248–50 (1958).

——— *et al.* "Soshō no sokushin to kōsei na saiban" 訴訟の促進と公正な裁判 (Acceleration of law suits and fair litigation), 31 *Hōritsu jihō* 4–51 (1959).

Kaneko Hajime 兼子一, Yanagawa Masao 柳川眞佐夫, and Kume Ai 久米愛. "'Chōtei' utagainaki ni shimo arazu" 「停調」疑なきにしもあらず (Conciliation is not without problems), *Jurisuto* (no. 20) 26–31 (Oct. 15, 1952).

Kanesue Tashio 金末多志雄, "Minji saiban chien to sono taisaku chōtei zenchi-shugi jisshi no teishō" 民事裁判遅延とその対策—調停前置主義実施の提唱 (Delay in civil trials and countermeasures therefore—a proposal to require preliminary conciliation), *Chōtei jihō* (no. 35) 15–19 (1963) and (no. 36) 14–16 (1963).

Katō Masaharu 加藤正治. "Kaisei minji soshōhō to shokken shugi" 改正民事訴訟法と職權主義 (The revised Code of Civil Procedure and the inquisitorial principle), 1 *Hōritsu jihō* 13–17 (1929).

Kawashima Takeyoshi 川島武宜, Kobori Kensuke 小堀憲助, Tanaka Hideo 田中英夫, Taira Ryō 平良 and Tanikawa Hisashi 谷川久. "Amerika no hōgaku kyōiku to shimin seikatsu ni okeru hōishiki" アメリカの法學教育と市民生活における法意識 (American legal education and legal consciousness in the life of the citizen), *Jurisuto* (no. 177) 42–51 (1959).

Kawashima Takeyoshi 川島武宜 *et al.* "Chōtei seido no jitsujō to kekkan, ichi, ni" 調停制度の實情と欠陥 (一), (二) (The actual condition and deficiency of the conciliation system [nos. 1 and 2]), 28 *Hōritsu jihō* (no. 2) 177–95; and (no. 3) 347–65 (1956).

———. "Kazoku seido no fukkatsu" 家族制度の復活 (The resurrection of the family system), *Jurisuto* (no. 73) 41–47 and 40 (1955).

———. "Shakai kōzō to saiban" 社會構造と裁判 (Social structure and litigation), *Shisō* (no. 432) 1–17 (1960).

Kikui Tsunahiro 菊井維大. "Tōjisha shugi no seigen—Kaisei Doitsu minji soshōhō gaikan" 當事者主義の制限—改正獨逸民事訴訟法概觀 (Limitation of the party-presentation principle—the general view of the revised German Code of Civil Procedure), 42 *Hōgaku kyōkai zasshi* 2009–46 (1924).

Kobayakawa Kingo 小早川欣吾. "Hōgen" 法源 (Sources of the law), *Zoku Meiji hōsei sōkō* 429–44 (1944).

This article deals with the law of security, but it gives interesting details on the influences from the customary as well as European law.

──── . "Kyūmimpōten hensan katei to kyūmimpōten ni taisuru ronsō ni tsuite" 舊民法典編纂過程と舊民法典に對する論争につ いて (Concerning the process of compiling the old Civil Code and the argument against the old Civil Code), *Zoku Meiji hōsei sōkō* 208–406 (1944).

──── . "Meyasubako ni tōnyū saretaru ni san no kempakusho" 目安箱に投入されたる二, 三の建白書 (Two or three petitions put in the plaint box), *Meiji hōsei sōkō* 214–57 (1945).

Koishi Hisao 小石壽夫. "Kaji chōtei ni kansuru hitotsu no chōsa hōkoku" 家事調停に關する一つの調査報告 (One research report concerning conciliation of family matters), *Hanrei taimuzu* (no. 6) 31–34 (1950).

Kokubo Yoshinori 小久保義憲. "Kaji chōtei ni arawareta tōjisha shuchō no shujusō" 家事調停に現われた當事者主張の種々相 (Various aspects of litigants' contentions as seen in the family conciliation), 9 *Jiyū to seigi* (no. 11) 35–36 (1958).

Kōno Tsutomu 河野力. "Saikin ni okeru kaji chōtei ni tsuite" 最近における家事調停について (Concerning recent family conciliation), 30 *Hōritsu jihō* (no. 3) 33–39 (1958).

Koyama Noboru 小山昇. "Chōteihō, chūsaihō" 調停法, 仲裁法 (Conciliation law, arbitration law), 38 *Hōritsugaku zenshū* 1–108 (1959).

──── . "Chōtei seido" 調停制度 (Conciliation system), *Jurisuto* (no. 100) 82–84 (1956).

──── . "Hanketsu igai no soshō shūryō gen-in" 判決以外の訴訟終了原因 (Causes other than trial judgment terminating lawsuits), 6 *Hōgaku seminā* 22–25 (1957).

──── . "Saiban jō no wakai" 裁判上の和解 (Compromise during trial), 3 *Sōgō hanrei kenkyū sōsho: minji soshōhō* 42–130 (1961).

──── . "Soshō jō no wakai to chōtei" 訴訟上の和解と調停 (Conciliation and compromise during suit), *Shihō* (no. 9) 104–15 (1953).

Kozeki Toshimasa 古關敏正. "Saibankan yori bengoshi e no chūmon" 裁判官より辯護士への注文 (A request from a judge to lawyers), 12 *Jiyū to seigi* (no. 8) 2–6 (1961).

──── . "Shinkembu no setchi" 新件部の設置 (Establishment of the new case section), 11 *Hōsō jihō* 1202–39 (1959).

Kurihara Yukio 栗原幸男. "Rikon chōtei jiken tōjisha ni taisuru tankikan no kaunseringu (Short-term counseling) no kokoromi" 離婚調停事件当事者に対する短期間のカウンセリングの試み ── ケ ース研究 (An attempt to do short-term counseling for persons concerned in a conciliation divorce case—case study), *Chōtei kiyō* (no. 5) 61–69 (1964).

Mabuchi Kenzō 馬淵健三. "Chōtei seido no kenkyū" 調停制度の研究 (A study of the conciliation system), 19 *Shihō kenkyū* (no. 9) (1935).

Maki Kenji 牧健二. "Meiji hachinen minji saiban no gensoku" 明治八年民事裁判の原則 (General principles of civil litigation in 1875), 17 *Hōgaku ronsō* 349–52 (1927).

———. "Meiji shonen ni okeru minji saiban no kannen" 明治初年に於ける民事裁判の觀念 (The concept of civil litigation in the first years of the Meiji period), 12 *Shirin* 85–93 (1927).

Makino Eiichi 牧野英一. "Chōteisei no tenkai" 調停制の展開 (Development of the conciliation system), 11 *Hōritsu jōhō* 388–89 (1939).

Matsuda Jirō 松田二郎. "Amerika yori kaerite" アメリカより歸りて (Coming home from America), *Shihō kenshūjohō* (no. 16) 2–58 (1955).

Matsui Yasuhiro 松井康浩. "Bengoshi no seikatsu to ishiki" 辯護士の生活と意識 (Life and thought of lawyers), 32 *Hōritsu jihō* (no. 5) 24–55 (1960).

Miyake Shōtarō 三宅正太郎. "Chōteihō" 調停法 (Conciliation law), 12 *Shin hōgaku zenshū* 1–83, separate paging (1937).

Miyazaki Sumio 宮崎澄夫. "Chōtei to yu koto" 調停ということ (The so-called conciliation), *Jurisuto* (no. 20) 2 (1952).

Miyazaki Toshiyuki 宮崎俊行. "Chūgoku chōteihō josetsu" 中國調停法序説 (Introduction to Chinese [Communist] conciliation law), 33 *Hōgaku kenkyū* 507–25 (1960).

Mizumoto Nobuo 水本信夫. "Chōteihō no bunkateki kachi" 調停法の文化的價値 (The cultural value of conciliation law), *Hōritsu shimbun* 2144 (1923).

Muramatsu Toshio 村松俊夫. "Shakumeiken" 釈明權 (Right to request elucidation), *Sōgō hanrei kenkyū sōsho*, 1 *Minji soshōhō* 98–161 (1958).

Nagashima Takeshi 長島毅. "Kaisei minji soshōhō ni okeru benron shūchū shugi" 改正民事訴訟法における辯論集中主義 (Principle of concentrated adversary principle in the revised Code of Civil Procedure), 1 *Hōritsu jihō* 7–10 (1929).

Nakada Kaoru 中田薫. "Furansuhō yunyū no senku" 佛蘭西法輸入の先驅 (A pioneer of importation of French law into Japan), 3 *Hōseishi ronshū* 905–21 (1943).

Nakagawa Tsuyoshi 中川毅. "Kyōsei chōtei no ikensei" 強制調停の違憲性 (Unconstitutionality of compulsory conciliation), 8 *Hanrei taimuzu* 42–45 (1957).

Nakajima Kōdō 中島弘道. "Chōtei jōkō to kore ni kansuru ichi kōsatsu" 調停條項とこれに關する一考察 (The conciliation provisions and a view concerning them), 12 *Hōritsu jihō* (no. 6) 602–12 (1940).

Nakajō Masayoshi 中條政好. "Bengoshigyō to zeirishigyō to no kengyō no rigai tokushitsu narabi ni genzai ni okeru sono jittai jissai ni tsuite" 辯護士業と税理士業との兼業の利害得失並びに現在におけるその實態實際について (Concerning present practice and actual conditions, and advantages and disadvantages of the overlap of lawyer business and tax practitioner business), 10 *Jiyū to seigi* (no. 3) 19–21 (1959).

Nakamura Hideo 中村英郎. "Saiban jō no wakai" 裁判上の和解 (Court compromise), *Minji soshō zasshi* (no. 7) 177–243 (1961).

Nakamura Kikuo 中村菊男. "Mimpōten ronsō" 民法典論爭 (Disputes on Civil Code), *Sōgō hōgaku* (nos. 22–27) (May-Oct. 1960).

Nakano Mineo 中野峰夫. "Shin minji soshōhō ni okeru tōjisha shugi to shokken shugi" 新民事訴訟法における當事者主義と職權主義 (The party-presentation and inquisitorial principles in the new Code of Civil Procedure), 7 *Hōsōkai zasshi* (no. 12) 1–18 (1929); and 8 *id.* (no. 2) 13–41; (no. 3) 39–62 (1930).

Nakata Junichi 中田淳一. "Chōtei ni kawaru saiban no gōkensei" 調停に代る裁判の合憲性 (Constitutionality of substitution of trial for conciliation), 35 *Minshōhō zasshi* (no. 4) 605–18 (1957).

―――. "Kaisei minsohō no shomondai—kaisei no yōten to sono kaisetsu narabi ni hihan" 改正民訴法の諸問題―改正の要點とその解説並に批判 (Various problems of the revised Code of Civil Procedure—essential points of revision and an interpretation and critique of them), 23 *Minshōhō zasshi* 350–76 (1948).

Nemoto Matsuo 根本松男. "Minji saiban seido no kaikaku to chōtei zenchi shugi" 民事裁判制度の改革と調停前置主義 (The reformation of the system of civil litigation and the principle of preliminary conciliation), 12 *Hōritsu jihō* (no. 1) 32–33 (1940).

Nibu Yurito 仁分百合人. "Minji soshō ga nagaku kakarisugiru koto to sono taisaku" 民事訴訟が長くかかり過ぎることとその対策 (Countermeasures against delays in civil litigation), *Jurisuto* (no. 265) 18–24 (1963).

Nojima Atsushi 野島厚志. "Gaikokujin no bengonin wa Nihon no hōtei ni tateruka" 外國人の辯護人は日本の法廷に立てるか (Can a foreign lawyer appear in the Japanese court?), 10 *Hōritsu no hiroba* (no. 9) 14–16 (1957).

Noma Shigeru 野間繁. "Shihō saiban to shihō gyōsei" 司法裁判と司法

行政 (Judicial adjudication and judicial administration), *Minji soshō zasshi* (no. 2) 23–69 (1955).

Nomura Satao 野村佐太男. "Bengoshikai e no yōbō" 護護士會への要望 (A demand to the Bar Association), 10 *Jiyū to seigi* (no. 3) 14-16 (1959).

Ogawa Yasuo 小川保男. "Chōtei no honshitsu" 調停の本質 (The essence of conciliation), 16 *Minshōhō zasshi* 229–39 and 358–78 (1942).

Ōhashi Seiichi 大橋誠一 *et al.* " 'Chōtei' o meguru zadankai" 調停を めぐる座談會 (A discussion meeting revolving around "conciliation"), *Jurisuto* (no. 20) 17–25 (Oct. 15, 1952).

Okuno Ken-ichi 奥野健一. "Minji soshōhō kaisei no kōsō" 民事訴訟 法改正の構想 (The structural principle of the revisions of the Code of Civil Procedure), *Hanrei taimuzu* (no. 2) 6–10 (1948).

Onogi Tsune 小野木常. "Chōtei tetsuzuki no kōzō" 調停手續の構造 (The structure of conciliation procedure), 43 *Hōgaku ronsō* 406– 31 and 511–35 (1940).

———. "Manshūkoku ni okeru junkai chōtei" 満州國における巡廻 調停 (The conciliation circuit in Manchuria), 48 *Hōgaku ronsō* 439–47 (1943).

———. "Meiji shoki no minji soshō" 明治初期の民事訴訟 (Civil procedure in the first part of the Meiji period), 49 *Hōgaku ronsō* 169–99, 313–30, 432–64, 605–32, and 659–85 (1943).

———. (reviewer). "Miyazaki kyōju 'Chōteihō no riron to jissai' " 宮崎教授調停法の理論と實際 (Professor Miyazaki's *The theory and practice of conciliation law*), 46 *Hōgaku ronsō* 646–61 (1942).

Osatake Takeshi 尾佐竹猛. "Mutsu Munemitsu no gōmon haishi no gi" 陸奥宗光の拷問廢止の議 (A discussion of the abolition of torture by Mutsu Munemitsu), 16 *Hōsōkai zasshi* (no. 3) 137–46; and (no. 4) 125–38 (1938).

———. "Shihōken no dokuritsu" 司法權の獨立 (Independence of the judicial power), 1 *Rekishigaku kenkyū* 321–27 (1934).

Phoenix. "Kanryō saibankan ze ka hi ka" 官僚裁判官是か非か (Are judges appointed by the government good or bad?), *Jurisuto* (no. 171) 29 (1959).

———. "Shihō chōki keikaku" 司法長期計畫 (A long-term judicial program), *Jurisuto* (no. 145) 55 (1958).

———. "Soshō e no izanai" 訴訟への誘い (Invitation to lawsuits), *Jurisuto* (no. 149) 11 (1958).

Saikō saibansho jimu sōkyoku minjikyoku 最高裁判所事務總局民事局. "Shōwa nijūhachinen-do minji jiken no gaikyō" 昭和二十八年度

民事事件の概況 (The general conditions of civil cases for the year 1953), 6 *Hōsō jihō* 1618–47 (1954).

Articles by the same author and title appear in *Hōsō jihō* each year.

———. "Shōwa sanjūgonen-do minji jiken no gaikyō" 昭和三五年度 民事事件の概況 (The general conditions of civil cases for the year 1960), 13 *Hōsō jihō* 1710–47 (1961).

Saikō saibansho minjikyoku kateikyoku 最高裁判所民事局家庭局 "Saikin ni okeru chōtei jiken no gaikyō ni tsuite" 最近における調 停事件の概況について (With respect to the general condition of recent conciliation cases), 28 *Hōritsu jihō* (no. 2) 61–67 (1956).

Saitō Hideo 齊藤秀夫. "Wagakuni no saibankan no tokushoku" わが 國の裁判官の特色 (The special characteristics of judges in Japan), *Jurisuto* (no. 245) 12–17 (1962).

Saitō Tsunesaburō 齊藤常三郎. "Chōtei narazaru baai no saiban" 調停成らざる場合の裁判 (Trials in cases where settlement is not reached), *Hōritsu shimbun* (no. 4607) 3 (1940).

Sasaki Yoshio 佐々木吉男. "Chihō ni okeru minji chōtei" 地方におけ る民事調停 (Civil conciliation in the rural districts), 32 *Hōritsu jihō* (no. 10) 59–73 (1960).

———. "Minji chōtei ni okeru 'gōi' ni kansuru ichi kentō" 民事調停 における合意に關する一檢討 (A view concerning agreements in civil conciliation), 11 pp. (1962).

This is a preliminary working paper showing the results of a poll taken in both Osaka and Shimane prefectures relating to the actual operations of the conciliation system.

———. "Minji chōtei ni okeru gōi no hōteki seishitsu ni kansuru ichi shiron" 民事調停における合意の法的性質に關する一試論 (An essay concerning the legal quality of agreements in civil conciliation), 7 *Shimadai hōgaku* 31–54 (1962).

———. "Minji chōtei ni okeru 'goi' no kentō" 民事調停における合 意の検討 (Inquiry in "agreements" in civil conciliation), 9 *Kanazawa hōgaku* 1–31 (Dec. 1963).

———. "Minji chōtei ni okeru hōteki handan to jian no kaimei" 民事調停における法的判断と事案の解明 (Fact determination and decisions in accordance with law in civil conciliation), *Minji soshō zasshi* (no. 7) 143–76 (1961).

Sawa Eizō 澤栄三. "Soshō no chien to hōsō jinkō" 訴訟の遅延と法曹 人口 (Delay of lawsuits and lawyer population), *Shōji hōmu kenkyū* (no. 94) 2–5 (1958).

Sekine Kosato 關根小郷. "Minji soshō kisoku to wakai" 民事訴訟規則

と和解 (The Rules of Civil Procedure and compromise), *Jurisuto* (no. 109) 26–28 (1956).

———. "Shihō seido no tōmen suru mondai" 司法制度の当面する問題 (Problems confronting the judicial system), *Jurisuto* (no. 265) 10–168 (1963).

Shimizu Makoto 清水誠. " 'Hōsō' no ishiki kōzō to sono henkaku" 法曹の意識構造とその變革 (The mental structure of "legal professionals" and its reformation), *Shisō* (no. 432) 753–69 (1960).

Shimomitsu Gunji 下光軍二. "Hikusugiru naien no tsuma no isharyō" 低過ぎる内縁の妻の慰籍料 (Too little alimony for informal wives), *Jurisuto* (no. 138) 24–32 (1957).

Shindō Kōji 新堂幸司. "Kyōsei chōtei o iken to suru kettei ni tsuite" 強制調停を違憲とする決定について (Concerning rulings declaring compulsory conciliation unconstitutional), *Jurisuto* (no. 209) 44–49 (1960).

———. "Soshō no sokushin to kōsei naru saiban" 訴訟の促進と公正 なる裁判 (Expediting lawsuits and a fair trial), 30 *Hōritsu jihō* 1248–93 (1958).

Suekawa Hiroshi 末川博 *et al.* "Chōtei ni kawaru saiban no gōkensei o megutte" 調停に代る裁判の合憲性をめぐって (Involving the constitutionality of trial substituted for conciliation), 35 *Minshōhō zasshi* 56–82 (1957).

Takanashi Kimiyuki 高梨公之 *et al.* "Kaji chōtei no kagakuka" 家事 調停の科學化 (Making a science of family conciliation), 30 *Hōritsu jihō* (no. 3) 276–349 (1958).

Takano Tsuruo 高野弦雄. "Nihon ni okeru bengoshi no rinri echiketto ni tsuite" 日本における辯護士の倫理エチケットについて (Concerning morals and etiquette of Japanese lawyers), 9 *Jiyū to seigi* (no. 12) 8–12 (1958).

Takayanagi Kenzō 高柳賢三. "Iken no shinsa, ichi, ni, san" 違憲の審査 (一) (二) (三) (Review for unconstitutionality, [1], [2], [3]), *Jurisuto* (no. 155) 22–30; (no. 156) 26–36; and (no. 157) 42–52 (1958).

Takiuchi Reisaku 滝内禮作 *et al.* "Hōtei gijutsu no kentō" 法廷技術の 検討 (Review of technique in the court), 33 *Hōritsu jihō* (no. 12) 4–87 (1961).

Tanabe Shigeko 田邊繁子 and Ōhama Eiko 大濱英子. "Kyōgi rikon no jittai chōsa" 協議離婚の實態調査 (An empirical study of divorce by agreement), 30 *Hōritsu jihō* (no. 3) 337–41 (1958).

Tanaka Kazuo 田中和夫. "Benron shugi" 辯論主義 (The adversary principle), 5 *Minshōhō zasshi* 315–40 (1937).

Tanaka Kōtarō 田中耕太郎. "Chōkan jūnen o kaerimite" 長官十年を顧みて (Reflecting upon the past ten years as Chief Justice of the Supreme Court), 120 *Hōsō* 1–6 (1960).

———. "Chōtei to saiban" 調停と裁判 (Conciliation and litigation), *Asahi shimbun* (Oct. 10, 1957).

Taniguchi Tomohei 谷口知平. "Kaji chōtei iin no shakai kaisō to shisō" 家事調停委員の社會階層と思想 (Social class and thought of committees of family conciliation), 30 *Hōritsu jihō* (no. 3) 21–26 (1958).

Taniguchi Yasuhei 谷口安平. "Junzentaru soshōjiken ni tsuki nasareta chōtei ni kawaru saiban no kōryoku" 純然たる訴訟事件につきなされた調停に代る裁判の効力 (The effect of substitution of trial for conciliation which was applied to a case which started as a pure lawsuit), 68 *Hōgaku ronsō* (no. 1) 120–35 (1960).

Terada Kumao 寺田熊雄. "Bengoshi gyōmu no hatten hōsaku" 辯護士業務の發展方策 (A plan for the development of lawyer business), 10 *Jiyū to seigi* (no. 3) 21–22 (1959).

Tsuneda Bunji 恒田文次. "Minji saiban seido ni okeru chōtei no shimei" 民事裁判制度における調停の使命 (Mission of conciliation in civil trial system), 1 *Aoyama hōgaku ronshū* (nos. 1 and 2, a bound volume) 113–34 (1959).

Udagawa Junshirō 宇田川潤四郎. "Katei saibansho no yakan chōtei" 家庭裁判所の夜間調停 (The night-time conciliation in the family court), *Jurisuto* (no. 89) 2–6 (1955).

Yamakido Katsumi 山木戸克己. "Kaji shimpan-hō" 家事審判法 (The Law for Adjustment of Domestic Affairs), 38 *Hōritsugaku zenshū* 1–124 (1959).

———. "Wakai tetsuzuki no taishō—wakai tetsuzuki to keiyaku no kōshō" 和解手續の對象—和解手續と契約の公証 (The object of compromise procedure—compromise procedure and notarization of contracts), 11 *Kōbe hōgaku zasshi* 1–24 (1952).

Yano Teruo 矢野照男. "Kaji chōtei to pāsonaritī rikai o meguru shomondai—sono shinriteki aprōchi" (shiryō) 家事調停とパーソナリティー理解をめぐる諸問題 — その心理的アプローチ — (資料) (Some problems centering around family conciliation and comprehension of personality—psychological approach to them [materials]), *Chōtei kiyō* (no. 5) 97–107 (1964).

Yasuda Mikita 安田幹太. "Shihō tenka no dankai to shite no chōtei" 私法轉化の段階としての調停 (Conciliation as a step in transforming the private law), 51 *Hōgaku kyōkai zasshi* 611–52, 909–45, 1015–45, and 1248–83 (1933).

Yokokawa Toshio 横川敏雄. "Soshō sokushin ni kansuru kisoku ni

tsuite, ichi, ni" 訴訟促進に關する規則について（一）（二）(Concerning rules for acceleration of lawsuits [1], [2]), 23 *Hōritsu jihō* (no. 2) 33–41; and (no. 3) 46–51 (1951).

Yoshimura Hiroyoshi 吉村弘義 and Horiuchi Setsu 堀内節. "Kaji chōtei wa mimpō o nashikuzushi ni hakai suru ka" 家事調停は民法をなしくずしに破壊するか (Will domestic conciliation gradually destroy the civil law?), 9 *Hōritsu no hiroba* (no. 4) 30–37 (1956).

PART II: WESTERN LANGUAGE SOURCES

17. *General References, Bibliographies, and Dictionaries*

A Bibliography on Foreign and Comparative Law Books and Articles in English. Compiled by Charles Szladits. New York: Columbia University Press, 1955. 508 pp.

"Congestion and Delay: A Selected Bibliography of Recent Materials." Compiled by Fannie J. Klein. *U.S. Attorney-General's Conference on Court Congestion and Delay in Litigation Proceedings* 212–45 (1958).

Dictionary of Philosophy. Ed. by Dagobert D. Runes. New York: Philosophical Library, Inc., no date. 342 pp.

Encyclopedia of World History. Compiled by William L. Langer. Cambridge, Mass.: The Riverside Press, 1952. 1243 pp.

A Guide to Japanese Reference and Research Materials in the Field of Political Science. By Robert H. Ward. Ann Arbor: University of Michigan Press, 1950. 104 pp.

Handbook of Oriental History. Ed. by C. H. Phillips. London: Royal Historical Society, 1951. 265 pp.

Historical and Geographical Dictionary of Japan. By E. Papinot. Ann Arbor, Mich.: Overbeck Company, 1948. 842 pp.

Historical Grammar of Japanese. By George B. Sansom. Oxford: Clarendon Press, 1946. 347 pp.

Japanese History: A Guide to Japanese Reference and Research Materials. By John W. Hall. Ann Arbor: University of Michigan Press, 1954. 165 pp.

Japan Science Review, Law and Politics. Ed. by Union of Japanese Societies of Law and Politics. Tokyo: Editor, from 1950. Annually.

Number 2 of this annual publication begins a practice of listing selected publications in various fields of law and politics. Annotations add to the convenience of these bibliographies. The coverage is very selective.

Judicial Administration and the Legal Profession; A Bibliography. Compiled by Fannie J. Klein. Dobbs Ferry, N.Y.: Oceana, 1963. 650 pp.

"Selected Annotated Bibliographies on Judicial Selection and Court Administration," 45 *J. Am. Jud. Soc'y.* (no. 8) 17–28 (1962).

Selected List of Books and Articles on Japan in English, French and German. Compiled by Hugh Borton, Serge Elisseeff, William W. Lockwood, and John C. Pelzel. Cambridge, Mass.: Harvard University Press, 1954. 272 pp.

18. *Japanese Government Publications in English*

Japan. Printing Office, National Diet. *The Official Gazette Extra.*
These extras include translations of the discussions on the floor of the Diet.

Japan. Supreme Court. *The Civil Code of Japan.* Tokyo: Author, 1959. 208 pp.

Japan. Supreme Court. *The Court Organization Law and Regulations Concerning the Departmental Organization of the General Secretariat of the Supreme Court.* Tokyo, 1950. 65 pp.

Japan. Supreme Court. General Secretariat. *The Family Court Jurisdiction in Japan.* By Junshirō Udagawa, Judge of Tokyo High Court and Director of Family Bureau. Tokyo: General Secretariat, 1954. 10 pp.

Japan. Supreme Court. General Secretariat. *A Guide to the Japanese Family Court.* Tokyo: General Secretariat, 1961. 27 pp.

Japan. Supreme Court. *Law for Adjustment of Domestic Relations* (1948). *EHS Law Bulletin Series* Vol. II (L-Z). 1954. 12 pp.

Japan. Supreme Court. *The Law of Civil Procedure.* Tokyo, 1959.

Japan. Supreme Court. Liaison Section, General Secretariat. *The Rules of Criminal Procedure.* Tokyo, 1948. 491 pp.

Japan. Supreme Court. *Organization and Procedure Chart of Japanese Courts.* Tokyo: General Secretariat, 1961. 5 pp.

Japan. Supreme Court. *Outline of a Civil Trial in Japan.* Tokyo: Supreme Court, 1955. 17 pp.

Japan. Supreme Court. *Outline of Japanese Judicial System.* Tokyo: General Secretariat, 1961. 76 pp.

19. *Miscellaneous*

Commerce Clearing House. *Labor Law Reporter.* 4th ed.

EHS Law Bulletin Series (Japan). Editor, Nakane Fukio. Tokyo: Eibun Hōreisha, from 1955.
This is comprised of several volumes of English translations of the Japanese codes and important other laws.

20. *Books, Pamphlets, and Monographs*

Adams, Henry *et al. Essays in Anglo-Saxon Law.* Cambridge: Wilson and Sons, 1876.

Akagi, Roy Hidemichi. *Japan's Foreign Relations.* Tokyo: Hokuseidō Press, 1936. 560 pp.

American Bar Association. *Lawyers' Economic Problems and Some Bar Association Solutions.* Chicago: Bancroft-Whitney Co. and The Lawyers Co-operative Publishing Co., Undated (about 1959). 32 pp.

American Bar Foundation. *The 1961 Lawyer Statistical Report.* Chicago: American Bar Foundation, 1961. 146 pp.

Ames, James B. *Lectures on Legal History.* Cambridge, Mass.: Harvard University Press, 1913. 553 pp.

Armstrong, Robert Cornell. *Light from the East.* Toronto, Ont.: University of Toronto, 1914. 326 pp.

Asakawa, Kan-ichi (ed. & tr.). *The Documents of Iriki.* Reprinted with the complete Japanese text. Tokyo: Japan Society for the Promotion of Science, 1955. 442 pp. Separate pagination in Japanese, 323 pp.

Association of American Law Schools. *Anatomy of Modern Legal Education.* St. Paul, Minn.: West Publishing Co., 1961. 517 pp.

Aung, Maung Htin. *Burmese Law Tales.* London: Oxford University Press, 1962. 157 pp.

Austin, John. *Lectures on Jurisprudence.* Ed. by Robert Campbell. 3rd ed., rev. London: J. Murray, 1889. 504 pp.

Barton, R. F. *Ifugao Law.* University of California Publications in American Archaeology and Ethnology, Vol. 15. Berkeley: University of California Press, 1919.

Beans, George H. *A List of Japanese Maps of the Tokugawa Era.* Jenkintown, Pa.: Tall Tree Library, 1951. 51 pp.

Beardsley, Richard K. *et al. Village Japan.* Ann Arbor: University of Michigan Press, 1959. 498 pp.

Bellah, Robert N. *Tokugawa Religion.* Glencoe, Ill.: Free Press, 1957. 249 pp.

Benedict, Ruth. *Chrysanthemum and the Sword.* Boston: Houghton Mifflin Co., 1946. 324 pp.

Bienenfeld, F. R. *Rediscovery of Justice.* London: George Allen & Unwin Ltd., 1947. 263 pp.

Bisson, T. A. *Prospects for Democracy in Japan.* New York: Macmillan Company, 1949. 143 pp.

Blakemore, Thomas L. (tr.). *The Criminal Code of Japan.* Tokyo and

Rutland, Vt.: Nihon Hyōron-sha Publishing Co. and Charles E. Tuttle Co., 1950. 186 pp.

Bloch, Marc. *Feudal Society.* Translated from the French by L. A. Manyon. Chicago: University of Chicago Press, 1962. 498 pp.

Blume, William Wirt. *American Civil Procedure.* Englewood Cliffs, N.J.: Prentice-Hall, Inc., 1955. 432 pp.

Bodenheimer, Edgar. *Jurisprudence.* Cambridge, Mass.: Harvard University Press, 1962. 402 pp.

Boxer, C. R. *The Christian Century in Japan, 1549-1650.* Berkeley and Los Angeles: University of California Press, 1952. 535 pp.

————. *The Great Ship from Amacon: Annals of Macao and the Old Japan Trade, 1555-1640.* Lisbon: Centro de Estudos Historicos Ultramarinos, 1959. 361 pp.

Brennan, William J., Jr. *Proceedings of the Attorney-General's Conference on Court Congestion and Delay in Litigation.* Washington, D. C.: Department of Justice, 1956. 87 pp.

Brown, Delmer M. *Money Economy in Medieval Japan.* New Haven, Conn.: Far Eastern Association, 1951. 127 pp.

————. *Nationalism in Japan.* Berkeley and Los Angeles: University of California Press, 1955. 336 pp.

Bruce, J. P. *Chu Hsi and His Masters.* London: Probsthain & Co., 1923. 336 pp.

Burdick, William W. *The Bench and Bar of Other Lands.* New York: Metropolitan Law Book Co., 1939. 652 pp.

Cairns, H. *The Theory of Legal Science.* Chapel Hill: University of North Carolina Press, 1941. 156 pp.

California. *Code of Civil Procedure.*

California. Judicial Council of California. *Annual Report of the Administrative Office of the California Courts: Judicial Statistics for the Fiscal Year 1962-1963.* San Francisco: California Office of State Printing, 1964. 128 pp.

California. Judicial Council of California. *California Manual of Pre-Capital Trial Procedures and Rules Relating to Pre-Trial Conferences.* San Francisco: California Office of State Printing, undated. 35 pp.

California. *Judicial Council of California to the Governor and the Legislature: Eighteenth Biennial Report.* San Francisco: California Office of State Printing, Jan. 1961. 204 pp.

Cardozo, Benjamin Nathan. *The Growth of the Law.* New Haven, Conn.: Yale University Press, 1924. 145 pp.

Carter, J. C. *The Proposed Codification of Our Common Law.* New York: Evening Post Job Printing Office, 1884. 117 pp.

————. *The Provinces of the Written and the Unwritten Law.* New York: Albany Banks and Brothers, 1889. 62 pp.

Chamberlain, Basil H. *Things Japanese.* 2nd ed., rev. London: L. Paul, Trench, Trubner & Co., 1891. 503 pp.

————, tr. *Women and Wisdom in Japan.* Translation of Kaibara Ekken, Onna Daigaku. London: J. Murray, 1914. 64 pp.

Chiang, Monlin. *Tides from the West.* New Haven, Conn.: Yale University Press, 1947. 282 pp.

Chinese Classics:

I. The Five Classics or Cannons (*Wu Ching* 五經):

1. *The Book of Changes.* (*I Ching* 易經; also known as *Chou I* 周易). *The I Ching or Book of Changes,* translated by Cary F. Baynes from the German version of Richard Wilhelm, 2 vols. New York: Pantheon Books, 1950. 395, 396 pp. *The Yi King,* translated by James Legge in *Sacred Books of the East,* F. Max Müller, Vol. 16. Oxford: Clarendon Press, 1882, 1899. 448 pp.

2. *The Book of History.* (*Shu Ching* 書經; also known as *Shang Shu* 尚書, *The Cannons of Yao and Shun*). *The Shoo King* (or *The Book of Historical Documents*), translated by James Legge in *The Chinese Classics,* Vol. 3, two parts. London, 1865; reprinted London: Oxford University Press, 1939; *ibid.* in *Sacred Books of the East,* ed. by F. Max Müller, Vol. 3. 2nd ed. Oxford: Clarendon Press, 1899; and Bernhard Karlgren, "The Book of Documents," *Bulletin of the Museum of Far Eastern Antiquities,* no. 22. Stockholm (1950), pp. 1–81.

3. *The Odes (The Book of Songs/Poetry)* (*Shih Ching* 詩經). *The Book of Songs,* translated by Arthur Waley. London: Allen & Unwin; Boston and New York: Houghton Mifflin Co., 1937. 358 pp. *The Book of Songs,* translated by Bernhard Karlgren. Stockholm: Museum of Far Eastern Antiquities, 1950. *The She King* (or *The Book of Poetry*), translated by James Legge in *The Chinese Classics,* Vol. 4, two parts. London, 1871.

4. *The Book of Rites* (*Li Chi* 禮記). *The Li Ki,* translated by James Legge in *Sacred Books of the East,* ed. by F. Max Müller, Vols. 27 and 28. Oxford: Clarendon Press, 1885, 1899; reprinted London: Oxford University Press, 1926. 480 and 491 pp.

5. *Spring and Autumn Annals.* (*Ch'un Ch'iu* 春秋); *The Ch'un Ts'ew, with Tso Chuen,* translated by James Legge in *The Chinese Classics,* Vol. 5, two parts. London, 1872.

II. The Four Books (*Szu Shu* 四書):

1. *Confucian Analects.* (*Lun Yü* 論語). Attributed to Confucius. *The Analects of Confucius,* translated by Arthur Waley. London:

Allen & Unwin, 1938, 1945. 268 pp.; New York: Vintage Books, n.d. 257 pp.; "Confucian Analects," translated by James Legge in *The Chinese Classics*, Vol. 1, pp. 137–354. 2nd ed. rev. Oxford: Clarendon Press, 1893; *The Analects of Confucius*, translated by William E. Soothill. Taiyuan, China, and Yokohama, Japan, 1910, reprinted in the *World's Classics*. London, 1937.

2. *Great Learning.* (*Ta Hsüeh* 大學). Chapter 39 of the *Book of Rites* (*Li Chi* 禮記). Attributed by Legge to Tsang Shan (Tseng Ts'an 曾參, or Tseng Tzu 曾子), disciple of Confucius. "The Great Learning," translated by James Legge in *The Chinese Classics*, Vol. 1, pp. 355–81. 2nd ed. rev. Oxford: Clarendon Press, 1893. Or see *The Li Ki*, translated by James Legge in *Sacred Book of the East*, ed. by F. Max Müller, Vol. 28, pp. 411–24. Oxford: Clarendon Press, 1885, 1899.

3. *Doctrine of the Mean.* (*Chung Yung* 中庸). Chapter 28 of the *Book of Rites* (*Li Chi* 禮記). Attributed by Legge to K'ung Chi (K'ung Chieh 孔伋, or Tzu Szu 子思), grandson of Confucius and disciple of Tseng Ts'an (曾參). "Central Harmony," translated by Ku Hung Ming, chapter 3 of *The Wisdom of Confucius*, ed. by Lin Yutang. New York: Random House, The Modern Library, 1938, pp. 104–34. "The Doctrine of the Mean," translated by James Legge, in *The Chinese Classics*, Vol. 1, pp. 382–434. 2nd ed. rev. Oxford: Clarendon Press, 1893. Or see *The Li Ki*, translated by James Legge in *Sacred Book of the East*, ed. by F. Max Müller, Vol. 28, pp. 301–29. Oxford: Clarendon Press, 1885, 1899.

4. *Mencius.* (Meng Tzu 孟子). Attributed to Mencius. *The Works of Mencius*, translated by James Legge in *The Chinese Classics*, Vol. 2. 2nd rev. ed. Oxford: Clarendon Press, 1895; *Mencius*, by Leonard A. Lyall. London and New York: Longmans, Green & Co., 1932. 242 pp.

Chu Hsi. *The Philosophy of Human Nature.* Translated from the Chinese, with note by J. Percy Bruce. London: Probsthain & Co., 1922. 444 pp.

Clark, Charles E. *Handbook of the Law of Code Pleading.* St. Paul, Minn.: West Publishing Co., 1947. 874 pp.

Clark, E.C. *Practical Jurisprudence.* Cambridge: Cambridge University Press, 1883. 403 pp.

Cohen, Jerome B. *Japan's Postwar Economy.* Bloomington: Indiana University Press, 1958. 262 pp.

————. *Japan's Economy in War and Reconstruction*. Minneapolis: University of Minnesota Press, 1949. 545 pp.

Coleridge, Samuel Taylor. *Essays on His Own Times*. Ed. by Sara Coleridge. London: W. Pickering, 1850. 1034 pp.

Conant, James B. *Modern Science and Modern Man*. Garden City, N.Y.: Doubleday and Company, Inc., 1954. 187 pp.

Corbett, Jim. *My India*. New York: Oxford University Press, 1952. 163 pp.

Cosenza, M. E., ed. *The Complete Journal of Townsend Harris*. Rev. ed. Tokyo: Tuttle, 1959. 616 pp.

Coulborn, Rushton, ed. *Feudalism in History*. Princeton, N.J.: Princeton University Press, 1956. 438 pp.

Craig, Albert M. *Chōshu in the Meiji Restoration*. Cambridge, Mass.: Harvard University Press, 1961. 385 pp.

Creel, H. G. *Confucius: The Man and the Myth*. New York: John Day & Company, 1949. 363 pp.

de Bary, William Theodore, ed. *Sources of the Japanese Tradition*. New York: Columbia University Press, 1958. 928 pp.

De Becker, Joseph Ernest. *Code of Civil Procedure of Japan*. London: Butterworth Company, 1928. 165 pp.

————. *Elements of Japanese Law*. Tokyo: 44 Asiatic Society of Japan, 1916. 473 pp.

————. *The Nightless City or The History of Yoshiwara Yukaku*. Yokohama: Maruya, 1899. 441 pp.

De Tocqueville, Alexis. *Democracy in America*. Ed. by Philips Bradley. New York: Alfred A. Knopf, 1945. 2 vols.

Dicey, A. V. *Introduction to the Study of the Law of the Constitution*. 10th ed. New York: St. Martin's Press, 1959. 535 pp.

Dore, R. P. *City Life in Japan: A Study of a Tokyo Ward*. London: Routledge & Kegan Paul, 1958. 472 pp.

Earl, David M. *Emperor and Nation in Japan*. Seattle: University of Washington Press, 1964. 270 pp.

Ehrlich, Eugen. *Fundamental Principles of the Sociology of Law*. Moll translation, first printed 1913. Cambridge, Mass: Harvard University Press, 1936. 541 pp.

Einstein, Albert. *The World As I See It*. New York: Covici, Friede, 1934. 290 pp.

Elkouri, Frank. *How Arbitration Works*. Washington, D.C.: Bureau of National Affairs, Inc., 1952. 271 pp.

Embree, John F. *A Japanese Village, Suye Mura*. London: Kegan Paul, Trench, Trubner & Co., 1946. 268 pp.

Field, Oliver P. *The Effect of an Unconstitutional Statute.* Minneapolis: University of Minnesota Press, 1935. 355 pp.

Field, Richard H. *Materials for a Basic Course in Civil Procedure.* Brooklyn, N.Y.: Foundation Press, 1953. 1166 pp.

Forkosch, K. *A Treatise on Labor Law.* Indianapolis: Bobbs Merrill, 1953. 1197 pp.

Frank, Jerome. *Courts on Trial.* Princeton, N.J.: Princeton University Press, 1950. 441 pp.

Freidrich, Carl J. *Constitutional Government and Democracy.* Ginn & Company, 1950. 688 pp.

Friedmann, Wolfgang. *Legal Theory.* 4th ed. London: Stevens & Sons, Ltd., 1960. 564 pp.

Fujii, Shin-ichi. *The Essentials of Japanese Constitutional Law.* Tokyo: Yūhikaku, 1940. 463 pp.

Fujisawa, Chikao. *Japanese and Oriental Political Philosophy.* Tokyo: Daitō Bunka Kyōkai, 1935. 296 pp.

Fukuzawa, Yukichi. *The Autobiography of Fukuzawa Yukichi.* Translated by Eiichi Kiyooka. First publication, 1934. Tokyo: Hokuseidō Press, 1961 ed. 401 pp.

Fuller, Lon L. *The Law in Quest of Itself.* Chicago: Foundation Press, Inc., 1940. 147 pp.

Fung, Yu-lan. *History of Chinese Philosophy.* Translated by Derk Bodde, Princeton, N.J.: Princeton University Press, 1952–53. 2 vols.

Gandhi, M. K. *Autobiography, the Story of My Experiments with Truth.* Translated by Desai. Washington, D.C.: Public Affairs Press, 1948. 640 pp.

Ganshof, F. L. *Feudalism.* 1st English ed. London, New York and Toronto: Longmans, Green and Co., 1952. 160 pp.

Garlan, E. N. *Legal Realism and Justice.* New York: Columbia University Press, 1941. 161 pp.

Gauntlett, John Owen, tr. *Kokutai no Hongi.* Cambridge, Mass.: Harvard University Press, 1949. 200 pp.

Goodman, Grant Kohn. *The Dutch Impact on Japan (1640-1853).* Ph.D. dissertation, University of Michigan, 1955. 316 pp.

Graf, Olaf. *Kaibara Ekken.* Leiden: E. J. Brill, 1942. 545 pp.

Gray, Alexander. *The Socialist Tradition.* London: Longmans, Green & Co., 1946. 523 pp.

Gubbins, John Harington, tr. *The Civil Code of Japan.* Tokyo: Maruya & Co., 1897 and 1899. 2 vols.

Gurvitch, Georges. *Sociology of Law.* New York: Philosophical Library and Albance Book Corporation, 1942. 309 pp.

Gutteridge, H. C. *Comparative Law*. Cambridge: Cambridge University Press, 1946. 208 pp.

Hall, John Whitney. *Tanuma Okitsugu, 1719-1788: Forerunner of Modern Japan*. Cambridge, Mass.: Harvard University Press, 1955. 196 pp.

Hartland, E. S. *Primitive Law*. London: Methuen & Co., Ltd., 1924. 222 pp.

Hayashi, Viscount. *For His People*. 1903.

Hegel, Wilhelm George Friedrich. *Philosophy of History*. Translated by J. Sibree. New York: Willey Book Co., 1944. 457 pp.

Henderson, Dan F. *The Pattern and Persistence of Traditional Procedure in Japanese Law*. Ph.D. dissertation, University of California at Berkeley, 1955. 513 pp.

Hiroshige. *Fifty-Three Stages of the Tōkaidō*. Tokyo: Takamisawa Mokubansha, no date. No paging.

Hobbes, Thomas. *Leviathan*. Reprint of 1651 ed. Oxford: Clarendon Press, 1909. 557 pp.

Hoebel, E. A. *The Law of Primitive Man*. Cambridge, Mass.: Harvard University Press, 1961. 417 pp.

Holdsworth, W. S. *A History of the English Law*. Boston: Little, Brown & Co., 1922–38. 13 vols.

Holmes, Oliver Wendell, Jr. *The Common Law*. Boston: Little, Brown & Co., 1881. 422 pp.

Honjō, Eijirō. *Economic Theory and History of Japan in the Tokugawa Period*. Tokyo: Maruzen Company Ltd., 1943. 350 pp.

Hozumi, Nobushige. *Ancestor Worship and Japanese Law*. 2nd ed. Tokyo: Hokuseidō Press, 1940. 205 pp.

———. *The New Japanese Civil Code as Material for the Study of Comparative Jurisprudence*. Tokyo: Maruzen, 1912. 166 pp.

Hsu, P. C. *Ethical Realism in Neo-Confucian Thought*. Ph.D. dissertation, Columbia University, 1933. 165 pp.

Hughes, E. R. *The Great Learning and the Mean-in-Action*. London: J. M. Dent & Sons, 1942. 176 pp.

Huizinga, Johan. *The Waning of the Middle Ages*. London: E. Arnold & Co., 1924. 329 pp.

Hurst, James Willard. *The Growth of American Law*. Boston: Little, Brown & Co., 1950. 446 pp.

Ike, Nobutake. *The Beginnings of Political Democracy in Japan*. Baltimore, Md.: Johns Hopkins Press, 1950. 246 pp.

Institute of Judicial Administration. *Compulsory Arbitration and Court Congestion; the Pennsylvania Compulsory Arbitration Statute—A Sup-*

plementary Report—1959. New York: Institute of Judicial Administration, 1959. 44 pp.

————. *Small Claims Courts in the United States*. New York: Institute of Judicial Administration, 1955. 48 pp. See also *1959 Supplement* by same title. 19 pp.

International Commission of Jurists. *The Rule of Law in a Free Society: A Report on the International Congress of Jurists, New Delhi, India, 1959*. Geneva: Author, no date. 340 pp.

Ishii, Ryōsuke. *Japanese Legislation in the Meiji Era*. Translated by William J. Chambliss. Tokyo: Pan-Pacific Press, 1958. 741 pp.

Jansen, Marius B. *Sakamoto Ryūma and the Meiji Restoration*. Princeton, N.J.: Princeton University Press, 1961. 423 pp.

Jhering, Rudolf. *Geist des Römischen Rechts*. 5th ed. Leipzig: Breitkopf and Härtel, 1898. 4 vols.

Jones, Stanleigh H., and John E. Lane, ed. *Researches in the Social Sciences on Japan: Volume 2*. Columbia University East Asian Institute Studies, No. 6. New York: Columbia University Press, 1959. 134 pp.

Kaempfer, Engelbert. *The History of Japan*. Glasgow: James Maclehose & Sons, 1906. 3 vols.

Written in 1690–92 by Kaempfer, a physician with the Dutch at Dejima.

Keene, Donald. *The Japanese Discovery of Europe*. London: Routledge and Kegan Paul Ltd., 1952. 246 pp.

Kelsen, Hans. *Allgemeine Staatslehre*. Berlin: Verlag von Julius Springer, 1925.

Kelsen, Hans. *General Theory of Law and State*. 20th-Century Legal Philosophy Series, Vol. 1. Cambridge, Mass.: Harvard University Press, 1945.

Kincaid, Clarence L. *A Study of Pre-Trial Usage in Nine Areas of the United States*. Unpublished report, 1955. 19 pp.

Kirk, Russell. *The Conservative Mind*. Chicago: Henry Regnery Co., 1953. 428 pp.

Lane, John E., ed. *Researches in the Social Sciences on Japan*. Columbia University East Asian Institute Studies, No. 4. New York: Columbia University Press, 1959. 84 pp.

Levi, Edward H. *An Introduction to Legal Reasoning*. Chicago: University of Chicago Press, 1948. 74 pp.

Llewellyn, Karl N. *The Bramble Bush: On Our Law and Its Study*. New York: Oceana Publications, 1960. 160 pp.

————. *The Common Law Tradition*. Boston: Little, Brown & Co., 1960. 565 pp.

————. *Jurisprudence-Realism in Theory and Practice*. Chicago: University of Chicago Press, 1962. 516 pp.

———— and E. A. Hoebel. *The Cheyenne Way*. Norman: University of Oklahoma Press, 1941. 360 pp.

Lockwood, William W. *The Economic Development of Japan: Growth and Structural Change, 1868-1938*. Princeton, N.J.: Princeton University Press, 1954. 603 pp.

Lombard, F. A. *Pre-Meiji Education in Japan*. Tokyo: Kyōbunkan, 1913. 271 pp.

MacIver, R. M. *The Web of Government*. New York: MacMillan Co., 1949. 498 pp.

McEwan, J. R. *The Political Writings of Ogyū Sorai*. Cambridge: Cambridge University Press, 1962. 153 pp.

McIlwain, Charles Howard. *The Growth of Political Thought in the West*. New York: Macmillan Co., 1932. 517 pp.

Maine, Sir Henry. *Ancient Law*. London: J. Murray, 1930. 440 pp.

————. *Dissertations on Early Law and Custom*. London: J. Murray, 1883. 402 pp.

————. *Lecture on the Early History of Institutions*. London: J. Murray, 1875. 421 pp.

Maitland, F. W. *Domesday Book and Beyond*. Reprinted ed. Cambridge: Cambridge University Press, 1907.

————. *The Forms of Action at Common Law*. Cambridge: Cambridge University Press, 1936. 92 pp.

Maki, John M. *Court and Constitution in Japan*. Seattle: University of Washington Press, 1964. 445 pp.

Malinowski, Bronislaw. *Crime and Custom in Savage Society*. New York: Harcourt, Brace & Co., 1926. 132 pp.

Meynard, Jean, et Brigitte Schröder. *La Mediation: Tendences de la recherche et bibliographie (1945-1959)*. In the series Confluence, Vol. 2. Amsterdam: North-Holland Pub. Co., 1961. 111 pp.

Millar, Robert Wyness. *Civil Procedure of the Trial Court in Historical Perspective*. New York: Law Center of New York University for the National Conference of Judicial Councils, 1952. 534 pp.

Mizuno, Sōji, tr. *Ihara Saikaku's Nippon Eitaigura; The Way to Wealth*. Tokyo: Hokuseidō Press, 1955. 133 pp.

Moore, Russell F. *Oriental Philosophies*. 3rd ed. rev. New York: R. F. Moore Co., 1951. 220 pp.

Murdoch, James. *A History of Japan*. London: Routledge & Kegan Paul, Ltd., 1949. 3 vols.

Nakamura Muneo. *A Comparative Study of "Judicial Process."* Waseda University Institute of Comparative Law, Publication No. 7.

Tokyo: Institute of Comparative Law of Waseda University, 1959. 74 pp.

Neville, Edwin Lowe, Jr. *The Development of Transportation in Japan: A Case Study of Okayama Han, 1600–1868.* Ph.D. dissertation, University of Michigan, 1959. 184 pp.

New York (State). *Sixth Annual Report of the Judicial Conference of the State of New York.* New York: State of New York, 1961. 263 pp.

New York (State). *Temporary Commission on the Courts.* New York: State Printer of New York, 1955. 107 pp.

Nims, Harry D. *Pre-Trial.* New York: Baker, Voorhis, 1950. 334 pp.

Nivison, David S., and Arthur F. Wright, ed. *Confucianism in Action.* Stanford, Calif.: Stanford University Press, 1959. 390 pp.

Norman, E. Herbert. *Andō Shōeki and the Anatomy of Japanese Feudalism.* 2 *T.A.S.J.* (3rd series) and supplement. 1949. 340+130 pp.

——. *Japan's Emergence as a Modern State.* New York: Institute of Pacific Relations, 1940. 254 pp.

North Dakota. *Supplement to the 1913 Compiled Laws of North Dakota.* (Annotated 1913–25), section 9192 (a) (1)–9192(a) (15) (passed 1921; repealed 1943).

Northrop, F. S. C. *The Complexity of Legal and Ethical Experience.* Boston: Little, Brown & Co., 1959. 331 pp.

——. *The Meeting of East and West.* New York: Macmillan Company, 1946. 531 pp.

——. *Philosophical Anthropology and Practical Politics.* New York: Macmillan Company, 1960. 384 pp.

Norway. Royal Norwegian Ministry of Justice. *Administration of Justice in Norway.* Oslo: Royal Norwegian Ministry of Justice, 1957. 145 pp.

Odegaard, Charles Edwin. *Vassi and Fideles in the Carolingian Empire.* Cambridge, Mass.: Harvard University Press, 1945. 166 pp.

Orfield, Lester Bernhardt. *The Growth of Scandinavian Law.* Philadelphia: University of Pennsylvania Press for Temple University Publications, 1953. 363 pp.

Paton, George Whitecross. *A Text Book of Jurisprudence.* Oxford: Clarendon Press, 1946. 528 pp.

Pfaff, Roger Alton. *The Conciliation Court of Los Angeles County.* Los Angeles, Calif.: Superior Court, 1960. 22 pp.

Pollock, Frederick, and F. W. Maitland. *The History of English Law Before the Time of Edward I.* 1st printed 1895, 2nd ed. reprinted. Cambridge: Cambridge University Press, 1952. 2 vols.

Pound, Roscoe. *Appellate Procedure in Civil Cases.* Boston: Little, Brown & Co., 1941. 431 pp.

———. *Interpretations of Legal History.* New York: Macmillan Company, 1930. 171 pp.

———. *The Lawyer from Antiquity to Modern Times.* St. Paul, Minn.: West Publishing Co., 1953. 404 pp.

———. *Outlines of Lectures on Jurisprudence.* Cambridge, Mass.: Harvard University Press, 1943.

———. *The Task of the Law.* Lancaster, Pa.: Franklin and Marshall College Press, 1944. 94 pp.

———, and Plucknett, tr. *Readings on the History of the System of the Common Law.* 3rd ed. Rochester, N.Y.: The Lawyers Co-Operative Publishing Co., 1927. 731 pp.

Radin, Max. *Anglo-American Legal History.* St. Paul, Minn.: West Publishing Co., 1936. 612 pp.

Reischauer, Edwin O., and John K. Fairbank. *East Asia: The Great Tradition.* Boston: Houghton Mifflin Co., 1960. 739 pp.

Robson, Robert. *The Attorney in Eighteenth-Century England.* Cambridge: Cambridge University Press, 1959. 182 pp.

Rosenberg, Leo. *Lehrbuch des Deutschen Zivilprozessrechts.* 4th ed. Berlin: C. H. Beck, 1949. 1054 pp.

Sadler, A. L. *The Maker of Modern Japan.* London: G. Allen & Unwin, Ltd., 1937. 429 pp.

Sakamaki, Shunzō. *Japan and the United States.* 18 *T.A.S.J.* (2nd series). 1939. 204 pp.

Sansom, George B. *A History of Japan to 1334.* Stanford, Calif.: Stanford University Press, 1958. 500 pp.

———. *A History of Japan, 1334–1615.* Stanford, Calif.: Stanford University Press, 1961. 442 pp.

———. *A History of Japanese, 1615–1867.* Stanford, Calif.: Stanford University Press, 1963. 258 pp.

———. *Japan: A Short Cultural History.* Rev. ed. New York: Appleton Century Crofts, Inc., 1943. 554 pp.

———. *The Western World and Japan.* New York: Alfred A. Knopf Inc., 1949. 504 pp.

Saris, John. *The First Voyage of the English to Japan.* Tokyo: Tōyō Bunko, 1941. 266 pp.

Scalapino, Robert A. *Democracy and the Party Movement in Prewar Japan.* Berkeley and Los Angeles: University of California Press, 1953. 471 pp.

———, and J. Masumi. *Parties and Politics in Contemporary Japan.* Berkeley and Los Angeles: University of California Press, 1962. 190 pp.

Schacht, Joseph. *The Origins of Mohammedan Jurisprudence.* Oxford: Clarendon Press, 1950. 348 pp.

Schlesinger, Rudolf B. *Comparative Law—Cases and Materials.* Brooklyn, N.Y.: Foundation Press, Inc., 1959. 635 pp.

Seagle, William. *The Quest for Law.* New York: Alfred A. Knopf, 1941. 439 pp.

Sheldon, Charles David. *The Rise of the Merchant Class in Tokugawa Japan, 1600–1868: An Introductory Survey.* New York: J. J. Augustin Inc., 1958. 194 pp.

Shinoda, Minoru. *The Founding of the Kamakura Shogunate, 1180–1185.* With selected translations from the Azuma Kagami. New York: Columbia University Press, 1960. 385 pp.

Shryock, J. K. *The Origins and Development of the State Cult of Confucianism.* New York, London: The Century Co., 1932. 298 pp.

Siebold, Philip Franz. *Manners and Customs of the Japanese in the Nineteenth Century.* English ed. London: J. Murray, 1841. 423 pp.

Sigur, Gaston Joseph, Jr. *A History of Administration in Bizen Han.* Ph.D. dissertation, University of Michigan, 1957. 177 pp.

Sindell, Joseph M. *Let's Talk Settlement by Joseph and David Sindell.* San Francisco, Calif.: Bender, 1963. 420 pp.

Smith, Thomas C. *Political Change and Industrial Development in Japan: Government Enterprise, 1868–1880.* Stanford, Calif.: Stanford University Press, 1955. 126 pp.

————. *The Agrarian Origins of Modern Japan.* Stanford, Calif.: Stanford University Press, 1959. 250 pp.

Smith, Warren W., Jr. *Confucianism in Modern Japan: A Study of Conservatism in Japanese Intellectual History.* Tokyo: Hokuseidō Press, 1959. 285 pp.

Sorley, W. R. *Tradition.* Oxford: Clarendon Press, 1926. 24 pp.

Spea, Joseph. *Itō Jinsai, a Philosopher, Educator and Sinologist of the Tokugawa Period.* Monumenta Serica, Monograph 12, 1948. 280 pp.

Statistik Sentralbyra. *Sivilrettsstatistikk 1960.* (Civil law statistics 1960). Oslo: Statistik Sentralbyra, 1961. 23 pp.

Stenton, F. M. *The First Century of English Feudalism, 1066–1166.* London: Oxford University Press, 1954. 311 pp.

Stern, Robert L., and Eugene Gressman. *Supreme Court Practice.* 2nd ed. Washington, D.C.: B. N. A. Inc., 1954. 544 pp.

Stone, J. *The Province and Function of Law.* Sydney: Associated General Publications Pty. Ltd., 1946. 918 pp.

Stumpf, Felix F. *et al.*, ed. *Family Law for California Lawyers.* Berkeley and Los Angeles; University of California Press, 1956. 779 pp.

Taeuber, Irene B. *The Population of Japan*. Princeton, N.J.: Princeton University Press, 1958. 461 pp.

Takayanagi, Kenzō. *Reception and Influence of Occidental Legal Ideas in Japan*. In series, Western Influences in Modern Japan. Tokyo: Japan Council of the Institute of Pacific Relations, 1929. 21 pp.

Takekoshi, Yosaburō. *The Economic Aspects of the History of Civilization of Japan*. 3rd ed. Tokyo: Heibonsha, 1930. 3 vols.

Ter Haar, B. *Adat Law of Indonesia*. Translated by E. Adamson Hoebel and A. Arthur Schiller. New York: Institute of Pacific Relations, 1948. 255 pp.

Timasheff, N. S. *An Introduction to the Sociology of Law*. Cambridge, Mass.: Harvard University Press, 1939. 418 pp.

Tsuchiya, Takao. *An Economic History of Japan*. 15 *T.A.S.J.* (2nd series) (Dec. 1937). 269 pp.

Tsukahira, George Toshio. *The Sankin Kōtai System of Tokugawa Japan*. Ph.D. dissertation, Harvard University, 1951.

United States Courts. *Annual Report of the Director of the Administrative Office of the United States Courts, 1961*. Washington, D.C.: Government Printing Office, 1962. 342 pp.

Van Alstyne, Arvo, and Harvey M. Grossman. *California Pretrial and Settlement Procedures*. Berkeley: California Continuing Education of the Bar, 1963. 383 pp.

Vanderbilt, Arthur T. *The Challenge of Law Reform*. Princeton, N.J.: Princeton University Press, 1955. 194 pp.

————. *Minimum Standards of Judicial Administration*. New York: National Conference of Judicial Councils, 1949. 752 pp.

van der Sprenkel, Sybille. *Legal Institutions in Manchu China*. London: The Athlone Press, 1962. 172 pp.

Vesey-Fitzgerald, S. G. *The Future of Oriental Legal Studies*. London: H. K. Lewis, 1948. 20 pp.

Vinogradoff, Sir Paul. *Outlines of Historical Jurisprudence*. London: Oxford University Press, 1920. 148 pp.

Virtue, Maxine B. *Survey of Metropolitan Courts Final Report*. Ann Arbor: University of Michigan Press, 1962. 523 pp.

von Mehren, Arthur (ed.). *Law in Japan*. Cambridge, Mass.: Harvard University Press, 1963. 706 pp.

Warnock, G. J. *Berkeley*. London: Penguin Books, 1953. 246 pp.

Washington Foreign Law Society. *Studies in the Law of the Far East and Southeast Asia*. Washington, D.C.: George Washington University Law School, 1956. 104 pp.

Washington (State) Courts. *Fifth Annual Report of the Administrator for the Courts*. Olympia, Wash.: State Printer, 1961. 74 pp.

Washington (State). Judicial Council. *Seventeenth Biennial Report, 1959–1960.* Olympia, Wash.: State Printer, 1961. 28 pp.

Weber, Max. *On Law in Economy and Society.* Translated by Edward Shils and Max Rheinstein. Cambridge, Mass.: Harvard University Press, 1954. 363 pp.

Wellman, Francis L. *The Art of Cross-examination.* New York: Macmillan Co., 1936. 479 pp.

White, R. J., ed. *The Conservative Tradition.* London: Nicholas Kaye Ltd., 1950. 256 pp.

Wigmore, John Henry. *Panorama of the World's Legal Systems.* St. Paul, Minn.: West Publishing Co., 1928. 3 vols.

————, ed. *Law and Justice in Tokugawa Japan.* Unpublished MSS in 10 vols.

Volumes 2 and 7 of these manuscripts were published in 1941 by the Kokusai Bunka Shinkōkai, but the outbreak of hostilities prevented further publication. They are presently at the K.B.S. Office in Tokyo. Some of these materials were also in 20 *T. A. S. J.*

Wright, Arthur F. *Studies in Chinese Thought.* Chicago: University of Chicago Press, 1953. 317 pp.

Yanaga, Chitoshi. *Japan Since Perry.* 1st ed. New York: McGraw-Hill Book Co., 1949. 723 pp.

Zeisel, Hans *et al. Delay in the Court: An Analysis of the Remedies for Delayed Justice.* Boston: Little, Brown & Co., 1959. 313 pp.

21. *Western Language Articles*

Albertsworth, E. F. "Leading Developments in Procedural Reform," 7 *Cornell L. Rev.* 310–33 (1921–22).

American Judicature Society, "State Federal Judicial Salary Summaries," 45 *J. Am. Jud. Soc'y* (no. 10) 255 (1962).

Anesaki, Masaharu. "Japanese Criticisms and Refutations of Christianity in the Seventeenth and Eighteenth Centuries," 7 *T.A.S.J.* (2nd series) 1–15 (1930).

Anonymous. "Act to Provide for Conciliation," 2 *J. Am. Jud. Soc'y* 151–57 (1918).

————. "Japanese Causes Celebres," 4 *Green Bag* 563–66 (1892).

————. "Zahl der Rechtsanwälte," 12 *Anwaltsblatt* (no. 5) 115–17 (1962).

Appleton, Richard B. "Reforms in Japanese Criminal Procedure under Allied Occupation," 24 *Wash. L. Rev.* 401–30 (1949).

Armstrong, R. C. "Ninomiya, Sontoku, the Peasant Sage," 38 *T.A.S.J.* (pt. II) 1–21 (1910).

Arnold, Thurman W. "The Role of Substantive Law and Procedure in the Legal Process," 45 *Harv. L. Rev.* 617–47 (1932).

Asakawa, Kan-ichi. "Notes on Village Government in Japan after 1600," 30–31 *Am. Oriental Soc'y* 151–216, 259–300 (1910–11).

———. "Some Aspects of Japanese Feudal Institutions," 46 *T.A.S.J.* (pt. 1) 76–102 (1918).

———. "Some of the Contributions of Feudal Japan to New Japan," 3 *Race Development* 1–32 (1912–13).

Beaseley, W. G. "Feudal Revenue in Japan at the Time of the Meiji Restoration," 19 *JAS* 255–72 (1960).

Biglia and Spinosa, "The Function of Conciliation in Civil Procedure," 10 *Unesco, Int'l. Soc. Sci. Bull.* 604, 605 (1958).

Blakemore, Thomas L. "Post-war Developments in Japanese Law," *Wis. L. Rev.* 632–53 (1947).

———, and Makoto Yazawa. "Japanese Commercial Code Revision Concerning Corporations," 2 *Am. J. Comp. L.* 12–24 (1953).

Bloch, Marc *et al.* "Feudalism," 6 *Encycl. of Social Science* 203–10 (1931).

Bodde, Derk. "Evidence for 'Laws of Nature' in Chinese Thought," 20 *Harvard Journal of Asiatic Studies* 709–27 (1957).

Bodenheimer, Edgar. "Reflections on the Rule of Law," 8 *Utah L. Rev.* (no. 1) 1–11 (1962).

Boorstin, D. T. "Tradition and Method in Legal History," 54 *Harv. L. Rev.* 424–36 (1940–41).

Borton, Hugh. "Peasant Uprisings in Japan of the Tokugawa Period," 16 *T.A.S.J.* (2nd series), 1–210 (1938).

Botein, Bernard. "Our Courts Face the Future," 139 *N.Y.L.J.* (no. 15) 4 (1958).

Brown, Ralph S. "Legal Research: The Resource Base and Traditional Approaches," 7 *American Behavioral Scientist* 3 (Dec. 1963).

Burtt, E. A. "How Can the Philosophies of East and West Meet?" 57 *Philosophical Review* 590–604 (1948).

Burke, Louis H. "Conciliation Court," in *Family Law for California Lawyers.* Berkeley and Los Angeles: University of California, 1956. Pp. 337–56.

———. "The Conciliation Court in Los Angeles," 42 *A.B.A.J.* 621–24 (1956).

Cantor, Daniel. "Improving the Lawyer's Income," 47 *A.B.A.J.* (no. 8) 768–71 (1961).

Cayton, N. "Small Claims and Conciliation Courts," 205 *Annals of the Am. Acad. Pol. and Soc. Sci.* 57–64 (1939).

Clement, Ernest W. "Chinese Refugees of the Seventeenth Century in Mito," 24 *T.A.S.J.* 12–40 (1896).

———. "The Tokugawa Princes of Mito," 18 *T.A.S.J.* 1–24 (1890).

———. "Yedo and Tokyo," 46 *T.A.S.J.* (pt. I) 49–69 (1918).

Cohen, Felix S. "The Problems of a Functional Jurisprudence," 1 *Mod. L. Rev.* 5–26 (1937).

———. "Transcendental Nonsense and the Functional Approach," 35 *Col. L. Rev.* 809–49 (1935).

Cohen, J. "Factors of Resistance to the Resources of the Behavioral Sciences," 12 *J. Legal Ed.* 67 (1959).

Coleman, Rex. "Japanese Family Law," 9 *Stan. L. Rev.* 132–54 (1956).

Comment, "California Pretrial in Action," 49 *Calif. L. Rev.* 909–30 (1961).

Crabb, J. H. "Positivism vs. Idealism: A Different Sort of Match; a Reply to Professor Jenkins, The Matchmaker," 12 *J. Legal Ed.* 548–52 (1960).

Dandō, Shigemitsu. "Interrelation of Criminal Law and Procedure," 2 *The Japan Annual of Law and Politics* 163–76 (1953).

Dening, Walter. "Confucian Philosophy in Japan," 36 *T.A.S.J.* 101–52 (1908).

Droppers, Garrett. "A Japanese Credit Association and Its Founder— Ninomiya, Sontoku (Kinjirō)," 22 *T.A.S.J.* (pt. 1) 69–102 (1894).

Edwin, Arnold. "Japanese Justice," 3 *Green Bag* 545–47 (1891).

Ehrenzweig, A. A. "Book Review of the Legal Philosophy of Lask, Radbruch and Dabin," 64 *Harv. L. Rev.* 355–59 (1950).

Ekvall, Robert B. "Mi sTong: Tibetan Custom of Life Indemnity," 4 *Sociologus* (no. 2) 136–45 (1954).

Embree, John F. "Standardized Error of Japanese Character," 2 *World Politics* 439–43 (1950).

Emerson, Rupert. "Paradoxes of Asian Nationalism," 13 *F.E.Q.* 131–92 (Feb. 1954).

Fisher, Galen M. "Kumazawa Banzan, His Life and Ideas," 16 *T.A.S.J.* 223–356 (1938).

———. "The Life and Teaching of Nakae Tōju," 36 *T.A.S.J.* 24–94 (1908).

Fisher, Harry M. "Judicial Mediation: How it Works through Pretrial," 10 *U. Chi. L. Rev.* 453–65 (1942–43).

Franklin, Marc A. *et al.* "Accidents, Money and the Law: A Study of the Economics of Personal Injury Litigation," 61 *Col. L. Rev.* 1–39 (1961).

Fuetō, Toshio. "The Discrepancy between Marriage Law and Mores in Japan," 5 *Am. J. Comp. L.* 256–67 (1956).

Fuller, Lon L. "The Case of the Speluncean Explorers," 62 *Harv. L. Rev.* 616–45 (1949).

Fung, Yu-lan. "The Philosophy of Chu Hsi," translated by Derk Bodde, 7 *Harvard Journal of Asiatic Studies* 1–51 (April 1962).

Gerhart, Eugene C. "The Case for the Individual Practitioner," 43 *A.B.A.J.* (no. 9) 793–96 (1957).

Graveson, R. H. "The Movement from Status to Contract," 4 *Modern L. Rev.* 261–72 (1941).

Green, L. C. "Law and Administration in Present-day Japan," 1 *Current Legal Problems* 188–205 (1948).

Grevstad, Nicolay. "Norway's Conciliation Tribunals," 2 *J. Am. Jud. Soc'y* 5–18 (1918).

Grinnell, F. W. "Congestion, Conciliation, Arbitration and the Berkshire Experiment," 38 *Mass. L. Q.* 38 (April 1953).

Gubbins, J. H. "The Feudal System in Japan under the Tokugawa Shoguns," 15 *T.A.S.J.* (pt. II) 3–142 (1887).

———. "Some Features of Tokugawa Administration," 50 *T.A.S.J.* 59–77 (1922).

Haga, P. "Note on Japanese Schools of Philosophy," 20 *T.A.S.J.* 134–47 (1892).

———. "Something More about Shushi's Philosophy," 20 *T.A.S.J.* 178–93 (1892).

Hall, John Carey. "Japanese Feudal Laws: Ashikaga Code," 36 *T.A.S.J.* 134–47 (1892).

———. "Something More about Shushi's Philosophy," 20 *T.A.S.J.* 178–93 (1892).

Hall, John Carey. "Japanese Feudal Laws: Ashikaga Code," 36 *T.A.S.J.* (pt. II) 3–25 (1908).

———. "Japanese Feudal Laws: The Institute of Judicature," 34 *T.A.S.J.* 1–44 (1906).

———. "Japanese Feudal Laws: III Tokugawa Legislation," 38 *T.A.S.J.* (pt. IV) 269–331 (1911).

———. "Japanese Feudal Laws: III Tokugawa Legislation," 41 *T.A.S.J.* (pt. V) 683–804 (1913).

Hall, John Whitney. "The Castle Town and Japan's Modern Urbanization," 15 *F.E.Q.* 37–56 (1955–56).

———. "Feudalism in Japan—A Reassessment," 5 *Comp. Studies in Soc. and History* (no. 1) 15–51 (1962).

———. "Foundations of the Modern Japanese Daimyo," 20 *JAS* 317–29 (1961).

―――. "Materials for the Study of Local History in Japan: Pre-Meiji Daimyo Records," 20 *Harvard Journal of Asiatic Studies* 187–212 (1957).

―――. "Tokugawa Bakufu and the Merchant Class," University of Michigan, Center of Japanese Studies, *Occasional Papers* (no. 1) 26–33 (1951).

Henderson, Dan F. "Japanese Legal History of the Tokugawa Period: Scholars and Sources." University of Michigan, Center of Japanese Studies, *Occasional Papers* (no. 7) 100–21 (1957).

―――. "Roles of Lawyers in U.S.–Japanese Business Transactions," 38 *Wash. L. Rev.* 1–21 (1963).

―――. "Settlement of Homicide Disputes in Sakya (Tibet)," 66 *American Anthropologist* 1099–1105 (1964).

―――. "Some Aspects of Tokugawa Law," 27 *Wash. L. Rev.* 85–109 (1952).

Hoebel, A. E. "Law and Anthropology," 32 *Va. L. Rev.* 835 (1945–46).

Holmes, Oliver W. "Path of the Law," 10 *Harv. L. Rev.* 457 (1897).

Hulse, Frederick S. "Status and Function as Factors in the Structure of Organizations among the Japanese," 149 *American Anthropologist* 154–57 (1947).

Hyde, James. Introduction to Jackson "Mediation and Conciliation in International Law," 10 *Unesco, Int'l. Soc. Sci. Bull.* 508–12 (1958).

Ike, Nobutaka. "The Political Role of Japanese Intellectuals," 5 *T.A.S.J.* (3rd series) 122–38 (1957).

Inoue, Tetsujirō. "Remarks by Prof. Inoue," 20 *T.A.S.J.* 155–56 (1892).

Jansen, Marius B. "New Materials for the Intellectual History of Nineteenth-Century Japan," 20 *Harvard Journal of Asiatic Studies* 567–97 (1957).

Jenkins, I. "Matchmaker or Toward a Synthesis of Legal Idealism and Positivism," 12 *J. Legal Ed.* 1–32 (1959).

Kaplan, von Mehren, and Schaefer. "Phases of German Civil Procedure," 71 *Harv. L. Rev.* 1193–1268 and 1443–72 (1958).

Kawashima, T. "Dispute Resolution in Contemporary Japan," in von Mehren (ed.), *Law in Japan: The Legal Order in a Changing Society.* Cambridge, Mass.: Harvard University Press, 1963.

Kawashima, Takeyoshi, and Kurt Steiner. "Modernization and Divorce Rate Trends in Japan," 9 *Econ. Dev. and Soc. Change* (no. 1, pt. 2) 213–39 (1960).

Knox, George Williams. "A Comment upon Shushi's Philosophy," 20 *T.A.S.J.* 148–56 (1892).

————. "A Japanese Philosopher," 20 *T.A.S.J.* 1–33 (1893).

————. "Ki, Ri and Ten," 20 *T.A.S.J.* 169–77 (1893).

————. "A Translation of the 'Hyō-chū-ori,' etc." [Oritaku-shiba-no-ki (Autobiography of Arai Hakuseki)], 30 *T.A.S.J.* (2nd series) 89–238 (1902).

Koyama, Matsukichi. "Yamaga Sokō and His Bukyō-shōgaku," 8 *Cultural Nippon* 67–88 (Dec. 1939).

Kumagai, Kaisaku. "Establishment of Theory of Japanese Law History" [*sic*], *Ōsaka L. Rev.* (no. 2) 25–45 (1953).

Langston, Eugene. "The Seventeenth Century Hayashi—A Translation from the *Sentetsu Sodan*," in Colorado University Asian Institute Series (no. 4) 1–32 (1957).

Lee, Otis. "Social Values and the Philosophy of Law," 32 *Va. L. Rev.* 802–17 (1945–46).

Llewellyn, Karl N. "Law and the Sciences—Especially Sociology," 62 *Harv. L. Rev.* 1286–1305 (1949).

————. "Legal Tradition and Social Science Method—A Realist's Critique," *Essays on Research in the Social Sciences* 89–120 (1931).

————. "The Normative, the Legal, and the Law Jobs—A Problem in Juristic Method," 49 *Yale L. J.* 1355–1400 (1940).

————. "Some Realism about Realism," 44 *Harv. L. Rev.* 1222–64 (1931).

Lloyd, Arthur. "Historical Development of Shushi Philosophy in Japan," 34 *T.A.S.J.* 5–80 (1906).

Longford, Joseph H. "Note on Ninomiya, Sontoku," 22 *T.A.S.J.* (pt. I) 103–8 (1894).

————. "A Summary of the Japanese Penal Codes," 5 *T.A.S.J.* (pt. II), 1–129 (1877).

MacClatchie, Thomas R. H. "The Castle of Yedo," 6 *T.A.S.J.* (pt. I) 119–50 (1878).

McAleavy, Henry. "The People's Courts in Communist China," 11 *Am. J. Comp. L.* 52–56, 61–63 (1962).

Malinowski, Bronislaw. "A New Instrument for the Interpretation of Law—Especially Primitive," 51 *Yale L. J.* 1237–52 (1942).

Matsuda, Jirō. "The Japanese Legal Training and Research Institute," 7 *Am. J. Comp. L.* (no. 3) 366–79 (1958).

Meyers, Howard. "The Japanese Inquest of Prosecution," 64 *Harv. L. Rev.* 279–86 (1950).

————. "Revision of the Criminal Code of Japan during the Occupation," 25 *Wash. L. Rev.* 104–34 (1950).

Michael, Franz. "The Role of Law in Traditional, National and

Communist China," *China Quarterly* 124–48 (Jan.-March 1962), or Modern Chinese History Project; Reprint Series No. 1.

Mill, John Stuart. "That the Ideally Best Form of Government is Representative Government," in *Considerations on Representative Government*. New York: H. Holt and Co., 1882. Chapter III.

Millar, Robert Wyness. "The Old Regime and the New in Civil Procedure," 14 *New York University Law Quarterly Review* 1–27, 197–226 (1936–37).

Mitsui, Takaharu. "Chōnin's Life under Feudalism," 8 *Cultural Nippon* 65–96 (1940).

———. "The System of Communications at the Time of the Meiji Restoration," 4 *Monumenta Nipponica* 88–101 (Jan. 1941).

Murdoch, James. "Chinese Philosophy as an Instrument of Government," 3 *History of Japan* 91–150.

Nathanson, Nathaniel. "Constitutional Adjudication in Japan," 7 *Am. J. Comp. L.* 195–218 (1958).

Needham, Joseph. "Human Laws and Laws of Nature in China and the West," 12 *Journal of the History of Ideas* 3–30 (Jan. 1951).

Nims, Harry D. "The Cost of Justice: A New Approach," 39 *A.B.A.J.* 455–58 (June 1953).

———. "New York's Hundred Years of Struggle for Better Civil Justice," 25 *N.Y.S.B.* 83 (1953).

Norman, E. Herbert. "Andō Shōeki and the Anatomy of Japanese Feudalism," 2 *T.A.S.J.* (3rd series) 340 pp. (1949).

Northrop, E. H. "Small Claims Courts and Conciliation Tribunals: A Bibliography," 33 *Law Lib. J.* 39–50 (1940).

Northrop, F. S. C. "A Comparative Philosophy of Comparative Law," 45 *Cornell L. Q.* 617–58 (1959–60).

———. "The Mediational Approval Theory of Law in American Legal Realism," 44 *Va. L. Rev.* 347–63 (1958).

———. "Review of E. A. Hoebel, *Law of Primitive Man*," 16 *La. L. Rev.* 455–64 (1955–56).

Oppler, Alfred C. "Japan's Courts and Law in Transition," 21 *Contemporary Japan* 19–55 (June 1952).

———. "The Reform of Japan's Legal and Judicial System under the Allied Occupation," 24 *Wash. L. Rev.* 290–324 (1949).

Ostenfeld, George H. "Danish Courts of Conciliation," 9 *A.B.A.J.* 747–48 (1923).

Phillips, Richard H. "Breaking the Judicial Log Jam: Connecticut's Blitz on Court Congestion," 45 *A.B.A.J.* 268–71 (1959).

Pike, L. O. "An Action at Law in the Reign of Edward III," 7 *Harv. L. Rev.* 266–80 (1893–94).

Pound, Roscoe. "The Call for a Realistic Jurisprudence," 44 *Harv. L. Rev.* 697–711 (1931).

——. "The New Feudal System," 19 *Ky. L. J.* 1–15 (1930).

——. "Scope and Purpose of Sociological Jurisprudence," 24 *Harv. L. Rev.* 591–619; 25 *id.* 140–68, 489–516 (1912).

Rabinowitz, Richard W. "The Historical Development of the Japanese Bar," 70 *Harv. L. Rev.* 61–81 (1956).

Radin, Max. "A Restatement of Hohfeld," 51 *Harv. L. Rev.* 1141–64 (1938).

Randell, Frank H. "Conciliation as a Function of the Judge," 18 *Ky. L. Rev.* 330–40 (1929–30).

Redmount, R. S. "Psychological Views in Jurisprudential Theories," 107 *U. of Pa. L. Rev.* 472–513 (1959).

Robson, W. A. "Sir Henry Main Today," in Ivor Jenning, ed., *Modern Theories of Law* 160–79 (1933).

Rudorff, Otto. "Tokugawa-gesetz-sammlung," 5 *Mittheilungen der deutschen Gesellschaft für natur-und-völkerkunde Ostasiens in Tokio.* Supp. (1889).

Saito, Hideo. "A Study of Concepts of Procedure from the Point of Comparative Jurisprudence," 1 *The Japan Annual of Law and Politics* 71–82 (1952).

Sakamaki, Shunzō. "Japan and the United States 1790–1853," 18 *T.A.S.J.* (2nd series) 1–204 (1939).

Salwin, Lester N. "The New Commercial Code of Japan," 50 *Geo. L. J.* 478–512 (1962).

Satow, E. M. "The Origin of Spanish and Portuguese Rivalry in Japan," 18 *T.A.S.J.* (pt. II) 133–56 (1890).

Schlossberg, Arnold. "Lawyers' Incomes and Professional Economics," 47 *A.B.A.J.* 968–70 (Oct. 1961).

Seely, James G. "California Pretrial in Action: Comment," 49 *Calif. L. Rev.* 909–30 (1961).

Segal, Robert M. "A New Look at the Economics of the Profession," 43 *A.B.A.J.* (no. 9) 789–92 (1957).

Shafer, George F. "North Dakota's Conciliation Laws," 9 *A.B.A.J* 748–49 (1923).

Sheldon, Charles David. "Some Economic Reasons for the Marked Contrast in Japanese and Chinese Modernization," 23 *Kyoto University Economic Review* 30–60 (1953).

Shively, Donald H. "Bakufu versus Kabuki," 18 *Harvard Journal of Asiatic Studies* 326–56 (1955).

——. "Chikamatsu's Satire on the Dog Shogun," 18 *Harvard Journal of Asiatic Studies* 159–80 (1955).

————. "Motoda Eifu: Confucian Lecturer to the Meiji Emperor," in *Confucianism in Action*. Ed. by David S. Nivison and Arthur F. Wright. Stanford, Calif.: Stanford University Press, 1959. Pp. 302–33.

Simpson, Sidney Post, and Ruth Field. "Law and the Social Science," 32 *Va. L. Rev.* 858–67 (1945–46).

Smith, Neil Skene. "An Introduction to Some Japanese Economic Writings of the 18th Century," 11 *T.A.S.J.* (2nd series) 33–107 (1934).

————. "Materials on Japanese Social and Economic History," 14 *T.A.S.J.* (2nd series) 1–176 (1937).

Smith, Reginald H. "The Danish Conciliation System," 11 *J. of Am. Jud. Soc'y* 85–93 (1927).

————. "The Place of Conciliation in the Administration of Justice," 9 *A.B.A.J.* 746–57 (1923).

Smith, Robert J. "Pre-Industrial Urbanism in Japan: A Consideration of Multiple Traditions in a Feudal Society," 9 *Economic Development and Social Change* (no. 1. pt. 2) 241–57 (1960).

Smith, Thomas C. "The Land Tax in the Tokugawa Period," 18 *JAS* 8 (1958).

————. "Old Values and New Techniques in the Modernization of Japan," 14 *F.E.Q.* 355–63 (1955).

Solomon, A. H. "Revision of Japanese Mining Law under the Occupation," 26 *Wash. L. Rev.* 232–46 (1951).

Spea, Joseph J. "Japanese Sinology," 5 *Monumenta Nipponica* 214–18 (1942).

Stammler, Rudolf. "Recht und Willkür," in 1 *Rechtsphilosophische Abhandlungen und Vorträge*. Charlottenburg: Pan verlag R. Heise, 1925. Chapter III.

Steiner, Kurt. "Post-war Changes in the Japanese Civil Code," 25 *Wash. L. Rev.* 286–312 (1950).

————. "The Revision of the Civil Code of Japan: Provisions Affecting the Family," 9 *F.E.Q.* 169–84 (Feb. 1950).

Stone, Julius. "Uncommitted Relativism in Modern Theories of Justice," 16 *Sw. L. J.* 171–215 (1962).

Sunderland, Edson R. "The English Struggle for Procedural Reform," 39 *Harv. L. Rev.* 725 (1925–26).

Symposium. "Law and Social Science," 5 *Vill. L. Rev.* 247 (1959–60).

Takayanagi, Kenzō. "The Common Law and Civil Law in Japan," 4 *Am. J. of Comp. L.* 60–69 (1955).

————. "Legal Education in Japan," 6 *Am. L. School Rev.* 161–67 (1927).

Tanaka, Kōtarō. "Democracy and Judicial Administration in Japan," 2 *Journal of International Commission of Jurists* (no. 2) 7–20 (1960).

Teisen, Axel. "The Danish Judicial Code," 65 *U. Pa. L. Rev.* 543–70 (1916).

Thode, E. W. "The Case for the Pretrial Conference in Texas Re-examined," 41 *Tex. L. Rev.* 545–66 (1963).

Timasheff, N. S. "The Sociologists' Contribution to the Law," 32 *Va. L. Rev.* 818–34 (1945–46).

Toussaint, Herdard. "Conciliation Proceedings in the Federal Republic of Germany, Switzerland, Austria, Scandinavia, England, and the United States," 10 *Int'l. Soc. Sci. Bull* 616–25 (1958).

Toyoda, Takeshi. "The Character of the Feudal Society in Japan," 8 *Annals of the Hitotsubashi Academy* 29–35 (1957).

Trollope. "The Carletti Discourse: A Contemporary Italian Account of a Visit to Japan in 1597–1598," translated by Mark Napier, 9 *T.A.S.J.* (2nd series) 1–35 (1932).

Tsuda, Sōkichi. "Survival of Ancient Customs in Modern Life," 7 *Cultural Nippon* 81–95 (1939).

Ukai, Nobushige. "The Individual and the Rule of Law under the New Japanese Constitution," 51 *Nw. U. L. Rev.* 733–44 (1956–57).

Veith, Ilza. "Englishman or Samurai: 'The Story of Will Adams,' " 5 *F.E.Q.* 5–27 (Nov. 1945).

von Mehren, Arthur T. "The Judicial Process: A Comparative Analysis," 5 *Am. J. Comp. L.* 197–228 (1956).

———. "The Legal Order in Japan's Changing Society: Some Observations," 76 *Harv. L. Rev.* 1170–1205 (1963).

———. "Some Reflections on Japanese Law," 71 *Harv. L. Rev.* 1486–96 (1958).

Wagatsuma, Sakae. "Democratization of the Family Relation in Japan," 25 *Wash. L. Rev.* 405–26 (1950).

———. "Guarantee of Fundamental Human Rights under the Japanese Constitution," 26 *Wash. L. Rev.* 145–65 (1951).

Wainwright, S. H. "Japan's Transition from the Rule of Persons to the Rule of Law," 47 *T.A.S.J.* 155–71 (1919).

Ward, Robert E. "The Origins of the Present Japanese Constitution," 50 *Am. Pol. Sci. Rev.* 980–1010 (April 1956).

———. "Patterns of Stability and Changes in Rural Japanese Politics," University of Michigan, Center of Japanese Studies, *Occasional Papers* (no. 1) 1–6 (1951).

————. "The Socio-Political Role of the Buraku (Hamlet) in Japan," 45 *Am. Pol. Sci. Rev.* 1025–40 (1952).

————. "Some Observations on Legal Autonomy at the Village Level in Present Day Japan," 12 *F.E.Q.* 183–202 (Feb. 1953).

Warren, Earl. "Delay and Congestion in the Federal Courts," 42 *J. Am. Jud. Soc'y* (no. 1) 9 (1958).

————. "The Problem of Delay: A Task for Bench and Bar Alike," 44 *A.B.A.J.* 1043–46 and 1069 (1958).

Watanabe, Yozo. "The Family and the Law," in von Mehren (ed.), *Law in Japan* 373 (1963).

Webb, Herschel F. "The Mito Theory of State," *Columbia University East Asian Institute Studies* (no. 4) 33–52 (1957).

Wigmore, John Henry. "Editing an Era's Archives of Justice in Japan," 21 *A.B.A.J.* 733–34 (1935).

————. "Japanese Causes Celebres," 3 *Green Bag* 359, 4 *id.* 563, and 5 *id.* 287 (1892–93).

————. "Legal Education in Modern Japan," 5 *Green Bag* 17–33 and 78–85 (1893).

————. "The Legal System of Old Japan," 4 *Green Bag* 403–11, 478–84 (1892).

————. "Materials for the Study of Private Law in Old Japan," separate paging:
part 1: Introduction, 192 pp.; part 2: Contract—Civil Customs, 138 pp.; part 3: Contract—Legal Precedents (sections 2 and 3 are not included) 426 pp.; part 5: Property—Civil Customs, 112 pp. 20 *T.A.S.J.* (pt. 2) (1892).

————. "Notes on Land Tenure and Local Institutions in Old Japan; Edited from Posthumous Papers of Dr. D. B. Simmons," 19 *T.A.S.J.* (pt. I) 37–270 (1891).

Winters, Glenn R., ed. "Lagging Justice," 328 *Annals of the American Academy of Political and Social Science* 1–227 (1960).

Woodruff, Judson S. "The Japanese Lawyer," 35 *Neb. L. Rev.* 429–57 (1956).

Woodsworth, K. C. "The Legal System of the Republic of China," 4 *Canadian Bar Journal* 299 (1961).

Wright, Arthur F. "Professor Northrop's Chapter on the Traditional Culture of the Orient," 10 *Journal of the History of Ideas* 143–49 (1949).

Yuasa, K. "The Revised Japanese Code of Civil Procedure," 24 *Ill. L. Rev.* 830–38 (1930).

INDEX